French Criminal Law

Catherine Elliott

WILLAN
PUBLISHING

Published by

Willan Publishing
Culmcott House
Mill Street, Uffculme
Cullompton, Devon
EX15 3AT, UK
Tel: +44(0)1884 840337
Fax: +44(0)1884 840251
e-mail: info@willanpublishing.co.uk

Published simultaneously in the USA and Canada by

Willan Publishing
c/o ISBS, 5824 N.E. Hassalo St,
Portland, Oregon 97213-3644, USA
Tel: +001(0)503 287 3093
Fax: +001(0)503 280 8832

First published 2001

ISBN 1-903240-31-X (cased)
ISBN 1-903240-30-1 (paper)

British Library Cataloguing-in-Publication Data
A catalogue record for this book is available from the British Library.

Printed and bound by T.J. International, Padstow, Cornwall

Contents

Acknowledgements

This book was written with the generous support of a Vivendi Award from the Franco British Lawyers Society, and the author would like to give her full thanks for this support.

The author would also like to thank Pearson Education for kindly agreeing to give copyright permission for the reproduction of material on French criminal procedure from the book *French Legal System*, which was co-written by the author and Catherine Vernon.

Preface

This book aims to provide a clear and accessible analysis of French criminal law in English. Where appropriate, at the end of each chapter a comparative analysis of the French and English law in the field is provided. There is a chapter on French criminal procedure, as an understanding of the structure of the French criminal system is important for an understanding of the substantive law.

The book will be of interest to people with an interest in French, criminal and comparative law.

Translation of French legal terminology

Where possible all French terms have been translated in the main body of the text and, if of legal interest, the original has been included in brackets or as a footnote. There are three terms which require a particular explanation here. French law uses a tripartite hierarchy of offences, determined according to the severity of the sentence that can be applied: *crime*, *délit* and *contravention*. Among other things, this division determines which court will hear the case. The English concepts of indictable, summary and triable-either-way offences are too different from these terms to provide acceptable translations. Instead the terms *serious offence*, *major offence* and *minor offence* have been preferred.

On the general issue of English/French legal translation use has been made of Catherine Elliott, Carole Geirnaert and Florence Houssais, *French Legal System and Legal Language. An introduction in French* (1998) (Harlow: Longman).

List of abbreviations

Ass. plén.	Arrêt de l'Assemblée plénière de la Cour de cassation (decision of the *Assemblée plénière* of the *Cour de cassation*)
B.	Bulletin des arrêts de la Cour de cassation
CA.	Cour d'appel (Court of Appeal)
C.civ.	Code Civile (Civil Code)
Ch. acc.	Chambre d'accusation
Ch. mixte	Arrêt de la chambre mixte de la Cour de cassation (decision of the *chambre mixte* of the *Cour de cassation*)
Chron.	Chronique
Comm.	Commentaire (commentary)
Crim.	Chambre criminelle de la Cour de cassation (Criminal Division of the *Cour de cassation*)
D.	Recueil Dalloz
D.H.	Recueil Dalloz Hebdomadaire
D.P.	Recueil Dalloz Périodique
Dr. pén.	Droit pénal
Gaz. Pal.	Gazette du Palais
Inf.Rap.	Informations rapides
J.C.P.	Jurisclasseur périodique, Semaine Juridique
J.O.	Journal officiel
Obs.	Observations (commentary)
Rev. sc. crim.	Revue de science criminelle
S.	Recueil Sirey
Somm.	Sommaires commentés
Th.	Thèse (thesis)

1

The evolution of French criminal law

The origins of criminal law: family justice

Human nature pushes the person who has been wronged to seek revenge against their aggressor. It is from this spontaneous revengeful reaction that criminal law is born. Though rudimentary and brutal, private revenge constituted a means of maintaining social order between clans. Fear of revenge acted as a deterrent against anti-social behaviour, such as murder. Thus the system of vendettas served to achieve respect for strangers and solidarity within each clan group, as the whole clan of the victim was ready to seek vengeance. Revenge would be sought not only against the individual aggressor but also against their family, their chief and the most important clan members. Thus, in its origins criminal liability was collective rather than individual. The focus was on the harm caused, and there was no interest in establishing the guilty mind of the aggressor. No distinction was drawn between voluntary and involuntary homicide and even a natural death could be attributed to an evil spell of a neighbouring clan.[1] The vendetta had no ambition to prevent criminality.

Revenge started to gain a new meaning when it began to have religious implications. Primitive societies believed that the crime attracted the anger of the gods. To appease the divine wrath, the priests, charged with the functions of judges, sought to expiate the guilty person. In this perspective, the suffering inflicted on the criminal was no longer merely the satisfaction of the harm suffered by the victim: it also contributed to re-establishing the balance in the human relations with the occult forces which governed the world.

---

[1] See Poirier, '*Les caractères de la responsabilité archaïque*,' in *La responsabilité pénale*, Travaux de l'Institut de Sciences criminelles et pénitentiaires de Strasbourg, Dalloz, 1961, p. 19 and seq.

Private justice

Private justice existed when there was a move away from mere brute force. It is the embryo of a legal system, having rules that establish limits on the use of repression. It is described as a system of private justice because the private party (the victim and their family) remain the instigators of the proceedings, often carrying out the sanction and being its principal beneficiaries. The public authorities only had a limited role, restricted to laying down rules of procedure rather than of substance, though this role would over time gradually increase. The victim and their family were still allowed to seek private revenge, but increasingly the public authorities applied limits on its exercise. Thus, the authorities would only allow close relations to the victim to carry out the revenge, and eventually prohibited revenge from being carried out on anybody other than the guilty person, particularly when the clan was not showing solidarity with the harmful behaviour of the guilty person and expelled them from the group or even handed them over to the victim's clan.

An element of subjectivism was introduced into the system, as offences that were committed unintentionally were subjected to a less stringent régime than that of private revenge. Gradually, a requirement of proportionality between the original harm and the revenge was developed, particularly where the victim did not die.

The appearance of the law of retaliation[2] marks a significant development. Under the law of retaliation the amount of revenge was limited, repression was individualised; retaliation was limited to crimes of intention. The resulting system was less draconian, frequently awarding the wronged party pecuniary compensation.

Public justice

As the State became more powerful, private justice fell into decline. Up to the thirteenth century the State primarily limited itself to controlling the procedures for carrying out private revenge. It sought to limit the excesses and the anarchic character of the vendetta.

Roman law had developed a system of public justice and France was inspired by this system and its legal texts. By the thirteenth century the system of private justice was transformed to one of public justice, with the State taking control of the system of repression, with the aim of repairing a social wrong rather than a private wrong. The private party was relegated to a secondary position, as a private claimant[3] to the proceedings. But still

---

[2] *le talion*, known in Latin as the *lex talionis*.
[3] *la partie civile*.

numerous institutions of private justice persisted for a long time under the regime of public justice. Private violence remained legitimate where the public authorities were not in a position to adequately ensure the protection of its citizens. The monarch sometimes took a vow when he came to power to maintain the peace of his kingdom and justice was seen as emanating from the monarch. When a crime was committed this represented a failure of the monarch to keep his oath, which then justified the monarch in instigating a criminal prosecution if the victim could not or dared not do so. This was the system in the duchy of Normandy, and was transported to England by William the Conqueror. Today the kings and queens of England continue to take this oath and they are known as the 'fountain of justice'.

In the sixteenth century special permission from the monarch[4] was required to approve the use of violence committed in legitimate defence. Today legitimate defence still exists where there is a danger requiring an immediate reaction.[5] Revenge was forbidden: only monarchs could seek revenge through their officers by virtue of the power they held from God.

The royal period (sixteenth to eighteenth centuries)

Pre-revolutionary law barely changed between the sixteenth and eighteenth centuries, apart from a slight reduction in the sentences handed down. The criminal law of this period presents in its sources a curiously international character. The renaissance of Roman law increasingly provided the basis for legal reasoning and the foundations for the systematisation of the criminal law. The Roman Digest, containing the writings of Roman lawyers,[6] was considered to be still in force and was followed unless there was a clear provision of custom or a written text.[7] Leading French criminal lawyers were inspired by the work of the Romans to gradually elaborate general principles of criminal law.[8] But the offences and the punishments had their roots in local customs which went back to feudal times.

The criminal law was also influenced by Christianity and canon law. In the Middle Ages the ecclesiastical courts played an important role in society. They had jurisdiction over matters which touched in any way the Church's interests. So they carried out trials involving crimes against holy

---

[4] *les lettres de grâce.*

[5] Art. 122–5 and 122–6 of the new Criminal Code.

[6] *Jurisconsultes.*

[7] On the sources of law under the *Ancien Régime*, see Ortolan, *Rev. crit.*, 1848, p. 21 et s.; 161 et s.

[8] Papon and Tiraqueau in the seventeenth century, Ayrault and Favre in the seventeenth century and Jousse, Muyart de Vouglans and Goursseau de la Combe in the eighteenth century.

places or the property of the Church, heresy, witchcraft, adultery, usury and perjury. They handed over to the secular courts the most serious offenders or those who were considered to be incorrigible and judged the others.

It is in the organisation of its own criminal system that the canon law developed a profoundly original view of repression in harmony with the notion of sin and penitence. Punishment under canon law has a retributive foundation: it is the sanction for the moral responsibility of the delinquent, the exact compensation necessary to expiate the fault. It is thus proportionate to the gravity of the fault and is not determined by the vindictive appetite of the victim or by an aim of deterrence. The aim is also to rehabilitate the offender following the idea of redemption. So, for the first time, the future of the condemned person was taken into account. The Church rejected the death penalty and amputations which were opposed to the principle of rehabilitation, and preferred imprisonment, or work in the monasteries.

It is clear that canon law has had a major influence on the development of modern criminal law. The concept of criminal liability was heavily influenced by canon law (itself influenced by Roman law) and the writings of the great theologians, in particular Saint Thomas Aquinas.[9] People identified the notion of crime with sin, that is to say of a willed and culpable fault of the individual, and the concept of punishment with penitence. The law generally required a voluntary act to show fault[10] of the person prosecuted. This subjective approach was the result of the influence of Roman and canon law. But often this fault was presumed from the gravity of the acts committed, though where it was only presumed a lighter sentence had to be imposed. Non-intentional acts were rarely incriminated. In the absence of fault, the matter was often treated as falling within the civil system, so that there was merely a civil trial for damages. If a prosecution was brought, it was quite easy for the guilty person to obtain a pardon.[11]

Pre-revolutionary law took into account the age of the offender, adopting the Roman distinctions of infant,[12] pre-pubescent,[13] *proximus infantiae*, almost pubescent,[14] pubescent,[15] and so forth. Minors only incurred the ordinary criminal punishment if they were judged *doli capax*, an approach very familiar to Anglo-Saxon lawyers. But *doli incapax* could

---

[9] Metz, '*La responsabilité pénale dans le droit canonique médiéval*', Colloque de philosophie du
      droit pénal tenu à Strasbourg en 1959, Paris 1961, p. 182.
[10] *le dol.*
[11] *une lettre de rémission.*
[12] *infans.*
[13] *impubère.*
[14] *impubère proximus pubertatis.*
[15] *pubère.*

be found simply from the gravity of the crime.[16] Children of 11 could be executed.

An order (*ordonnance*) of 1670 unified and codified criminal procedure, though much of the criminal law continued to vary depending on the region. One exception was the law on theft which was the subject of a royal declaration of 13 March 1731.[17] Under pre-revolutionary law[18] the offences resulted from custom, and as most of these customs were not written, their content and exact scope was sought in the Roman texts, opinions of authors and legal precedents. Custom also determined the maximum punishment applicable to the offence and the mode of its execution.

Pre-revolutionary law had two key characteristics: it was arbitrary and the sentences were harsh. Looking at the first characteristic, the judges held wide arbitrary powers. Under the maxim 'all punishments are arbitrary' judges were sometimes authorised to impose a sanction they thought appropriate to the case. This allowed the judges to graduate the punishment according to the responsibility of the guilty person, but the power could be abused. The Royal Order of 1670, which regulated criminal procedure, did not provide a list of potential offences or their sentences. So, the activities that could give rise to a criminal penalty remained uncertain, as well as the type of sentence that would be imposed. The judges thus benefited from a wide discretion to decide according to their conscience whether to convict a defendant, and to order any punishment provided it was 'in use in the realm'.

As all justice emanated from the monarch, he or she could issue an order under the King's private seal[19] to terminate a prosecution or, without relying on the judges, convict or imprison an individual without a trial and without even an offence having been committed.

The nobility and clerics enjoyed procedural guarantees and privileges which meant that a gentler regime was applied to them. This inequality in the system has been heavily criticised.

Looking at the second characteristic of the pre-revolutionary system, from the seventeenth century France was dominated by the philosophy of retribution. The criminal system did not therefore try to cure criminals, and showed no interest in their personal future: the philosophy was that it was necessary to save the healthy part of the population while sacrificing the unhealthy part.

---

[16] Castaing, '*L'enfance délinquante à Lille au XVIIe siècle*', thesis, Lille, 1960.
[17] M. Privost, '*Introduction à l'étude du vol et sa répression en France, à la fin de l'ancien régime*', thesis, Paris II, 1973.
[18] *l'ancien régime.*
[19] *une lettre de cachet.*

Heavy sentences were imposed. Alongside capital punishment (which could be by the gallows,[20] quartering[21] or decapitation,[22] for example), there were also corporal punishments such as flogging[23] and the amputation of a hand or tongue. There existed a wide range of public humiliations which were intended to imprint in the popular consciousness the shameful character of the criminal conduct. These included the iron-collar,[24] public exposure,[25] pillory,[26] branding with a red-hot iron[27] and public confession.[28] A person's freedom could be restricted by banishing them from a town, province or kingdom. Imprisonment was not considered a true punishment: it was frequently used, but either administratively or pending a trial. The death sentence was common and applied even to offences such as theft and it was often combined with terrible tortures. Some of the methods of torture were so horrific that the judges sometimes inserted a proviso[29] in their judgement that the convict should be secretly strangled before the end of the torture. Women as well as men could be subjected to the death penalty (though they were spared torture on the wheel).[30]

The evolution of ideas in the eighteenth century

It is only since the end of the eighteenth century that criminal theories, strengthened by the birth of criminology, started to play an important role in the evolution of criminal policy.

The classical theory of criminal law[31] was born between 1748, date of the publication of *L'Esprit des Lois* by Montesquieu, and 1813 when the Bavarian Criminal Code was passed, directly inspired by the German lawyer Feuerbach. This classical theory was developed by the writings of Feuerbach, Montesquieu, Rousseau, the Italian Beccaria, and the Englishman Bentham.

Montesquieu recommended a general softening of punishments, but this philosophy had little influence on the actual law until the sensational

---

[20] *la potence.*
[21] *l'écartèlement.*
[22] *la décolation.*
[23] *le fouet.*
[24] *le carcan.*
[25] *l'exposition publique.*
[26] *le pilori.*
[27] *le marque au fer rouge.*
[28] *une amende honorable.*
[29] *retentum.*
[30] *le supplice de la roue.*
[31] *le droit pénal classique.*

success of the work of Cesare Beccaria.[32] In 1764, when he was 26, this young man, who had studied in Paris and was an admirer of Montesquieu, published in Milan his famous *Treaty on offences and punishments*.[33] This book was a major success and contributed to the French Revolution. It was written following discussions with his friend Alexandre Verri who was inspector of prisons in Milan, and influenced the whole of Europe. Beccaria heavily criticised the severity of the existing punishments and the use of torture. He fought against capital punishment, and argued that a moderate but certain punishment would be more effective in preventing crime than a frightening but arbitrary punishment. He emphasised the need to rehabilitate offenders so that they could return to a normal and honourable place in society. On the other hand, he accorded less importance to the intention of the guilty party than to the social harm that they had caused when determining the appropriate punishment. He was opposed to arbitrary systems and advocated that everyone should be treated equally by the criminal system. He developed the principle of the statutory basis of offences, according to which offences and their punishments needed to be contained in a legal text rather than be left to the arbitrary decisions of an individual judge.

On 7 May 1788 Louis XVI held at Versailles a meeting, known as a *lit de justice*, during which he developed a plan to reform the criminal law. The envisaged reforms would have constituted major progress towards removing arbitrary and overly severe punishments from the system. Unfortunately, the royal edicts issued to introduce the reforms were badly received by the senior courts.[34] The high judicial court of Paris went on strike and in Grenoble a leaflet was written criticising the reforms, and triggered riots.

Revolutionary law[35]

Translated into French in 1766, Beccaria's book was received with enthusiasm by Voltaire and Diderot. Influenced by his and Montesquieu's ideas, the Revolutionary Assemblies made considerable reforms to the criminal law. They passed two Acts dated 19–22 July 1791 and 24 September–6 October 1791, which amounted to a criminal code.[36] Thus, the criminal law moved away from being a custom-based system. The sentences were generally reduced, corporal punishments were abolished

---

[32] Jacomella, 'L'actualité de Cesare Beccaria', *Rev. inter. crim.*, 1964, p. 84.

[33] *Traité des délits et des peines.*

[34] *les parlements.*

[35] *le droit intermédiaire.*

[36] Plawski, 'Le Peletier de Saint-Fargeau, auteur du Code pénal de 1791', *Rev. sc. crim.*, 1957, p. 619.

and capital punishment was only preserved for a few offences. The legislation posed the principle of equality and took this to an extreme by imposing fixed sentences and abolishing pardons. In addition, the Declaration of the Rights of Man of 1789 outlawed arbitrary decision making. The principle of the statutory basis of offences was included in the Declaration which stated in article 6:

> All that is not forbidden by the law cannot be prevented and no one can be forced to do what it does not order.[37]

Article 7 added:

> [T]he law can only lay down punishments that are strictly and obviously necessary and a person can only be punished by virtue of a law established and promulgated prior to the wrongful conduct and legally applicable.[38]

The Declaration now forms part of the French constitution.

As regards criminal procedure, the legislation was inspired by the English accusatorial system, and a jury system was introduced. It was at this stage that the distinction between serious,[39] major[40] and minor[41] offences was developed.

The Criminal Code of 1810

The Napoleonic Code of 1810 mixed aspects of the Revolutionary law with the law that had existed before the Revolution. On the one hand, the ideas of Beccaria and Montesquieu, which had directly inspired the revolutionary Criminal Code of 1791, left their traces on the imperial code. Thus, the principle of legality was included in the Criminal Code of 1810 at article 4 which stated:

> No minor, major or serious offence can be punished with sentences that were not laid down by legislation before they were committed.[42]

---

[37] '*Tout ce qui n'est pas défendu par la loi ne peut être empêché et nul ne peut être contraint de faire ce qu'elle n'ordonne pas.*'

[38] '*la loi ne peut établir que les peines strictement et évidemment nécessaires et nul ne peut être puni qu'en vertu d'une loi établie et promulguée antérieurement au défit et légalement applicable.*'

[39] *le crime.*

[40] *le délit.*

[41] *la contravention.*

[42] '*Nulle contravention, nul délit, nul crime, ne peuvent être punis de peines qui n'étaient pas prononcées par la loi avant qu'ils fussent commis.*'

There was, however, a move away from fixed sentences which had proved to be impractical; instead maximum and minimum sentences were specified and the judge could choose the sentence within these boundaries. The 1810 Code imposed an egalitarian system founded on the mental responsibility of the offender.

On the other hand, social unrest at the time had given rise to lawless behaviour and led to the imposition of a fairly harsh criminal system, which reflected the severity of the pre-Revolutionary law. The Code was influenced by the work of the English philosopher Jeremy Bentham, founder of the utilitarian doctrine. He supported the use of severe punishments where these would serve as an effective deterrent. A range of offences could incur the death penalty, particularly those that threatened public order, and brutal corporal punishments such as branding with a red-hot iron and the amputation of a hand were reintroduced. It was only for the least serious offences that there appeared to be a clear aim of re-habilitation. Attempts were punished as severely as the complete offences and accomplices were treated as if they were the principal offender. The severity of the system was gradually weakened by subsequent governments. Reforms introduced by the Act of 28 April 1832 reduced some of the severity of the punishments and on 9 August 1981 the death penalty was abolished.

The Code was adopted in Belgium and Luxembourg and served as a model for criminal codes of other countries in Europe.

It was generally accepted that the Criminal Code of 1810 was not the best of the Napoleonic codes. Its structure was criticised as illogical since it dealt with the sentence before defining the offence, and the general defences were scattered throughout the Code in parts relating to specific substantive offences. There had been talk of reforming it ever since 1832, and until 1992 various unsuccessful attempts had been made to replace it. Numerous amendments were made to the Code in an effort to modernise and improve it. After the Second World War there was a move to take into account the personality and age of the offender, and a community sentence was developed that was inspired by the English use of probation. The Code was eventually replaced in 1994.

The Criminal Code of 1992

The process of creating a new criminal code started with the Commission for Revision of 1974, which was composed of practising lawyers and university academics. It prepared a draft Bill in 1978 which was heavily criticised and was not adopted by the Government. In 1981 the process started again under the new Minister of Justice, Robert Badinter. In 1989, the President of the Republic, François Mitterrand, announced that the preparation of a new Criminal Code would be a priority of his second term in office. It seems that the President had spent his Christmas holidays with Robert Badinter and this might have influenced his decision.

The new Code was prepared as four Acts of Parliament which were passed on 22 July 1992. A further Act was passed on 16 December 1992 to amend the existing law to take into account the provisions of the new Code. A decree was passed on 29 March 1993 containing the minor offences to be included in the Code. A further Act amending the existing law and to correct minor details in the Code was passed on 1 February 1994. The Code had the support of most of the elected representatives, with only the communists voting against it. As a result the legislation was not referred to the *Conseil constitutionnel*.

The Code finally came into force on 1 March 1994. It is divided into two parts, the first legislative and the second regulatory. The substantive offences concerning major and serious offences are contained in books II to V of the legislative part. The regulatory part is found in book VI and contains the minor offences. The numbering of the Code has changed. Each article has four numbers. The first corresponds to the relevant book of the Code, the second to the relevant part[43] of the Code, and the third to the chapter where the article can be found. The fourth number refers to the position of the article in the chapter. So the first article in the Code is not article 1 but article 111–1. This method of numbering was preferred because it is easier to insert new articles as the criminal law develops.

The main aim of the Code was to group together the criminal law in a form that was accessible to the general public. It does not represent a major reform of the law. Its primary aim was to modernise the drafting and layout of the Code, by simplifying the language and providing clearer definitions of some of the offences. The basic principles of the criminal law have remained unchanged. The new Code provided an opportunity for the legislation to take into account some of the case law developments in the field. The major changes made by the Code were to introduce corporate liability and to create a new offence of deliberately putting another person in danger.

The Code starts with the general principles of the criminal law, criminal liability and sentencing. It deals with these matters in more detail than the old Code. It then moves on to the study of the offences against the person, property, the nation, the State and public peace. In following this order, in preference to that of the Napoleonic Code which had started with the offences against the State before dealing with those against the individual, the new Code seeks to prioritise the value of human life over other interests.

Some important legislation remains outside the Code, including the Act of 21 July 1881 on the freedom of the press.

---

[43] *Titre.*

2

Criminal procedure

The sources

French criminal procedure was originally codified in the *Code d'instruction pénale* of 1808. This was replaced in 1958 by the Code of Criminal Procedure which is currently in force. Any articles referred to in this Chapter will be to this Code unless specified otherwise. Under the 1958 Constitution, criminal procedure falls within the legislative domain of article 34, and therefore regulations play only a limited role in this area, primarily applying parliamentary legislation. Because of article 55 of the Constitution, legislation must conform with international treaties, which is particularly significant in this context due to the 1950 European Convention for the Safeguard of Human Rights. This Convention therefore makes an important contribution to the rules on criminal procedure. In particular, article 6 of the European Convention protects the right to a fair trial in the criminal field. This right is available from the time of the person being charged to the end of the prosecution, and procedures such as on-the-spot penalty fines breach this protection. In considering this right, the courts look at the fairness of the procedures globally, allowing the absence of one guarantee to be counterbalanced by the existence of another. In practice, the Criminal Division of the *Cour de cassation* generally takes the view that for matters of criminal procedure its principal source is the Code, and the Convention is only of secondary importance. An Act of 31 May 2000[1] made some important changes to criminal procedure with a view to strengthening the rights of the accused and the victim. This introduced a new opening article for the Code of Criminal Procedure, laying down the general principles that underpin the criminal system. This article states:

---

[1] *Loi no. 2000–516 du 15 juin 2000 renforçant la protection de la présomption d'innocence et les droits des victimes.*

Art. 1.

I. The criminal procedure must be fair and give due hearing to the parties and preserve the balance between the parties' rights. It must guarantee the separation of the authorities responsible for the prosecution and the trial. People finding themselves in similar conditions and prosecuted for the same facts must be judged according to the same rules.

II. The judicial authority watches over the investigation and the guarantee of the victims' rights during the whole of the criminal procedure.

III. Any person suspected or prosecuted is presumed innocent as long as their guilt has not been established. Attacks on the presumption of innocence are prevented, remedied and sanctioned according to the conditions laid down by the law. He has the right to be informed of the charges against him and to be represented by a defence lawyer. Measures of constraint that this person can be subjected to are taken by a decision, or under the effective control, of the judicial authority. They must be strictly limited to the needs of the procedure, proportionate to the gravity of the offence reproached and not attack the dignity of the person. The accusation made against this person must be definitively ruled on within a reasonable period of time. Any convicted person has the right to have their conviction examined by another court.[2]

Three stages

In order to protect the citizen from abuses of power it is felt to be important to prevent too much power being given to one individual, and instead to allow one group of people to have the power to carry out only one type of function. Thus the criminal process can be divided into three stages, with different officials responsible for each stage of the procedure:

---

[2] 'Art. 1er.

I. *La procédure pénale doit être équitable et contradictoire et préserver l'équilibre des droits des parties. Elle doit garantir la séparation des autorités chargées de l'action publique et des autorités de jugement. Les personnes se trouvant dans des conditions semblables et poursuivies pour les mêmes infractions doivent être jugées selon les mêmes règles.*

II. *L'autorité judiciaire veille à l'information et à la garantie des droits des victimes au cours de toute procédure pénale.*

III. *Toute personne suspectée ou poursuivie est présumeé innocente tant que sa culpabilité n'a pas été établie. Les atteintes à sa présomption d'innocence sont prévenues, réparées et réprimées dans les conditions prévues par la loi. Elle a le droit d'être informée des charges retenues contre elle et d'être assistée d'un défenseur. Les mesures de contraintes dont cette personne peut faire l'objet sont prises sur décision ou sous le contrôle effectif de l'autorité judiciaire. Elles doivent être strictement limitées aux nécessités de la procédure, proportionnées à la gravité de l'infraction reprochée et ne pas porter atteinte à la dignité de la personne. Il doit être définitivement statué sur l'accusation dont cette personne fait l'objet dans un délai raisonnable. Toute personne condamnée a le droit de faire examiner sa condamnation par une autre juridiction.'*

- the police investigation and the prosecution;
- the judicial investigation;
- the trial.

The distinction between the first two stages is slightly artificial, as in practice the investigating judge delegates most of the tasks of investigation to the police, so the police play a key role during both phases.

The rules of criminal procedure are developed around the distinction between the three classes of offences: serious[3], major[4] and minor offences.[5] In particular, a judicial investigation only tends in practice to be used where a serious offence has been committed.

Inquisitorial and adversarial

A distinction can be drawn between inquisitorial and adversarial criminal systems. An inquisitorial system is characterised by a process that is not open to the public, the parties do not automatically have a right to be heard, the judges play an important and active role in collecting the evidence and an emphasis is placed on collecting written documentation to prove or disprove the case. Adversarial systems put an emphasis on public procedures, oral hearings, giving an opportunity to the parties to put forward their case, while the judge is primarily limited to the role of an arbitrator ensuring that there is fair play. The first two stages of the French criminal procedure have traditionally been inquisitorial in nature, with particular emphasis being placed in the building up of a written file of the case containing all the statements, expert reports, and records of investigative procedures carried out. Elements of the adversarial process have been added in recent years, in an effort to give greater protection to the rights of the citizen. The trial hearing has always mixed elements of the inquisitorial and adversarial system as it usually takes place in public with a limited opportunity for the parties to put their case orally, but the written file on the case prepared during the pre-trial investigations is central to the hearing.

Reform

Criminal procedure is an area that attracts considerable political attention, and is frequently the subject of legislation. Most recently, President Chirac established the *Commission de réflexion sur la Justice* which was presided

---

[3] *le crime.*
[4] *le délit.*
[5] *la contravention.*

over by the president of the *Cour de cassation*, Pierre Truche, and reported
in July 1997 (the Truche Report). There were two main themes to its report:
the protection of the presumption of innocence and the relationship
between the Public Prosecutor's Office and politicians. As a result several
pieces of legislation were presented to Parliament during 1998 and 1999
which adopt many of the recommendations made in the Truche Report.
The legislation aims to increase the openness and transparency of the
system, reduce the powers of the investigating judge, and strengthen
the independence of the Public Prosecutor. These changes are felt to be
vital in order to regain the confidence of the French public, which had been
lost in the aftermath of various political and financial scandals. In 2000
much of this legislation was blocked by the opposition, on the ground that
they were concerned that too much power was going to be given to the
judges, but the Government still hopes that it will be able to successfully
progress this legislation through Parliament at a future date. Some
significant reforms were, however, introduced with the passing of the Act
of 15 June 1995 reinforcing the presumption of innocence and the rights of
victims.

Secrecy

Traditionally, the police and judicial investigations and the judicial
deliberations take place in secret, leaving only the trial hearing open to the
public. It is felt that the democratic principles of freedom of information
and freedom of the press have to be balanced by the need to achieve
justice. The secrecy of the early stages of the criminal procedure means
that investigations can be carried out without prior communications
taking place between accomplices, relevant evidence being destroyed and
pressure being placed on witnesses. It is claimed that it protects the
presumption of innocence, by preventing the media from declaring guilt
before a court has reached its judgment. The dangers of too much publicity
were highlighted in 1997, when a high-profile operation was launched to
arrest suspected members of a paedophile ring, where several of those
arrested subsequently committed suicide. Article 11 of the Code of
Criminal Procedure provides:

> Except in cases where the law provides otherwise, and without prejudice to the
> rights of the defence, the procedure during the police and judicial investigation
> is secret.
>   Any person who participates in this procedure is bound by professional
> secrecy and if breached can be punished under articles 226–13 and 226–14 of the
> Criminal Code.

In fact, only a limited number of people are bound by this secret, as article

11 refers simply to those who 'participate' in the procedure. This has been interpreted as referring to people whose profession or status mean they have a duty to be involved in this process, such as the public prosecutor, the investigating judge, the police, experts, interpreters, court clerks and defence lawyers. The *Cour de cassation* had suggested that because of their duty of confidentiality, the defence lawyers could not pass to their clients documents from the case file that had been given to them for their exclusive use.[6] This had been strongly criticised as preventing the defendant from effectively preparing their defence. The Act of 30 December 1996, amending article 114 of the Code of Criminal Procedure, was therefore passed allowing lawyers to give their clients copies of any documents from the file that they receive.

Article 11 does not bind the private claimant and ordinary witnesses to keep the criminal procedures secret, as they are not treated as 'participating' in the procedure. In addition, the secret only applies to certain elements of the file. For example, facts which are visible to the public, such as arrests and re-enactments, cease to be covered by the secret, so that a witness is free to tell other people what they have seen. Certain acts, like police custody and the holding of a person on remand, cannot be covered by the secret, as it would be dangerous to allow a person to be detained without another being informed. Information can be released to the public where this is in the interests of the investigation, such as where there is a call for witnesses or a photo of the suspect is issued.

The principle of secrecy is protected by both criminal, civil and disciplinary sanctions. There is, for example, an offence of violating the duty of confidentiality.[7] A journalist can be convicted of the offence of handling if they are found to have obtained documents in breach of a duty of confidentiality.[8] Proving the commission of these offences can be difficult as journalists are not bound to reveal their sources.[9] The courts have, however, been prepared to convict journalists for handling when the exact identity of their source is not known, but the court is confident that the original transfer of the information to the journalist must have been by a police officer in breach of article 11.[10] The offence of defamation is also available.[11] If no criminal investigation has been commenced, and the media have suggested that a person has committed a crime, they are free to bring an action for defamation to clear their name. Such an action was successfully brought by the leading politician, François Léotard, when a

---

[6] *Ass. Plén.* 30 juin 1995.
[7] Art. 226–13 and 226–14 of the Criminal Code.
[8] Crim. 3 avr. 1995, *B*. p. 397.
[9] Art. 109 of the Code of Criminal Procedure.
[10] Crim. 13 mai 1991, *B*. p. 514.
[11] Act on the Freedom of the Press of 29 July 1881.

book was published suggesting that he was involved in the murder of an MP in the south of France.

Public revelations in breach of the principle of secrecy during the police and judicial investigation do not, however, render the relevant procedure void[12] unless this breach was detrimental to the interests of one of the parties.[13]

In recent years it has been accepted that too great an emphasis on secrecy during the criminal investigation can lead to an abuse of power, since it places the suspect in a very vulnerable position. As a result the legislator has been progressively intervening to introduce greater openness and transparency to the system.

In practice the media have obtained information on these early criminal procedures and have been prepared to publish this, despite possible infringements of the criminal law. Sometimes the investigating judges are themselves responsible for the diffusing of information, most markedly in the case of Jean-Michel Lambert, who was an investigating judge looking into the mysterious murder in 1984 of Gregory Villemin; he brought out a book about the murder while the criminal investigations were still ongoing. On the other hand, the investigating judges sometimes use media publicity to ensure that their investigations are not summarily curtailed by corrupt decision makers higher up, in an attempt to prevent political and financial scandals coming to light. It has been suggested that such publicity about the contaminated blood scandal (allegations that blood contaminated with the AIDS virus had been used by the medical services for financial reasons) ensured that criminal procedures were pursued.

While the Truche Report accepted that the press played an important democratic function, it also felt that further restrictions on its powers needed to be imposed to encourage the press to behave ethically. It recommended that to protect the presumption of innocence, the names of people who have been charged or held in police custody should not be revealed by journalists. The Commission was divided over whether publication of the names of suspects who had been elected to public office or had made public requests for funds (usually where there has been an abuse of charitable funds) would be justified; the majority felt that the principle of equality between citizens would prevent such a revelation. In any case, such restrictions would be progressively lifted during the judicial investigation. It also proposed that the publication of images of suspects in handcuffs should be strictly prohibited. This recommendation was adopted by the Act of 15 June 2000.[14] The Act created an offence where such a picture was published without the consent of the suspect.[15] The

---

[12] Crim. 24 avr. 1984.
[13] Crim. 25 janv. 1996.
[14] Art. 803 of the Code of Criminal Procedure.
[15] Art. 35 Act of 29 July 1881.

recommendation of the Truche Report that a media watchdog should be created has caused the most controversy. This was seen by the National Union for Journalists as an attempt to prevent journalists revealing future political and financial scandals.

The Truche Report recommended that generally there should be greater openness during the criminal investigation, with public hearings being held where important decisions affecting the freedom of individuals had to be made, which all the parties could attend. It also wanted the courts to establish communications services, so that the public and journalists could receive more information about criminal cases through official channels.

While secrecy has in the past been the norm for the initial stages of the criminal procedure, it has been accepted that the trial hearing should take place in public. However, a recent decision of the Criminal Division of the *Cour de cassation* of 15 June 1999 refused to annul a decision of the Court of Appeal of Grenoble that was reached behind closed doors. In that case, the defendant had been ordered in January 1990 to demolish within six months an illegal building. A fine was imposed of FF 100 a day for each day that the defendant failed to do this after that date. When the defendant failed to demolish the building, in a private hearing the Court of Appeal increased the fine to FF 500 a day. The *Cour de cassation* accepted that it had been a mistake to hear the case behind closed doors, but the decision was allowed to stand as it had neither been established nor argued that the interests of the defendant had been violated.

The police investigation and the prosecution

There are two types of police in France: the crime prevention police[16] and the criminal investigation police.[17] The former aim to stop the commission of offences, while the latter are responsible for finding the criminal after an offence has been committed. It is the criminal investigation police that we are concerned with in this chapter. They are made up of two different kinds of police officer. Firstly, the national police who work primarily in urban areas and belong to the Home Office. Secondly, the *gendarmes* who carry out their functions in the suburbs and in rural areas and are attached to the Ministry of Defence. The senior Public Prosecutors are responsible for watching over police investigations and must be kept informed by the police of the procedures carried out.

As regards the methods of investigation, there are rules against entrapment, so that the police cannot themselves play a part in the commission of the offence in order to detect its commission, though there are exceptions for drug and customs offences.

[16] *la police administrative.*
[17] *la police judiciaire.*

Having been informed of the commission of an offence, the police can carry out either an ordinary[18] or an expedited[19] investigation.

The expedited investigation

Serious and major offences can give rise to an expedited investigation if:

- the suspect was caught red handed or shortly after the commission of the offence;

- the suspect was found in possession of incriminating objects soon after the commission of the offence; or

- the offence was committed in a private home[20].

The advantage for the police of an expedited investigation is that they have increased powers which do not require the consent of those who are subjected to them. They can, for example, search property without the owner's consent,[21] seize any object capable of revealing the truth,[22] hear witnesses, and place a suspect in police custody.[23]

Having been informed of an offence, the police must immediately inform the Public Prosecutor[24] and then go directly to the scene of the crime to take all measures necessary to preserve any evidence. A suspect must be arrested where serious incriminating evidence justifies them being charged. A person's home can be searched without their consent where the occupier appears to have participated in the commission of an offence or to have documents or objects relating to an offence.[25] Any place can be searched where objects can be found whose discovery would be useful for revealing the truth.[26] Certain places, such as diplomatic buildings and university premises, enjoy special protection. In principle, the searches cannot be started before 6 o'clock in the morning and after 9 o'clock in the evening.[27] Night searches are possible for investigations concerning terrorism, drug trafficking and the procuring of prostitutes.[28] The search must take place in the presence of the person in whose home it

---

[18] Art. 75 to 78 of the Code of Criminal Procedure.
[19] Art. 53 to 74 of the Code of Criminal Procedure.
[20] Art. 53 of the Code of Criminal Procedure.
[21] Art. 56 of the Code of Criminal Procedure.
[22] Art. 54 and 56 of the Code of Criminal Procedure.
[23] Art. 63 to 65 of the Code of Criminal Procedure.
[24] Art. 54 of the Code of Criminal Procedure.
[25] Art. 56 of the Code of Criminal Procedure.
[26] Art. 94 of the Code of Criminal Procedure.
[27] Art. 59 of the Code of Criminal Procedure.
[28] Art. 706–28 and 706–35 of the Code of Criminal Procedure.

is carried out, or where this is impossible, by a representative of their choice. Failing this, two independent witnesses must be appointed by the police.[29] The police must seize everything that could serve to reveal the truth.[30] A statement describing the whole of the operation must be drawn up, if possible at the place where the search took place. The witnesses must sign the statement of operations and where there is a refusal to sign, this is mentioned in the statement. Only the police and the qualified participants in the search can look at the papers and documents before they are seized.

Searches carried out in certain places can only be performed by a judge in the presence of a representative of the profession to which the subject of the search belongs. This is the position for searches of the offices of doctors, *notaires*, *avoués* and court bailiffs.[31] Searches in the offices or home of an *avocat* can only be carried out by a judge in the presence of the President of the local Bar or a delegated person. The Act of 15 June 2000 tried to reinforce the role of the President of the local Bar so that they are able to contest the removal of documents where they consider the search to have been carried out illegally. The matter will then be referred to the *juge des libertés et de la détention*[32] who will decide whether the documents can be lawfully removed.

In order to protect the principle of freedom of information, searches of the offices of a newspaper or broadcaster can only be carried out by a judge. This judge makes sure that the investigations carried out do not attack the free exercise of the journalist's profession, and do not lead to an unjustified delay in the diffusion of information.[33] If the rules on search are breached the search is illegal and invalid.[34]

The ordinary police investigation

When the police carry out an ordinary police investigation, they only have two coercive powers: to order witnesses to come to the police station to be questioned[35] and to place suspects in police custody.[36] Any other measures restricting the freedom of an individual (such as the search and seizure of their property) require that person's consent, and in particular the police have no power of arrest. In relation to terrorism, the president of the *tribunal de grande instance* or the judge assigned by him or her can, on the

---

[29] Art. 57 of the Code of Criminal Procedure.
[30] Art. 54 and 56 of the Code of Criminal Procedure.
[31] Art. 56 of the Code of Criminal Procedure.
[32] Art. 56–1 of the Code of Criminal Procedure, inserted by art. 45 of the Act of 15 June 2000.
[33] Art. 56 of the Code of Criminal Procedure.
[34] Art. 59 of the Code of Criminal Procedure.
[35] Art. 78 of the Code of Criminal Procedure.
[36] Art. 77 of the Code of Criminal Procedure.

request of the state prosecutor, decide that the searches can be carried out without the agreement of the person in whose home they take place.[37]

Police custody

The placing of a person in police custody is considered a vital part of the criminal process, providing an opportunity to interrogate a suspect, while preventing them from being able to communicate with members of the public, particularly possible accomplices. Until 1958 there was no legal text regulating police custody. This was a dangerous situation as it left scope for abuse by the police, and the passing of the 1958 Code of Criminal Procedure provided an opportunity to lay down a legal framework for this stage of the police investigation. The rules relating to police custody are the same whether it is carried out under an ordinary or an expedited investigation. Initially, both suspects and witnesses could be subjected to police custody, but since the Act of 4 January 1993, its use is now limited to suspects.[38] Witnesses can only be held for the time necessary to take their statement.

A person can be placed in police custody for the purposes of interrogation for 24 hours. In certain circumstances this can be extended to 48 hours by the public prosecutor.[39] Exceptionally, a person can be held in police detention for 98 hours, if they are suspected of having been involved in a terrorist or serious drug offence.[40]

There have been concerns over police violence during this stage of the criminal process. The Committee for the Prevention of Torture, an organ of the European Council, pointed in 1993 and again in 1998 to the persistence of bad treatment inflicted on people held in police stations.

Between 25 and 29 November 1991 Ahmed Selmouni was held in police custody in Bobigny, which is on the outskirts of Paris. He had been arrested and was later convicted of being involved in the international traffic of heroin. It seems that during his detention he suffered serious abuse at the hands of five police officers. His hair was pulled, he was punched and kicked and received blows to his head with a baseball bat. As a result he had to be taken to hospital as an emergency patient. On his return to the police station the next day, he again suffered ill-treatment.

The case was taken to the European Court of Human Rights by Ahmed Selmouni. He has joint Moroccan and Dutch nationality and the Netherlands took the exceptional decision of joining itself to the proceedings. Relying on the medical evidence, and in the absence of any plausible alternative explanation for the injuries he had suffered, France was condemned for torture, inhuman and degrading treatment under

---

[37] Art. 706–24 of the Code of Criminal Procedure.
[38] Art. 63 of the Code of Criminal Procedure.
[39] Art. 63 and 77 of the Code of Criminal Procedure.
[40] Art. 706–23 and 706–29 of the Code of Criminal Procedure.

article 3 of the Convention on 28 July 1999 by a unanimous verdict of 17 judges of the European Court. It is only the second country in Europe, the first being Turkey, to be condemned for torture by the European Court. Ahmed Selmouni was awarded 500,000 francs damages.

France was also condemned by the European Court for not having given him a fair trial within a reasonable time. He had submitted his formal complaint on 15 March 1993. The police were only brought before the Court of Versailles five-and-a-half years later. They were convicted and given prison sentences but submitted an appeal. This was heard by the Court of Appeal in March 1999. The Court of Appeal of Versailles upheld their convictions but significantly reduced their sentences. The sentence of the senior police officer, Bernard Hervé, was changed from four years in prison to 18 months, with 15 months suspended. The three months remaining had been covered by the time spent on remand and the automatic sentence reductions, so Bernard Hervé did not have to return to prison. All the other sentences to prison were reduced to suspended sentences. A further appeal could have been made to the *Cour de cassation* and normally the European Court will not hear cases until all available proceedings before the national courts have been completed. However, case law has been developed in relation to the Kurds in Turkey that the European Court will only wait for the completion of these proceedings if they are 'efficient' and available in practice and not just in theory. This case law was applied to France which was found to have been too dilatory in prosecuting this matter.

The case has been deeply embarrassing to France, which prides itself on being a country which protects human rights, and raises questions not just about the violence in the police force but also about the relationship between the police and the judiciary, as the judges should be playing a key role in detecting and prosecuting such cases. Fabien Jobard, a researcher in the field of police violence, has commented on the problem of prosecuting the police for violence, unless it is very serious, as they can claim that injuries were caused by the victim violently resisting arrest.[41] The *Ligue des Droits de l'Homme* has asked for the creation of an independent administrative authority that would investigate police violence.

Following the Acts of 4 January 1993 and 15 June 2000, a person held in police custody enjoys a certain number of rights to protect them from abuse during their period in detention. They can have a close person informed by telephone immediately that they are being held in police custody unless there is a contrary decision of the Public Prosecutor.[42] To reduce the risk of physical abuse, they can be examined by a doctor.[43]

---

[41] *Le Monde*, 3 July 1999.
[42] Art. 63–2 of the Code of Criminal Procedure.
[43] Art. 63–3 of the Code of Criminal Procedure.

The right to see a lawyer during police custody has been the subject of considerable parliamentary debate. The Act of 4 January 1993 originally provided that a lawyer could be contacted at the beginning of the police detention, but this was subsequently reformed by the Act of 1 March 1993 which only gave the suspect a right to see a lawyer after 20 hours' detention for a period of 30 minutes – though this in itself represented a minor revolution in criminal procedure. Following the Act of 15 June 2000, the suspect now has a right to see a lawyer within an hour, and then after 20 hours, and 36 hours.[44]

The lawyer will be informed by the police of the nature of the offence concerned, but is not allowed to consult the file on the case, attend the formal acts of the police investigation, or to tell anyone about the interview while the person is held in police custody. They can simply provide written observations to be added to the file. The lawyer is not present during the actual interrogation.

The *Conseil constitutionnel* considers that the right to see a lawyer during police custody is an absolute right of the defence, though different rules can be laid down by the legislator according to the facts of the case, provided any differences do not arise from unjustified discrimination and do not affect the rights of the defence.[45] Thus, in relation to conspiracy, living off immoral earnings or aggravated forms of extortion and organised crime, a person is only allowed to see a lawyer after 36 hours. For terrorist and serious drug offences a lawyer can only be seen after 72 hours.[46]

Affidavits must be prepared stating the time spent in police custody, the duration of the police questioning and the detainees' rest periods.[47] Though there are no fixed time limits for police questioning, a circular specifies that the law aims to avoid questioning for lengthy periods. Research carried out in 1993 on behalf of the Royal Commission of Criminal Justice in the UK suggested that in practice such questioning could take place for oppressive lengths of time, until the detainee was emotionally broken. The researchers questioned the reliability of any confession that was obtained in these circumstances.

Under article 41 of the Code of Criminal Procedure the whole process of police custody is placed under the control of the Public Prosecutor's Office. Thus, when a person is placed in police custody, the police must inform a senior state prosecutor at the start of the police custody[48] and they can subsequently authorise, where appropriate, its prolongation for a further

---

[44] Art. 63–3 of the Code of Criminal Procedure as amended by art. 5 of the Act of 15 June 2000.
[45] *Conseil constitutionnel* 11 aôut 1993.
[46] Art. 63–4 of the Code of Criminal Procedure.
[47] Art. 64 of the Code of Criminal Procedure.
[48] Art. 63 and 77 of the Code of Criminal Procedure.

period of 24 hours. The role of the prosecutor is considered to provide an important protection for the detainee, but it may not satisfy the requirements of the European Convention. Article 5(3) of this Convention requires that a person who is arrested or detained must be immediately transferred before a judge who is empowered by the law to exercise judicial functions. Members of the Public Prosecutor's Office are technically judges, being members of the same professional body and receiving the same training as the judges on the bench. The Criminal Division of the *Cour de cassation* has therefore held that articles 63 and 77 of the Code of Criminal Procedure are not incompatible with the Convention, considering that the senior Public Prosecutor is a judge 'empowered by the law to exercise judicial functions'.[49] However, the European Court of Human Rights ruled that local state prosecutors in Switzerland did not satisfy the criteria of article 5(3), as their impartiality could be questioned since they could subsequently bring a prosecution against the person placed in custody.[50] This judgment has influenced subsequent legislation so that the extension for a further 48 hours' police custody in relation to terrorist or drug offences must be authorised either by the president of the *tribunal de grande instance* or a designated member of the bench.

In the past the suspect was not informed of their right to remain silent and there was no obligation to inform a suspect why they were being detained in police custody. These weaknesses in the rights of the suspect have been remedied by the Act of 15 June 2000.[51]

The Truche Report recommended that police interrogations should be recorded, with the recordings being placed under seal, and then referred to where there is subsequently a conflict between the written statements and later declarations. This recommendation was only adopted by the Government in the Act of 15 June 2000 for young offenders.

The Public Prosecutor's Office

Once the police investigation is completed, a prosecution can be brought by a civil servant, who is normally the Public Prosecutor.[52] The prosecutor competent to bring a prosecution is the one who has jurisdiction in the area where the crime was committed, where the suspect lives, where they were arrested,[53] or occasionally where they are being detained.[54]

---

[49] Crim. 10 mars 1992, *B.* p. 272.
[50] *Huber v Suisse* (1990).
[51] Art. 63–1 para 1 of the Code of Criminal Procedure as amended by art. 8 of the Act of 15 June 2000; art. 63–4 of the Code of Criminal Procedure as amended by art. 11 of the Act of 15 June 2000.
[52] Art. 1 of the Code of Criminal Procedure.
[53] Art. 43 of the Code of Criminal Procedure.
[54] Art. 663 and 664 of the Code of Criminal Procedure.

The Public Prosecutor's Office is organised on a hierarchical basis with the Minister of Justice at its head. In the *Cour de cassation* the chief prosecutor is known as the *Procureur général près de la Cour de cassation* who is assisted by *avocats généraux*. Each court of appeal has a *Procureur général* who is assisted by *avocats généraux* and *substituts généraux*. The *Procureur de la République* is based in the *Tribunal de grande instance* and is assisted by *procureurs adjoints* and *substituts*. Where a court of first instance has no automatic representative of the Public Prosecutor's office the *Procureur de la République* can fulfil this role for courts falling within his or her jurisdiction.

As well as playing an important role in criminal proceedings, the Public Prosecutor's Office also represents the interests of society in civil proceedings. It oversees the proper and uniform application of the law in civil cases by making submissions, usually in writing, on the relevant law and its application to the case.

In criminal proceedings, before deciding whether or not to prosecute, Public Prosecutors often in practice seek to apply intermediary solutions. Thus, they can issue warnings which will only be followed by a prosecution if the person re-offends; or they can temporarily classify the case as requiring no further action, with an order for the suspect to put the situation right by, for example, paying their road tax. In recent years efforts have been made towards criminal mediation. Legislation to provide a legal framework for this practice was passed on 4 January 1993. With their agreement, the victim and the author of the crime are brought together, and if the mediation is successful the Public Prosecutor's Office can decide not to pursue the prosecution. When it is unsuccessful, the prosecution will be commenced.[55] Legislation was passed on 18 December 1998 and 9 June 1999 to expand the use of mediation when an offence has been committed. In order that the rights of the defence are fully respected during a mediation, the legislation organises new procedural guarantees: every person engaged in a mediation has to be informed that they have a right to a lawyer, and a system of remuneration for lawyers is organised in this context in order that even the poorest people can benefit from legal advice. The legislation also promotes the development of *Maisons de justice et du droit* where these mediations often take place in practice. As part of the mediation package, the prosecutor has the power to order *compensation judiciaire*, which can be a fine of up to FF10,000, the return of property, the removal of a driving or hunting permit for up to four months, or the carrying out of up to 60 hours of work in the community. Any such order has to be validated by the president of the court.

The Public Prosecutor's Office disposes of different means of instituting criminal proceedings according to the gravity of the offence:

---

[55] Art. 41 of the Code of Criminal Procedure.

- a request for the setting up of a judicial investigation into the case;[56]

- a summons to appear before the trial court, served by the court bailiff.[57] This is the normal procedure for bringing a person before the *tribunal de police*, and it cannot be used for serious offences as a prior judicial investigation is required;

- a notice to attend a court voluntarily.[58] This is not available for the *Cour d'assises*;

- a formal order to attend the *tribunal correctionnel* in relation to a major offence;

- an immediate court attendance (which will take place the same day) before the *tribunal correctionnel* in relation to either a major offence with a maximum sentence of 1 to 7 years which has been subjected to an expedited investigation; or a straight forward case where the maximum sentence is between 2 and 7 years, if it appears that the evidence is sufficient and the case ready to be judged.[59]

A matter that has caused considerable public debate in recent years is that prosecutors have a discretion whether or not to bring a prosecution. They are perfectly entitled to decide that, although an offence has been committed, no further action should be taken. This is because article 40 para. 1 states:

> The senior state prosecutor receives complaints and denunciations and decides the action to be taken.

They may, for example, decide that though a crime has been committed, it is not in the public interest to bring a prosecution as it was a minor offence which posed no real threat to society. A decision to take no further action has no legal effect, in that it does not extinguish the right to bring a prosecution in the future. As a result, if new evidence should come to light or the prosecutor simply realises that their earlier decision was wrong, they can subsequently decide to commence a prosecution. There is no right of appeal against the prosecutor's decision.

At the moment there is little effort to provide any real guidance and direction in the exercise of this discretion. Prosecuting policies are developed at random at a national, regional and local level. At a national level, the Ministry of Justice (particularly its Section for Criminal Matters and the Award of Pardons) issues circulars on the matter, indicating general priorities. Examples are the directive on the prosecution of

---

[56] Art. 80 of the Code of Criminal Procedure.
[57] Art. 394 of the Code of Criminal Procedure.
[58] Art. 388 of the Code of Criminal Procedure.
[59] Art. 395 of the Code of Criminal Procedure.

foreigners of 11 July 1994, and the directive for the centralising of prosecutions involving counterfeit money of 19 February 1997. But there is little supervision of the application of these circulars in practice, and where such control occurs, the Truche Report considered it to be insufficient and sporadic. At the regional level, the senior Public Prosecutors, responsible for 'watching over the application of the criminal law in the whole of the jurisdiction of the Court of Appeal'[60] have 'the same prerogatives as those given to the Minister of Justice'.[61] Relying on these provisions, several local Public Prosecutor's Offices have for some years regularly called their members together with a view to harmonising their prosecuting policies. At a local level, individual Public Prosecutors have consulted with local organisations to determine prosecuting priorities in the area. They can then rely on article 12 of the Code of Criminal Procedure to direct the police on which offences to target.

There are three main justifications for allowing the Prosecutor to have this discretion to decide whether or not to prosecute. Firstly, more and more cases are coming to their attention, due to an increased crime rate, legislation creating more offences, and the development of legal aid which facilitates access to justice. By selecting which cases to prosecute, the Prosecutor reduces delays and their discretion allows them to regulate the flow of cases according to the resources available. Secondly, there are other solutions available beyond the criminal solution to deal with wrongful conduct, such as disciplinary proceedings and mediation. Finally, a decision to prosecute could aggravate public order problems, for example where there has been rioting in a neighbourhood.

However, the use of the decision to take no further action has caused considerable controversy. Public Prosecutors are unusual in that they are both judges and civil servants; they both belong to the professional body of the judiciary and are subordinated to the Minister of Justice. They can receive instructions to prosecute a particular case from the Minister of Justice, though orders not to prosecute are technically excluded.[62] Following the Act of 24 August 1993, such instructions must be written and placed in the file of the case. But the Truche Report comments that in practice less formal communications take place coming from the top to those lower down the hierarchy, which often resemble instructions or are felt to be such. The current Minister of Justice Elisabeth Guigot has decided to repeal the relevant article 36, and in the meantime has promised not to issue individual instructions herself.

It has been felt that the Prosecutors have ordered no further action to be taken in too many cases. In 1995, of 5.2 million crimes formally referred to the prosecutors of the *Tribunaux de grande instance*, 4.2 million (that is to

---

[60] Art. 35 of the Code of Criminal Procedure.
[61] Art. 37 of the Code of Criminal Procedure.
[62] Art. 36 of the Code of Criminal Procedure.

say, 80 per cent) were classified for no further action. This may be acceptable where it has not been possible to trace the author of the offence, but 50% of cases were classified for no further action where there was a named suspect.

In addition, there have been strong suspicions that in ordering no further action in cases that risked causing political embarrassment, Prosecutors have been directly influenced by politicians. Secret interventions have been made by the Ministry of Justice in favour of political friends. Revelations of such practices have seriously discredited both the political class and the judiciary. The Public Prosecutors' subordination to the politicians was highlighted by research carried out by Alain Bancaud and presented at a conference on François Mitterrand in January 1999. This revealed how frequent and routine Mitterrand's interventions were in matters of justice between 1981 and 1984. He did not hesitate to directly intervene in sensitive cases. A confidential note written in June 1981 by a senior member of staff to the President indicated that 'it seems desirable that the President conserves – as he has always done – a minimum of control over what happens in judicial matters'.

The public became increasingly concerned about this behaviour as certain highly remunerative, corrupt practices by politicians and heads of business, involving the siphoning off of public funds, had eventually come to the attention of the legal system. As case after case was classified for no further action, the suspicions of the public were raised. For example, in the Urba scandal, the Public Prosecutor for the court of appeal of Aix-en-Provence contacted the Ministry of Justice on 8 May 1989, to let it know that he was proposing to open an investigation that would look into the financing of the Socialist Party in the south of France. The socialist Minister of Justice of the time, Henri Nallet, has written a book 'Tempête sur la Justice' which discusses this matter. He states that the Ministry of Justice understood that this investigation would have 'unfortunate and unforeseen consequences for a number of political representatives'. He wrote to the Public Prosecutor instructing him to classify the case for no further action to block the investigation. He has justified this decision as being necessary to protect the State. An amnesty law was subsequently passed to avoid a large number of elected people of all political persuasions from being incriminated.

The Longuet scandal concerned the funding of a project organised by Gérard Longuet, a Minister in the Government of Edouard Balladur. The then Minister of Justice, Pierre Méhaignerie, is reported to have said that he would ask the opinion of the Prime Minister to see what course of conduct he would prefer in relation to that criminal investigation.[63] He then delayed by one month the opening of the judicial investigation, by

[63] *Le Monde*, 12 July 1997.

prolonging unnecessarily a preliminary police investigation which had already been completed. This allowed M. Longuet to discreetly resign from office before being charged. He subsequently benefited from a decision that there was no case to answer in this matter.

The Tiberi scandal occurred in 1996 when Jacques Toubon, the then Minister of Justice, learnt that the Public Prosecutor for Evry was preparing to open a judicial investigation on the case of the salary of FF 200,000 received by Xavière Tiberi, the wife of the leading politician, for a report she was supposed to have written. A helicopter was sent to Katmandu, in Nepal, where the senior Public Prosecutor was on holiday, in order to give him a document to sign that would have ordered the inquiry to be limited to an initial police investigation. In fact, the helicopter's mission was unsuccessful as the senior Public Prosecutor had already left when it arrived.

Jean-Claude Bouvier, Pierre Jacquin and Alain Vogelweith have written that in sensitive cases, the Director of Criminal Affairs and Pardons in the Ministry of Justice, Marco Moinard, had oral communications with the relevant Public Prosecutors, in breach of the Code of Criminal Procedure that requires such communications to be in writing. They point out that M. Moinard had in the past also been director of judicial services which is responsible for determining promotions within the judiciary, and claim that he still retains considerable influence over this matter. The authors suggest that he exploited this power to put pressure on the Public Prosecutors to accept his oral communications on what steps to take in relation to a particular case, which the judges' union (*Syndicat de la magistrature*) accept is a very powerful tool in relation to the judiciary.[64] M. Moinard has vigorously contested these accusations, stating that while his Section has always given advice on technical matters, it has never given individual instructions to drop a prosecution, and that in this day and age the Public Prosecutors would not accept such approaches.

It was these mounting suspicions that led to the establishment of the Truche Commission, as suspected abuses of power by politicians to put an end to sensitive prosecutions were undermining the country's respect for the whole legal system. The independence of the judges of the bench was being thrown into doubt due to the fact that they were members of the same professional body as the Public Prosecutors, and also dependent in part on the Ministry of Justice for the progress of their career.

Reform

Michel Jéol, a leading lawyer before the *Cour de cassation*, commented in 1994 'Like the administrative courts and the Eiffel Tower, the Public

---

[64] *Le Monde*, 6 May 1997.

Prosecutor is one of those monstrosities which doubtless one would no longer build today, but which no one can seriously envisage demolishing'.[65] While no government is prepared to abolish the Public Prosecutor altogether, it is likely to undergo significant changes over the next few years. Some have argued that the Prosecutor's discretion should be removed so that a prosecution would have to be brought if an offence appeared to have been committed. This is the approach that applies most strictly to the rule of law and is the practice in Italy and Germany. However, it does not allow for regulating the flow of cases to take into account the availability of resources.

The Truche Report favoured retaining the prosecution discretion, but would place greater restrictions on its exercise. The Report pointed out that the decision to refer a case to an independent and impartial court, which offers the judicial guarantees of a public hearing and reasoned judgements, does not give rise to suspicion. Nor does criminal mediation as this is a negotiated solution which implies the agreement of the parties. It felt that the decision to classify for no further action needed to be surrounded by equivalent guarantees.

Instructions on individual cases from the Ministry of Justice to the Public Prosecutor's Office would be banned, with article 36 being repealed. But it considered that some communications between the Public Prosecutor's Office and the Ministry of Justice needed to remain. These were necessary to ensure that like cases were being treated alike, and to tackle problems arising from particularly sensitive situations, such as those which threatened public order or diplomatic relations. These communications should all be in writing and placed on any criminal files concerned.

The Commission accepted that in a democracy it was the role of the Minister of Justice, as part of the Government, to determine the judicial policy of a country. It therefore felt that it was inappropriate to give the Public Prosecutor's Office complete autonomy from the Ministry of Justice. Instead it favoured allowing the Ministry of Justice, in consultation with other interested ministries, to establish a clear prosecution policy, which would serve to guide the Public Prosecutors in the exercise of their discretion on whether to prosecute. This policy would be the subject of a regular debate before Parliament. In order to assist the government in the development of this policy, the current *ad hoc* feedback provided by the Public Prosecutors should be replaced by two types of formal feedback. Firstly, an annual report provided by the local Public Prosecutor's Offices of the work carried out over the previous year. Secondly, *ad hoc* reports which could be provided automatically or on demand summarising the cases which were being handled at the time by a Public Prosecutor's Office

[65] *Le Monde*, 4 June 1998.

which are of particular interest to the development of the prosecuting policy, and the reasons for any decisions they proposed to take in relation to those cases. While the Truche Report states that no instructions could be issued, the danger is that such a procedure could be used to place pressure on the Prosecutors where there is a high profile defendant, such as a politician. The resulting prosecution policy would be published in the form of circulars in the Official Journal.

The prosecution policy would seek to fix priorities, taking into account the contemporary problems facing society. By placing the exercise of the prosecutor's discretion within a clear framework, its exercise would reflect a coherent and consistent application of the law. Citizens would be treated equally before the law and the accusation of arbitrary decision making would become unfounded. The decision to classify for no further action would have to contain reasons.

In the light of the national prosecution policy, senior Public Prosecutors will hold regular consultation meetings with those interested in the workings of the criminal system in their region, to determine how to apply that policy in the light of the specific needs of the area. For this to work effectively, they recommended that the Prosecutors would need to be evenly distributed around the country, which would require some changes to the locations of the Court of Appeals and some closures.

The Truche Report favoured the establishment of a right to appeal against a decision to classify for no further action. An appeal could be founded on a failure to comply with the national prosecuting policy. It proposed that these appeals be heard by a body composed and designated in a similar way as the *Commission des requêtes* of the *Cour de justice de la République*, though the mandate of its members would not be renewable. The appeal would be open to any interested person, with the exception of those able to act as civil parties. To prevent this body being overworked, it was suggested that it would only be seized through the intermediary of the Public Prosecutor for the *Cour de cassation*, but this restriction could render the appeal process completely ineffective as the Prosecutor could filter out any sensitive cases. The body would be able to undertake its own investigations where appropriate. Should it conclude that a prosecution was necessary it would be able to order the Prosecutor to act. Should it conclude that the original decision was correct this would stand, unless new evidence should arise within the time limits for the bringing of a prosecution.

In the context of a reinforced statutory independence of the Public Prosecutor and a strengthened *Conseil supérieur de la magistrature*, the Truche Report would allow the link between the Public Prosecutor's Office and the executive to remain.

As the law currently stands, the Minister of Justice cannot directly seize the criminal court, but can only act through the intermediary of the Public Prosecutor. The Truche Report recommended that where a case had been classified for no further action, the Minister of Justice would be able to seize either the court overseeing the judicial investigation or the trial court. The Minister would be represented by a lawyer.

The proposals of the Truche Commission in relation to the independence of the Public Prosecutor have essentially been accepted by the Government and in 1998 they prepared a Bill to be presented to Parliament which encapsulated their main proposals on the subject. In particular, it would abolish individual instructions on cases, while seeking to strengthen the development of general guidance on prosecution policy. The Government originally intended that this would be done through 'directives' but, following criticism, it changed this to circulars laying down 'general orientations'. These circulars would be more detailed than in the past and would state, for example, whether criminal mediation should be developed, prosecutions for the use of drugs should be pursued, or the fight against street crime should be prioritised. These orientations, which would be made public, would be the object, every year, of a debate in Parliament. The links between the Public Prosecutor and the Ministry of Justice would, in this respect, be made tighter. Originally it was suggested that a failure to follow these general instructions would constitute a disciplinary fault, but in the light of heavy criticism this proposal has been withdrawn.

Controversially, the proposed Bill would give the Minister a new power, described as a 'right of action'. This would allow the Minister, when the general interest so required, to start a prosecution by seizing the competent court. The *Conseil Supérieur de la Magistrature* has argued that the power of the Minister to open a prosecution after the Public Prosecutor has refused to do so would undermine the position of the latter. It would also make it very difficult for the Public Prosecutor to make independent decisions on the subsequent prosecution as whatever they did would be seen as showing either obstinacy or submission. Initially it had also been proposed that the Minister would have the power to replace the Prosecutor by, for example, ordering a person to be placed in detention on remand, but this latter proposal has been abandoned in the face of heavy criticism. The proposal as it stands still leads to a confusion between the executive authority and the judicial authority, which the reform was aimed to put an end to but which would instead find itself symbolically reinforced. The Minister of Justice up to now hardly appears in the Code of Criminal Procedure, but through this legislation his role would be reaffirmed. Madame Delmas-Marty, a leading criminal law academic, has commented that the Government appears to be taking back with one hand what they abandoned with the other. She has pointed out that while in

England Attorney Generals do have a right to start proceedings, they are not a member of the Cabinet and their powers are limited to a narrow range of very serious offences.[66]

The Public Prosecutor's Office would remain hierarchised and the Public Prosecutors would continue to be placed 'under the direction and control of their hierarchical heads and under the authority of the Minister of Justice', according to the formula of the statute of 1958.

The Public Prosecutor would keep the power to classify a case for no further action, but they would in the future have to give reasons for their decision. Individuals who could not act as civil parties, but showed a sufficient interest in the case, would have the right to contest such an order, and ultimately a power to apply to a Commission of Appeals made up of several judges from the Public Prosecutor's Offices attached to the court of appeals. If an abusive appeal was made the individual could be heavily fined.

In Parliament some MPs expressed their concern that the removal of the controls by the politicians over the Public Prosecutors would give too much power to the judges, and a return to the bad old days before the Revolution, an interpretation which the Prime Minister, Lionel Jospin, has not hesitated to mock.[67] However, the Bill was successfully opposed in Parliament, though the Government hopes to re-introduce this legislation at a later date.

The civil action

The prosecution can be initiated not only by the Public Prosecutor's Office, but also by the victim or their legal representatives when they bring a civil action for damages before the criminal courts (art. 2 and 3). There are two ways in which this can be done. Firstly, they can issue a summons to a known suspect to attend a trial court. This will be served by the process server and is possible for minor or major offences where a judicial investigation is only discretionary. Secondly, they can make a complaint to an investigating judge. This procedure will be used where there is no known suspect or where a judicial investigation is either compulsory (see below) or felt to be useful on the basis of the facts.

If the criminal prosecution has already been commenced, the victim, or their representative, can simply add their civil claim for damages. They can do this either orally or in writing during the judicial investigation, or at the trial hearing before the Public Prosecutor has presented the oral submissions. Such an application cannot be made at an appeal.

---

[66] *Le Monde,* 16 April 1998.
[67] *Le Monde,* 22 June 1999.

To be able to commence civil proceedings the individual must have suffered a personal and direct harm – including psychological harm – as a result of the offence. Where a crime causes no harm to an individual, but simply endangers public order, such as possession of a drug or a forbidden weapon, only a Public Prosecutor will be able to initiate the prosecution, as there will be no right to bring a civil action.

Should the victim die, their heirs can act in their personal capacity or as the legal successor. If the victim dies without having started proceedings, they can bring the action in their capacity as heirs for both the material and psychological harm suffered by the victim.[68]

There is always the option of bringing the civil action before the civil courts,[69] though once the civil court has been chosen, the case cannot be withdrawn and presented to a criminal court.[70] The advantages of bringing the civil action before a criminal court are that this can be cheaper, simpler and quicker; the private claimant can benefit from the evidence gathered by the Public Prosecutor's Office or by the investigating judge; and it avoids the risk of conflicting judgements from the civil and criminal courts, as an award of damages will only normally be made if the defendant is found guilty. Unlike the public prosecution, which can only be brought against the principal offender and accomplices of the crime, the civil action can also be brought against their heirs and third parties bearing civil liability for the principal offender and accomplices, such as their parents. A disadvantage is that the private claimant, being a party in the criminal proceedings, cannot be heard as a witness. As the victim would frequently be the principal prosecution witness, this can considerably weaken the prosecution case, leading to acquittals which could otherwise have been avoided.

Should the exercise of the independent action for damages be found to have been abusive or time wasting, its author can be ordered to pay a fine.[71]

Though the private claimant may have started the prosecution, once commenced it is the Public Prosecutor's Office that is responsible for continuing that prosecution, and the private claimant has very little influence over it. If the Public Prosecutor's Office decides that the prosecution is ill founded, it can call for a finding of no case to answer by the investigating judge or for an acquittal by the trial court. Civil parties can only exert a limited influence over the prosecution. They can ask the investigating judge to carry out certain investigations or demand the annulment of acts which breached the law.[72] They are notified of any

---

[68] Crim. 30 avril 1976.
[69] Art. 4 of the Code of Criminal Procedure.
[70] Art. 5 of the Code of Criminal Procedure.
[71] Art. 91 and 392–1 of the Code of Criminal Procedure.
[72] Art. 89–1 of the Code of Criminal Procedure.

important decisions that have been made in relation to the case,[73] and sometimes have a right to appeal against such decisions.[74]

The judicial investigation

The key practical difference between the police investigation and the judicial investigation is that the investigators are given greater coercive powers, such as to place a person on remand in custody or to tap telephones. A judicial investigation can only take place once a prosecution has been commenced. There are only two possible ways that a judicial investigation can be opened: either following a request from the Public Prosecutor's Office;[75] or, alternatively, and less frequently, through an application by the victim or their representative for damages to be determined by the criminal courts.[76] The investigating judge can refuse to open a judicial investigation and issue a decision to this effect where it is evident from the documentation that no offence has been committed or that the prosecution is inadmissible.[77]

The judicial investigation seeks to build on the work undertaken during the police investigation, in an effort to discover the truth and determine whether the case should be referred for trial. It is compulsory in relation to serious offences[78] and discretionary for all other offences. In practice it is only used in about 10 per cent of all cases, and only very exceptionally for minor offences. For a major offence, a Public Prosecutor will tend to request a judicial investigation where particular measures purely open to the investigating judge prove to be indispensable. This will be the case where expert reports are required, investigations need to be carried out abroad, or a warrant for arrest needs to be issued for a fugitive suspect. In 1995, only 7.3 per cent of cases submitted to the *Tribunaux correctionnel* were preceded by a judicial investigation. While statistically such cases are rare, these are actually the most important ones due to their gravity, complexity, international nature or threat to social order.

This stage of the criminal procedure is directed by the investigating judge. This judge is a member of the bench and is nominated to their position for three years.[79] There is no equivalent to these judges in the English and Welsh system. They do not decide the guilt or innocence of the accused, this is done by the trial court. When making judicial decisions,

---

[73] Art. 183 of the Code of Criminal Procedure.
[74] Art. 186 of the Code of Criminal Procedure.
[75] Art. 80 of the Code of Criminal Procedure.
[76] Art. 51 of the Code of Criminal Procedure.
[77] Art. 87 of the Code of Criminal Procedure.
[78] Art. 79 of the Code of Criminal Procedure.
[79] Art. 50 of the Code of Criminal Procedure.

such as whether or not to award bail, the investigating judge is technically sitting as a court. They are competent where the crime, the suspect's residence, the arrest or the detention takes place within their jurisdiction,[80] and such cases are allocated to them by the president of the *Tribunal de grande instance*. Usually a single investigating judge works alone, but where a case is particularly serious or complex, additional investigating judges can be attached to the case.[81] For example, four additional investigating judges have been attached to the inquiry into the collapse of Crédit Lyonnais. Some of these investigating judges have become extremely well known by the public due to the high profile cases they have been responsible for. This is particularly true of the eleven judges in the specialist financial section of the Public Prosecutor's Office in Paris, including Judge Eva Joly who has been in charge of the investigations into Crédit Lyonnais and Elf Aquitaine.

The role of the investigating judges is firstly to watch over the regularity of investigations carried out in their name, to prevent abuse of the broad coercive powers available at this stage. In addition to their role of investigator, the investigating judge also technically acts as a court of first instance when taking judicial decisions, such as whether to refer a person's case to a trial court. These judicial decisions are then controlled by the formation of the Court of Appeal which used to be known as the *Chambre d'accusation*, but which was renamed by the Act of 15 June 2000[82] as the *Chambre de l'instruction*, to reflect the legislative efforts to strengthen the presumption of innocence.

The original *Code d'instruction criminelle* of 1808 had conceived the procedure of judicial investigation as an inquisitorial process, being written (all the acts of the judicial investigation and all the decisions which it gave rise to were, and still are, collected in the file) and taking place out of the public's view and without automatically allowing the parties to present their case. But in recent years elements of the adversarial procedure have been introduced. For example, the person charged and the victim who has commenced a civil action before the criminal courts can be kept informed of the procedure by their lawyer who is informed of the contents of the file at all times.

The request to investigate may either refer to a suspect by name, or where the police investigation has not found a clear suspect, it will be left to the investigating judge to identify the offender. A judicial investigation is required in practice if the author of the crime is unknown. Where the suspect is referred to by name the judicial investigation must commence with that person being formally charged,[83] that is to say the person is

---

[80] Art. 52 and 663 of the Code of Criminal Procedure.
[81] Art. 83 of the Code of Criminal Procedure.
[82] Art. 83 of the Act of 15 June 2000.
[83] Art. 80 of the Code of Criminal Procedure.

formally designated as the probable author of the offence. A person can be charged when there exists significant evidence suggesting they participated in the offence.[84] Once a person has been charged they can be represented by a lawyer, who will be allowed to see the file on the case.

The Truche Report has suggested that the presumption of innocence would be better protected if the decision to charge were delayed, with the investigating judges relying in the meantime on the legislative provisions allowing them to hear the interested parties as witnesses in the presence of a lawyer who has access to the file.[85] The Act of 15 June 2000 has adopted these recommendations regarding 'represented witnesses'.[86] There is no appeal against a decision to charge, and the Truche Commission does not recommend that one should be introduced.

Investigating judges aim to discover the objective truth, rather than the guilt of the particular suspect. A social investigation destined to shed light on the personality of the offender is compulsory for serious offences, it is simply discretionary for major offences.[87] This involves looking at the suspect's personality, sometimes through a psychologist's examination, and the environment where they live.

Investigating judges can only investigate the criminal conduct referred to in the request or complaint. They cannot extend their investigation to other criminal acts. If they discover such acts during the investigation, they must inform the Prosecutor. If the latter considers it appropriate, he can instruct an investigating judge, through a supplementary order, to widen the field of their investigations. The Truche report has proposed that if the Prosecutor refused to extend the jurisdiction of the investigating judge an appeal could be made to the new body that it has recommended should be set up to hear appeals of a Prosecutor's decision to take no further action, as such a refusal can also give rise to suspicion.

By contrast, investigating judges are not bound to limit their investigation to the people referred to in the order or complaint; they can extend the charge to all those who appear to them to have participated in the criminal conduct of which they are seized.

According to article 81 of the Code of Criminal Procedure:

> The investigating judge carries out, in accordance with the law, all acts of investigation that he considers useful for the establishing of the truth.

These judges have wide powers. They can visit the scene of the crime,[88] carry out a reconstruction of the offence (when the accused and their

---

[84] Art. 80 of the Code of Criminal Procedure.
[85] Art. 104 and 105 of the Code of Criminal Procedure.
[86] *les témoins assistés.*
[87] Art. 81 para. 6 of the Code of Criminal Procedure.
[88] Art. 92 of the Code of Criminal Procedure.

lawyer will normally be present), hear witnesses, search and seize property, arrest the person charged and, most importantly, place them on remand in custody,[89] or release them on bail with conditions imposed.[90] The main conditions applied aim to prevent the suspect from becoming a fugitive, for example by imposing that they must not go outside a fixed geographical area.

The investigating judge can interrogate the parties and the judge cannot end the investigation without having questioned the suspect, unless they conclude there is no case to answer. To avoid abuse of the right to interrogate, this process is now regulated by articles 114 onwards of the Code of Criminal Procedure.

Following the Act of 24 August 1993, article 114 provides that the suspect and the private claimant have access to the file four days before any questioning. After the first interrogation, the file is always available to their lawyer, provided it does not cause too much disruption to the judicial investigator's office, and the lawyer can provide a copy to their client. At any stage of the judicial investigation, the Public Prosecutor's Office can demand to see the file on the case and request an investigating judge to carry out any acts which it considers would be useful for the revelation of the truth and to take all necessary security measures.[91] Following the Act of 15 June 1998, a person charged and the civil parties can ask the investigating judge to carry out 'any act that they consider necessary for the revelation of the truth'. The investigating judge can agree or not to these requests, but their decision is subject to the control of the *Chambre de l'instruction*.

Telephone tapping

An order can be issued for telephones to be tapped, something that cannot be carried out during a police investigation. A distinction must be drawn between telephone tapping during a judicial investigation for the detection and investigation of crime, and that by the administration for reasons of security – national security, the prevention of terrorism and the prevention of organised crime. The latter are authorised by the Prime Minister and controlled by a national Commission for security inter-ceptions. These have been the subject of some controversy as it appears Mitterrand ordered the telephones of his political rivals to be intercepted. Here we are concerned with telephone tapping carried out during a judicial investigation. In the past there was no legislation controlling this activity, but the Act of 10 July 1991 now regulates this important

---

[89] Art. 144 to 148 of the Code of Criminal Procedure.
[90] Art. 138 of the Code of Criminal Procedure.
[91] Art. 82 para.1 of the Code of Criminal Procedure.

infringement of a person's right to privacy, whose provisions are found in article 100 onwards of the Code of Criminal Procedure.

Two conditions have to be satisfied to be able to tap a telephone:

• the maximum sentence of the offence investigated must be for at least two years;

• the measure is necessary, in other words traditional means of investigation are insufficient.

To tap the line of an *avocat* the investigating judge must inform the president of the local bar, and to tap the phone of an MP or a senator the president of their House of Parliament must be informed.[92]

The decision to allow a telephone to be tapped is valid for four months and is renewable. It is not considered to be of a judicial nature, and therefore there is no right of appeal. Any recordings of conversations must be placed under seal and communications which are useful to the investigation will be transcribed as affidavits.

Criticism of the judicial investigation process

One difficulty facing investigating judges is that it is impossible for them to carry out most of the investigative procedures themselves. Instead, they have to delegate this activity to police officers, over whom they have no direct control. While investigating judges can fix the time limits for the execution of their orders by the police,[93] the Truche Report points out that they cannot ensure that such orders are fully complied with. Given that the police are answerable to either the Minister of the Interior or the Minister of Justice, the Truche Report suggests that this position feeds the suspicion that the judiciary are dependent on politicians. There is also a danger that the police will communicate information about an investigation in breach of the principle of secrecy.

The conflicts that can result from the dependency of the investigating judge on the police was highlighted by the case of Olivier Foll, who is at the head of the criminal investigation police in Paris. Eric Halphen was an investigating judge who was carrying out a judicial investigation into corrupt practices involving council flats in Paris. As part of this investigation he decided to carry out a search of the home of Jean Tiberi who was both an MP and the mayor of Paris. Jean Tiberi was suspected of having given his son a council flat at a low rent and then arranging for it to be renovated at vast expense to the State. Eric Halphen asked for the assistance of three police officers to carry out the search without specifying the nature of the operation. Once they arrived at the building, the judge

---

[92]   Art. 100–7 of the Code of Criminal Procedure.
[93]   Art. 151 of the Code of Criminal Procedure.

informed the police what he wanted them to do. The police officers telephoned Olivier Foll, who ordered them not to participate in the search. Olivier Foll was subsequently condemned by the *Chambre d'accusation*[94] for failing to carry out his duties as a senior police officer and, thereby, obstructing the course of justice. As punishment it forbade him from carrying out the functions of a senior police officer for the next six months. His appeal was dismissed by the *Cour de cassation* on 26 February 1997. Though he was temporarily not allowed to exercise the functions of a senior police officer, he was not removed from his position as director of the investigating police in Paris, so to members of the public his punishment seemed rather hollow.

One solution would be to place a certain number of investigators directly under investigating judges for particularly sensitive cases. This has been done in Italy for the investigation of Mafia-related offences. The Truche Report favoured experimenting with improvements to the current system, and considered that only if these failed should more radical solutions such as these be resorted to. It proposed that within the Ministry of Defence and the Ministry of Home Affairs a judge should work alongside the chief police administrator, in order to ensure the political independence of the police when carrying out investigations. The position of chief police administrator would also be open to a judge. They recommended that there should be judges among the teaching personnel for police training to encourage tighter links between the two. On being accepted to the profession, the police should be made to take an oath promising to respect human rights and the secrecy of investigations and to carry out investigations according to the Code of Criminal Procedure. Where there is an incident that gives rise to an inquiry, it should be headed by a judge and judges should form part of the team of inspectors.

The judicial investigation tends to be slow. On average this procedure will take fifteen months to complete and certain investigations take over three years. Some investigating judges have complained that they suffer from a lack of resources, particularly in relation to financial crime.[95] Until the 1980s, financial corruption involving state funds was rarely prosecuted. From 1984 to 1994 the number of convictions for corruption and abuse of power increased from 44 to 104. In relation to abuse of public funds, the number increased by over 50 per cent, passing from 198 in 1990 to 310 in 1994. It has been argued that the rise in large cases, such as that of Crédit Lyonnais, requires an increase in funding for the investigators to confront the challenge. It has also been suggested that more specialist training should be provided for investigating judges working in this field, due to their particular complexity.

---

[94] now known as *La chambre de l'instruction*: art. 83 of the Act of 15 June 2000.
[95] *Le Monde*, 15 November 1997.

Remand in custody

The basic principle is that a suspect must remain free until they have been convicted, and an order to place them in custody must be the exception.[96] Article 137 of the Code of Criminal Procedure[97] states:

> The person charged, presumed innocent, remains free. However, he can be subjected to conditional bail where this is necessary for the judicial investigation or as a security measure. When this is insufficient with respect to these objectives, he can, exceptionally, be placed on remand.[98]

A person can only be placed on remand in custody where they are accused of a serious or major offence. Where they are accused of a major offence the maximum sentence must be at least three years or, except where the person has already been convicted to at least one year's imprisonment, five years for property offences.[99] In addition it must be shown that detention is the sole means of:

- preserving the evidence, stopping pressure being placed on a victim or witness, or avoiding communications taking place between suspects and their accomplices;
- protecting suspects, guaranteeing their availability to the courts, putting an end to the crime or preventing its repetition;
- putting an end to persistent and exceptional public disorder caused by the seriousness of the offence, the circumstances of its commission or the importance of the harm which it has caused. However, this ground cannot justify an extension of the remand period unless the maximum sentence for the offence is at least ten years.[100]

Suspects can also be placed in custody where they have breached their bail conditions. While one of these conditions may be satisfied when a person is first placed on remand, with time this may cease to be the case, for example there may no longer be a risk of public disorder, at which point the person should be released on bail.

Until recently, investigating judges had the power to remand suspects in custody during the whole or part of the judicial investigation. There were, however, concerns that these judges were placing too many people

---

[96] Art. 137 of the Code of Criminal Procedure.
[97] As amended by the Act of 15 June 2000.
[98] '*La personne mise en examen, présumée innocente, rest libre. Toutefois, en raison des nécessités de l'instruction ou à titre de mesure de sûreté, elle peut être astreinte à une ou plusieurs obligations du contrôle judiciaire. Lorsque celles-ci se révèlent insuffisantes au regard de ces objectifs, elle peut, à titre exceptionnel, être placée en détention provisoire.*'
[99] Art. 143–1 and 144 of the Code of Criminal Procedure.
[100] Art. 144 of the Code of Criminal Procedure.

on remand. On average, 44 per cent of the prison population is made up of remand prisoners. In 1995, 23,979 people were placed on remand, while 18,042 were given bail by the investigating judge. For 30 years its average duration has increased: in 1970 to 1995 it went from 2.1 months to more than 4 months, and in 1996 32.5 people were being held on remand for every 100,000 inhabitants. Today France holds more people on remand than most of its European neighbours despite the fact that it has a comparable rate of criminal activity. Statistics of the Council of Europe show that in 1996 the only countries of Western Europe which had higher levels than those of France were Moldavia, Poland, Portugal, and Turkey. These figures are all the more worrying as remand in custody goes against the presumption of innocence and increases the likelihood of a conviction.

Concerns existed that investigating judges had too much power. They were accused of abusing their powers, by placing a suspect on remand in custody to put pressure on them to provide a confession, despite the fact that this was not included within the grounds legally permitted for making such an order. It has been suggested that this was the case for M. Miara, who was a suspect placed on remand in custody during the investigation of the high profile Elf Aquitaine affair, involving the misuse of large amounts of public funds.[101] The research carried out for the Royal Commission for Criminal Justice in 1993 in the United Kingdom also considered that the legislative terms were too widely drafted. The research pointed in particular to the broad interpretation that was possible for the third condition concerned with 'public disorder' and the Act of 15 June 2000 has tried to tighten up this last condition.

Reform of the remand procedure has been a recurrent feature of the political agenda since 1789, and there has been considerable legislation on the subject under the fifth Republic. Since the two main laws of 1970 and 1975 establishing conditional bail and obliging judges to give reasons for their decisions to place on remand, Parliament has not ceased to re-consider the question: the rules on remand were changed in 1984, 1985, 1987, 1989, 1993 and 1996. Two of these laws, the Act of Badinter of 1985 and the Act of Chalandon of 1987, were repealed before they were even brought into force. These two Acts would have given the decision to hold on remand to three judges rather than a single judge, but these Acts were both repealed before being implemented due to a lack of resources. The Act of 4 January 1993 conferred for several months the decision to place someone on remand in custody on a judge belonging to the bench,[102] but this Act was repealed on 24 August 1993.

The Truche Commission proposed that the powers of the investigating judge should be restricted. It pointed out that the presumption of innocence needs to be respected first and foremost by the judiciary. In-

---

[101] *Le Monde*, 29 December 1997.
[102] *le juge délégué*.

vestigating judges have to gather evidence of a crime without presuming guilt. They have to search as much for what proves as for what disproves the guilt of the suspect. This presumption does not cease until an official declaration of guilt by a court. But, for example, when an order is made to place someone on remand in custody, this may suppose that there is already proof that the suspect committed the crime where the person is to be detained 'to put an end to the offence or to prevent its renewal'.[103] It recommended that the power to place on remand in custody should be conferred to a collegial body of three judges which would not include the investigating judge and which would hear cases in public. This body would also consider applications contesting the regularity of a procedural act, the duration of the criminal process and a refusal to carry out certain acts of investigation. We have seen that the creation of a collegial body had been accepted by Parliament in the past, but then abandoned for lack of resources. The Commission also favoured restricting the use of the public order criteria for allowing remand in custody, to where the maximum sentence for the relevant offence was more than three years' imprisonment.

The Act of 15 June 2000 has now removed the power to detain on remand from the jurisdiction of the investigating judge and given it to a new judge, called the *juge des libertés et de la détention*. He or she will be a senior member of the judiciary. The decision of whether or not to place someone on remand or release them from remand will be taken after a public hearing where all parties will have an opportunity to put their case on the matter, unless the judge has to hold it in private due to the requirements of the investigation or the risk of attack on a third party.[104]

The reduction in the powers of the investigating judges has been seen by some as a cynical move to punish them for having revealed, in the recent scandals, the failings of a section of the ruling class. It has been argued that there is no reason why the new judges should be any more effective at protecting liberties than their predecessors, and that in fact the best person to decide the question of remand is the one who knows the case best – who will inevitably be the investigating judge. Indeed, faced with the complexity of certain files, the delegated judge that was established in 1993 was sometimes content to simply accept the advice of the investigating judge.[105] In Marseilles, during this brief experiment with the delegated judge, only 7 per cent of requests to place on remand in custody were refused, though often the investigating judge exercised a form of self-censure, hesitating to submit cases which would have been

---

[103] Art. 144 of the Code of Criminal Procedure.
[104] Art. 145 of the Code of Criminal Procedure.
[105] *Le Monde*, 30 October 1997.

contested. In any case, the reform will require an increase in the number of judges, and the provision in the 1998 budget for the creation of 70 additional judges may not prove to be sufficient.

An application to appeal against an order to place someone on remand must be submitted by the end of the next day, and this has the effect of suspending the order. The appeal is heard by the *Chambre de l'instruction*. It is possible to ask the president of this court to hear the application within three days. If the president considers that the conditions of article 144 have been satisfied then the matter will be sent to a full hearing of the *Chambre de l'instruction* to rule on the matter.[106]

The detention cannot exceed a reasonable length of time given the gravity and the complexity of the case and is limited to six months for major offences.[107] An application to be released can be submitted at any time. After one year for serious criminal matters, the rejection of the application to be released must contain specific reasons for the continuation of the judicial investigation and state its probable duration.[108] Investigating judges are not bound to indicate the nature of the investigations which they intend to carry out when such a revelation might jeopardise their success.[109]

A person can be refused a right to communicate with people outside the prison for a maximum of 20 days. After a month the detainee can only be refused the right to a visit from a member of their family if this refusal is necessary for the judicial investigation and the investigating judge issues a written decision to this effect.[110]

Detention on remand creates a right to damages when the suspicions which had given rise to it prove to be completely ill-founded.[111] The Act of 30 December 1996 repealed the requirement of a loss 'manifestly abnormal and of a particular gravity', leaving simply a requirement to prove harm. The award of damages is made by a decision of a president of a court of appeal.[112]

The closing order

Once the investigating judge has carried out all the acts of investigation

---

[106] Art. 187 of the Code of Criminal Procedure.

[107] Art. 144–1 of the Code of Criminal Procedure

[108] Art. 145–3 of the Code of Criminal Procedure, as amended by the Act of 30 December 1996.

[109] Art. 145–1 and 145–2 of the Code of Criminal Procedure.

[110] Art. 145–4 of the Code of Criminal Procedure.

[111] Art. 149 of the Code of Criminal Procedure as amended by art. 70 of the Act of 15 June 2000.

[112] The Act of 15 June 2000 removed this power from the *Commission Nationale près la Cour de cassation*.

that could be useful in revealing the truth, he or she issues a closing order which brings the investigation to an end.[113] This order states either that the case should be transferred for trial or that there is no case to answer when the judge feels that it is inappropriate to proceed with the prosecution.[114] Of the 63,942 people who had been subjected to a judicial investigation and whose cases came to an end in 1995, 7,801 (12.2 per cent) benefited from a ruling that there was insufficient evidence to proceed. If the case concerns a serious criminal offence it is not automatically transferred to the *Cour d'assises*. Instead, the file is sent to the Public Prosecutor who asks the *Chambre de l'instruction* to examine it, to decide whether to go ahead with the transfer or not.[115] The *Chambre de l'instruction* exercises judicial control over the work carried out by the investigating judge. It can refer the case to the *Cour d'assises* if it finds that there is sufficient evidence to support the charges and that the earlier procedure was complete and lawful. The referral will be not only for the serious offence itself, but also for other offences which are linked to it.[116]

To reduce the length of judicial investigations, the Truche Commission recommended that after a fixed period a trial court must automatically be seized for a public hearing. Only this trial court would be able to order the continuation of the judicial investigation if it felt it had insufficient evidence before it to judge the case.

The trial

At the trial the judge often simply rubber stamps the findings of the pre-trial investigation, while in England and Wales all decisions as to both fact and law are made at the trial itself where the parties present their own version of events. While the first stage of the criminal procedure takes place outside the court system, both the second and third stages have their own hierarchy within the court system.

First instance criminal trial courts

There are three courts of general jurisdiction: the *Tribunal de police*, the *Tribunal correctionnel* and the *Cour d'assises*. These have jurisdiction to hear criminal cases depending on the gravity of the offence.

---

[113] Art. 175 of the Code of Criminal Procedure.
[114] Art. 177 of the Code of Criminal Procedure.
[115] Art. 181 of the Code of Criminal Procedure.
[116] Art. 214 of the Code of Criminal Procedure.

The Tribunal de police

All minor offences, known as *contraventions*, are heard by a *Tribunal de police*, which is a special formation of the *Tribunal d'instance*. This court has limited sentencing powers, it cannot impose a prison sentence and the maximum fine it can impose is FF20,000. There is no right of appeal against conviction for the most minor offences, but both the accused and the Prosecutor have a right of appeal in other cases.

The Tribunal correctionnel

Major offences, known as *délits*, are heard by the *Tribunal correctionnel*, which is a special formation of the *Tribunal de grande instance*. It can impose fines of FF25,000 or above and can order imprisonment. The more serious offences must be tried by three judges.[117] A number of less important offences (about half of cases heard) must normally be tried by a single judge.[118] These include many traffic offences, the misuse of credit cards or cheques, and the possession of soft drugs.

To cope with complex cases involving business and financial matters, legislation[119] provides for such matters to be tried in a specialised division of certain designated *Tribunaux de grande instance*. These divisions operate in practice as separate courts, but the French legal system is wary of establishing special courts to deal with particular categories of crime. Precedents, mostly connected with periods of unrest, such as the fight for Algerian independence, have acquired a poor reputation. Nonetheless, considerable press interest and the character of the persons involved have made some of the investigating judges attached to these divisions into celebrities.

The Cour d'assises

The most serious offences, known as *'crimes'*, are tried in the *Cour d'assises*. It has the power to impose life imprisonment. This is the only court that uses a jury, which was introduced by the law of 16–26 September 1791. This was inspired by the practice in the United Kingdom, though it has developed in a unique way.

There is one *Cour d'assises* in each department,[120] though it does not usually have its own buildings but tends to share premises with the court of appeal or the *Tribunal de grande instance* in the department's chief town. The court has jurisdiction to hear a case when the defendant either lives in the department where the court is situated, or committed the crime or was

---

[117] Art. 398–3 of the Code of Criminal Procedure.
[118] Art. 398 of the Code of Criminal Procedure.
[119] Art. 704 of the Code of Criminal Procedure.
[120] Art. 232 of the Code of Criminal Procedure.

arrested in that department. It sits in sessions normally of 15 days duration, so that jurors are not prevented from carrying out their usual occupations for too long. In Paris the court sits nearly continuously, but in other towns it only convenes once a quarter.

The court has a president and judges known as *assesseurs* whose work is assisted by a jury. The jurors are French citizens complying with certain minimal qualifications, and are chosen at random.

Specialised criminal courts

A number of specialised courts exist which have the jurisdiction to judge the President of the Republic if he or she is suspected of high treason, and members of the government suspected of committing offences. Specialised courts exist to try members of the armed forces and minors. Young people also have the benefit of a specialised criminal system. Serious crimes committed by young persons aged 16 or 17 are tried in a special juvenile formation of the *Cour d'assises*. This follows a similar procedure to that for adults though they are not always open to the public. There are restrictions on the members of the public who are allowed to attend: even the minor can be excluded and simply be represented by their lawyer. Custodial sentences are lighter but similar to adult sentences.

Where the juvenile formation of the *Cour d'assises* does not have jurisdiction, the court system for criminal charges against young people under the age of 18 runs parallel to that for adults, and uses the same court buildings. The adult system has been carefully adapted for young people, except for very minor offences tried in the police court, where there is no special procedure. Following an investigation, the judge can refer the matter to trial or can decide to deal with the case outside the courts and pronounce a non-custodial sentence such as a warning or a supervision order.

The court hearing

The procedural rules applied to the trial proceedings are generally the same for all criminal courts, except the *Cour d'assises* which will be discussed below.

Criminal trials are relatively short. Cases are generally heard by a minimum of three judges to reduce the risk of judicial error, bias and corruption. With a view to saving money, there is an increasing number of exceptions to this general principle. A single judge in the *Tribunal de police* can hear all minor offences. Though three judges may officially be allocated a case in the *Tribunal correctionnel*, in practice frequently only one judge will study the file in detail. The law also provides for certain major offences to be tried by a single judge, the matter is regulated by article 398–1 of the Code of Criminal Procedure.

If there is a suspicion of bias a judge can be challenged[121] and transferred from a case where there is a legitimate suspicion that he will not be impartial.[122] Failure to verify an accusation of bias constitutes a violation of article 6 of the European Convention, which protects the right to a fair trial. Such a violation of the European Convention was found to have occurred in the case of *Rémilly v France* where the *Cour d'assises* refused to act upon a suggestion of racism.

The Code of Criminal Procedure, like the Code of 1808, organises the hearing in accordance with the adversarial model. It bears the three fundamental characteristics of such a system, as it is public, oral and with a due hearing of the parties. The judges are not, therefore, allowed to pronounce judgement after simply reading the file, they must have first gained a personal experience of the human reality of the parties and witnesses at the trial. Though the hearing is primarily oral,[123] it is centred around the written file prepared during the earlier investigations. If a public hearing would cause public disorder or be harmful to public morals, the court can order that the matter be heard *in camera*.[124] For serious sexual offences involving torture and inhumane acts, the private claimant can request for the case to be heard *in camera*. In other cases the public can be excluded provided the private claimant does not object. The court hearing cannot be filmed or recorded,[125] except, for example, to keep archives of important judicial cases. Thus, the trial of Maurice Papon for crimes against humanity in 1998 (discussed on p. 135) was recorded.

In accordance with article 6.3 of the European Convention the parties have a right to be represented by a lawyer. The *Cour de cassation* has acknowledged the constitutional nature of the right to a defence lawyer.[126] The defendant must be represented before the *Cour d'assises*, for minors and for those suffering from an infirmity preventing them from defending themselves.[127]

Following a recommendation made in 1990 by the Commission on Criminal Justice and the Rights of Man, presided over by the leading criminal law academic Mme Delmas-Marty, the Act of 15 June 2000 inserted an express reference to the presumption of innocence in article 1 of the the Code of Criminal Procedure. It can also be found in article 6 of the European Convention on Human Rights of 1950 and article 9 of the Declaration of the Rights of Man of 1789.

---

[121] Art. 668 of the Code of Criminal Procedure.
[122] Art. 662 of the Code of Criminal Procedure.
[123] Art. 427 of the Code of Criminal Procedure.
[124] Art. 306 of the Code of Criminal Procedure.
[125] Art. 308 of the Code of Criminal Procedure.
[126] Crim. 30 juin 1995.
[127] Art. 114 and 274 of the Code of Criminal Procedure.

Because of the presumption of innocence, the burden of proof rests with the prosecution, though the defence must prove the existence of a defence. Occasionally presumptions of law exist where defendants are presumed to have committed the offence unless they prove the contrary. For example, following public concern that gangs of children were being ~~ouraged~~ by their parents to commit street robberies, if children ~~ally~~ commit property offences, the parents will be presumed to be ~~~ior handling.[128]

All evidence legally obtained is, in principle, admissible. If someone claims to have been physically abused in police custody, the Court of Strasbourg has stated that the burden of proof is on the State to show that this is untrue. The trial judge will be given details of the defendant's criminal record to determine both questions of sentencing and guilt. The Truche Commission justified this approach as allowing the court to fully understand the person on trial, but the English courts would normally exclude such evidence as being dangerously prejudicial to the defendant. For serious offences and some major offences, the court will also be provided with information on the personality of the accused, and their family or social background.[129]

The judges take an active role throughout the hearing, with the president responsible for directing proceedings. There is no system for the entering of a guilty plea. The full investigation and trial automatically take place, regardless of whether the accused has confessed. The Truche Report considered whether it would be desirable to introduce a system of guilty pleas, where defendants would get a sentence reduction for entering a guilty plea, as is the case in Anglo-Saxon systems. The benefit would be a reduction in costs and delay, but the Report rejected this proposal because they considered that it undermined the principle that the burden of proof was on the prosecution. They also feared that suspects might later retract the confession, having already prevented a full investigation from taking place.

The hearing normally starts with the cross-examination of the defendant. The evidence is presented by the reading of statements and the hearing of witnesses. Witnesses must swear on oath to say 'the truth, nothing but the truth'; in addition, before the *Cour d'assises* they swear to 'speak without hate and without fear'. Defendants have the right to question the prosecution witnesses.[130]

The hearing provides the final stage in the investigation where the file on the case is re-examined, the witnesses are heard and there is a final opportunity to fill any gaps remaining in the earlier investigations. The court can order new measures of investigation to be carried out, for

---

[128] Art. 321–6 of the Criminal Code.
[129] Art. 81 of the Code of Criminal Procedure.
[130] European Convention, art. 6 para. 3(d).

example, by summoning a witness for a later hearing, or ordering the production of certain documents.

Where there is a civil action brought by the victim or their representatives, their claim will be heard and the amount of damages sought will be specified. The parties then make their closing speeches. At the end of the hearing, the president of a trial of major and minor offences will tell those present of the date when the judgement will be delivered.[131] The judicial deliberations take place in private and verdicts are reached according to their personal conviction.[132] The judgement will be both read to the court, and handed down in writing. The judgement for major and minor offences must contain the judges' reasons for reaching the decision.[133] Following a conviction, the private claimant will be awarded damages provided that the court is satisfied that the harm suffered by the victim was caused by the offences committed by the defendant. If the defendant is acquitted, the court cannot usually grant damages on the civil action.

The trial hearing before the *Cour d'assises* is different in certain respects from that in the other courts due to the existence of a jury. The *Cour d'assises* consists of three professional judges and nine jurors chosen at random from an election list. In addition, substitute jurors attend court and hear the case, but are only called to participate in the decision if one of the jurors is forced to withdraw. At the start of the trial they take an oath promising to examine and decide the case according to their conscience and their personal conviction.[134] This oath was amended by the Act of 15 June 2000 so that it now makes direct reference to the presumption of innocence. Unlike the English system, the judges and jurors deliberate and vote together on the facts, the law and the sentence. The judges and jurors retire together to reach their decision, using a list of questions which the presiding judge establishes before they retire. The deliberations on the verdict take place immediately after the court debates, and must not be interrupted, but continue until a decision is reached. In order to convict a defendant, eight votes are required so a majority of five jurors must agree with the conviction.

Appeals

As a general rule, a person has a right to an appeal on both the facts and law of a case. However, there is currently no right of appeal on the facts for very minor offences. The exercise of the right of appeal is itself surrounded

[131] Art. 462 of the Code of Criminal Procedure.
[132] Art. 353 and 427 of the Code of Criminal Procedure.
[133] Art. 353 of the Code of Criminal Procedure.
[134] Art. 304 of the Code of Criminal Procedure.

by a certain number of guarantees, in particular that the appeal judge cannot amend the decision which is the subject of the appeal in a way that runs against the interests of the appellant.[135] Thus, the sentence cannot be increased on appeal, unless the appeal is made by the prosecution.

Appeals by way of a full retrial are heard by the local court of appeal. Each court of appeal hears appeals from *Tribunaux de police* (except for very minor offences), and the *Tribunal correctionnel*. The larger courts of appeal have specialised criminal divisions,[136] while the smaller courts sit on alternate days as civil or criminal courts. Appeals relating to young offenders are heard by a specialised division of the court of appeal, presided over by a specialist judge.

Appeals on points of law from decisions of all the lower criminal courts can be submitted to the criminal division of the *Cour de cassation*. Appeals are heard by five judges, unless it is a straightforward case, when only three judges will hear the matter. The lower court decision will either be quashed or confirmed. If it is quashed the decision will be referred back to another lower court to reconsider. If, owing to new evidence of fact, there is a *prima facie* case that a judicial error has been committed the *Cour de cassation* can exceptionally act as a full appeal court.

There was in the past no ordinary appeal to a court of appeal from a decision of the *Cour d'assises*. This was because the French considered the jury to be the voice of the French people, which should not be overturned in the way ordinary lawyers' decisions can be. The absence of a right of appeal on the facts of a case may have been in breach of the European Convention on Human Rights, to which France is a signatory. The European Convention specifies that 'every person declared guilty of a criminal offence by a court has the right to have examined by a higher court the declaration of guilt or the conviction'. Three justifications were given for the absence of an ordinary appeal. Firstly, it was pointed out that through the jury the verdict has been reached by the people, who are sovereign. Secondly, rights of appeal to the *Chambre de l'instruction* exist in relation to the judicial investigation that preceded the trial. Finally, Protocol 7 of the European Convention provides that there need be no right of appeal where a person has been tried by the highest court, and it was argued that the *Cour d'assises* was such a court.

Various proposals for reform had been made in the past. In 1982 it was suggested that the *Cour d'assises* should be replaced by two permanent courts. The first tier was to be modelled on the current court and the second tier was to be a specialised appeal court, on the same model, using the jury system but with a greater number of jury members. Political steps were taken in 1995 towards the creation of a new court to hear serious

---

[135] Art. 515 of the Code of Criminal Procedure.
[136] Art. 510 of the Code of Criminal Procedure.

criminal cases at first instance. This would have been made up of three professional judges and five jurors. The *Cour d'assises* would have become the court of appeal against the decisions given at first instance. This right of appeal against the trial court judgement would have replaced the right of appeal against the decision of the investigating judge to refer the case to trial.

The Act of 15 June 2000 has at last introduced a full right of appeal against decisions to convict of the *Cour d'assises*. The appeal will be heard by another *Cour d'assises* designated by the Criminal Division of the *Cour de cassation*. This second *Cour d'assises* will have 12 jurors sitting alongside the professional judges, and a decision on appeal will require a majority of 10 votes.[137] It had been argued that the first *Cour d'assises* should be obliged to give reasons for their decision. These reasons could then form the basis of an appeal, and would also be a means of obliging the jury to reach a rational decision, which avoids mistakes of law. This proposal was not adopted.

There is a right to make an appeal on a point of law to the *Cour de cassation*.

Sentencing

A judge disposes of the power to order a wide range of sentences following the conviction of a defendant. Where imprisonment is imposed by the trial judge, the convicted person is sometimes allowed to spend part of their sentence outside prison, under various schemes aimed at rehabilitating the offender. This lead to concerns that the system was becoming dangerously lenient. As a result an Act of 22 November 1978 introduced a system whereby the trial judge could state that during a certain period, known as *la période de sûreté*, the convict could not benefit from any measures of leniency in their sentence.[138]

The maximum sentence that can be imposed on an offence depends on whether it has been classified as a serious, major or minor offence.[139]

Serious offences

The sentences incurred for serious offences are laid down in articles 131–1 and 131–2 of the Criminal Code. The death penalty was abolished on 9

---

[137] Art. 231, 296, 297, 298, 359, 360, 362, and 380–1 onwards of the Code of Criminal Procedure.

[138] The relevant legislative provisions are now contained in art. 132–23, 221–3 and 221–4 of the Criminal Code and art. 720–2 to 720–5 of the Code of Criminal Procedure.

[139] Art. 131–1 to 131–18 of the Criminal Code.

October 1981. Article 131–1 lays down four levels of imprisonment that can be imposed as follows:

1. Imprisonment for life;

2. Imprisonment for 30 years;

3. Imprisonment for 20 years;

4. Imprisonment for 15 years.

These are maximum sentences and a court can always choose to impose a lighter sentence, though the minimum sentence that can be imposed for a serious offence is ten years.[140] In 1996 there were 510 people condemned to life imprisonment in France, considerably fewer than in England.

A person convicted of a serious offence can also be subjected to a fine and a range of complementary punishments.[141] The possible complementary sentences are outlined in article 131–10 of the Criminal Code, though it does not attempt to provide a definitive list as these sentences are numerous. Article 131–10 states:

> When the legislation so provides, a serious or major offence can be sanctioned by one of several complementary punishments which, being imposed on physical people, involve the banning, disqualification, incapacity or removal of a right, freezing or confiscation of assets, closure of an establishment or publication of the decision given or diffusion of this either through the written press, or by any means of audiovisual communication.[142]

Several common or very serious complementary punishments are defined in article 131–19 onwards of the Criminal Code, including the confiscation of assets, the removal of civic and family rights, the banning from the territory of France and the compulsory closure of an establishment.

Major offences

According to article 131–3 of the Criminal Code, sentences for major offences are:

---

[140] Art. 131–1 of the Criminal Code.
[141] *les peines complémentaires.*
[142] '*Art. 131–10. Lorsque la loi prévoit, un crime ou un délit peut être sanctionné d'une ou de plusieurs peines complémentaires qui, frappant les personnes physiques, emportent interdiction, déchéance, incapacité ou retrait d'un droit, immobilisation ou confiscation d'un objet, fermeture d'un établissement ou affichage de la décision prononcée ou diffusion de celle-ci soit par la presse écrite, soit par tout moyen de communication audiovisuelle.*'

1. *Imprisonment*

2. *Fine*: The minimum fine that can be imposed is FF25,000.[143] The definition of the individual offences frequently state the maximum fine that can be imposed.

3. *Daily fine*:[144] for this punishment the judge fixes a daily sum that must be paid for a certain number of days. The total amount is not due until the expiry of this period. If the person fails to pay the full sum they will spend half the equivalent number of unpaid days in prison instead.[145] In practice this sentence has not proved popular with the judges due to difficulties in enforcing it. Thus if a person is ordered to pay FF300 for 50 days, they will have to pay a total of FF15,000 at the end of the 50-day period. The amount to be paid must be fixed by taking into account the resources and expenses of the defendant and can be no more than FF2,000 per day and the maximum number of days permitted is 360. Thus the total possible fine that could be payable is FF720,000.

4. *Work in the community*:[146] this sentence can only be imposed with the defendant's consent.[147] It must be for a minimum of 40 hours and a maximum of 240 hours over a period of no more than 18 months.

5. *Punishments depriving or restricting rights laid down in article 131–6*: there are 11 such punishments listed, about half of which are concerned with restricting a person's right to drive.

6. *Complementary punishments laid down in article 131–10*: These are discussed above.

As regards imprisonment, article 131–4 of the new Code lays down seven levels of imprisonment that can be imposed:

1. 10 years imprisonment;

2. 7 years imprisonment;

3. 5 years imprisonment;

4. 3 years imprisonment;

5. 2 years imprisonment;

6. 1 year imprisonment;

7. 6 months imprisonment.

[143] Art. 381 of the Code of Criminal Procedure.
[144] *le jour amende.*
[145] Art. 131-5 of the Criminal Code.
[146] *le travail d'intérêt général.*
[147] Art. 131–8 para. 2 of the Criminal Code.

Under the old Criminal Code the maximum sentence that could be imposed on a major offence was five years, this was increased to ten years by the new Code. This change meant that more offences could be classified as major offences and thereby avoid the more stringent rules of procedure required for serious offences including the use of a jury in the *Cour d'assises*. Judges are entitled to impose sentences of less than six months, though they are discouraged from doing so due to the major social disruption caused by short prison sentences.

Minor offences

According to article 131–12 of the Criminal Code, the sentences that can be imposed following a conviction for a minor offence are a fine or one of the sentences depriving or restricting a person's rights which are laid down in article 131–14. In addition one of the complementary punishments laid down in articles 131–16 and 131–17 can be imposed. Under the old code minor offences could also be the subject of a prison sentence, but this power was removed by the new Code.

Minor offences are divided into five different classes, depending on their gravity. The maximum fine that can be imposed depends on the class of the minor offence:[148]

1. 250 francs for minor offences of the 1st class;

2. 1,000 francs for minor offences of the 2nd class;

3. 3,000 francs for minor offences of the 3rd class;

4. 5,000 francs for minor offences of the 4th class;

5. 10,000 francs for minor offences of the 5th class (and 20,000 francs in the case of reoffending).

Under articles 131–14 and 131–15 of the Criminal Code the criminal courts can replace the fine incurred for a minor offence of the fifth class by one of six alternative sentences.

The execution of the sentence is watched over by the *juge de l'application des peines*.

The limitation period

While English law only applies a limitation period to civil proceedings, French law applies this restriction to criminal proceedings as well. In the criminal context there are two types of limitation period: the limitation

---

[148] Art. 131–13 of the Criminal Code.

period that applies to the bringing of a prosecution and the limitation period that applies to the punishment. The former takes effect before an offender has been convicted, while the latter takes effect after conviction. Each of these will be considered in turn.

The limitation period for the bringing of prosecutions

If the prosecution has not been brought within a certain time after the commission of the offence, then the limitation period will prevent a future prosecution. The relevant legislative provisions can be found in the articles 7, 8 and 9 of the Code of Criminal Procedure. These state:

> *Art. 7*: For serious offences and with the exception of the provisions of article 213–5 of the Criminal Code the prosecution is subject to a limitation period of 10 whole years counting from the day when the serious offence has been committed if, in this interval, no act of investigation or prosecution has been done.
>
> If such an act has been carried out in this period, the limitation period does not take effect until after ten whole years have passed counting from the last act. It is thus even with respect to people who would not be implicated in this act of investigation or prosecution.
>
> When the victim is a minor and the serious offence has been committed by legitimate, natural or adoptive ascendants or by a person having authority over him, the limitation period only starts to run from the time of his majority.[149]
>
> *Art. 8*: For major offences, the limitation period for the bringing of the prosecution is three whole years; it is complete according to the distinctions specified in the preceding article.[150]
>
> *Art. 9*: For minor offences, the limitation period for the bringing of the prosecution is one whole year: it is complete according to the distinctions specified in article 7.[151]

Thus, the limitation period for serious offences is ten years, for major offences it is three years and for minor offences it is only one year. The time runs from the day that the offence was committed. For certain particularly

---

[149] '*Art. 7: En matière de crime et sous réserve des dispositions de l'article 213–5 du Code pénal l'action publique se prescrit par dix années révolues à compter du jour où le crime a été commis si, dans cet intervalle, il n'a été fait aucun acte d'instruction ou de poursuite.*

S'il en a été effectué dans cet intervalle, elle ne se prescrit qu'après dix années révolues à compter du dernier acte. Il en est ainsi même à l'égard des personnes qui ne seraient pas impliquées dans cet acte d'instruction ou de poursuite.

Lorsque la victime est mineure et que le crime a été commis par un ascendant légitime, naturel ou adoptif ou par une personne ayant autorité sur elle, le délai de prescription ne commence à courir qu'à partier de sa majorité.'

[150] '*Art. 8: En matière de délit, la prescription de l'action publique est de trois années révolues; elle s'accomplit selon les distinctions spécifiée à l'article précédent.*'

[151] '*Art. 9: En matière de contravention, la prescription de l'action publique est d'une année révolue; elle s'accomplit selon les distinctions spécifiées à l'article 7.*'

odious offences there is either no limitation period (such as crimes against humanity referred to in article 213–5 of the Criminal Code) or an extended limitation period (such as for terrorism and drug trafficking which have a limitation period of 30 years for serious offences and 20 years for major offences). Where it is in the public interest to forget, the limitation period has also been shortened, for example for the offence of defamation by the press which has a limitation period of only three months.[152]

The limitation period can be either stopped altogether or temporarily suspended. It will be stopped by the commission of any act of investigation or prosecution in relation to the offence. This has been widely interpreted by the courts to include acts relating to the preliminary police investigation.[153] After this act has been completed the limitation period recommences from the beginning and the time that has already elapsed is ignored. There is no general legislative provision stating when the limitation period will simply be suspended, but the case law takes the view that the limitation period is suspended where there has been an obstacle of fact or law to the bringing of the prosecution. An example of suspension of fact is where the defendant has suffered from serious mental ill health after the commission of the offence. The limitation period will be suspended until the offender's mental health improves. Where there is a mere suspension of the limitation period, the earlier lapse of time will be taken into account when calculating whether the limitation period has expired.

It has been noted earlier in this chapter that the civil action is often brought alongside the criminal proceedings. Civil actions are also subject to limitation periods. In the past, because the traditional view has been that the criminal prosecution must always take priority, where the criminal proceedings could no longer be brought due to the completion of the limitation period, the civil proceedings could not be brought either. The problem with this was that where an action was founded on a simple civil fault the ordinary civil limitation period of 30 years applied; but if the action was based on a criminal fault, which was by its nature much more serious, the maximum limitation period would normally be ten years. As car accidents increased the need to reform this area of law became apparent. Thus article 10 para. 1 of the Code of Criminal Procedure now states:

> *Art. 10.* The civil action is subject to the limitation rules of the Civil Code. However, this action can no longer be brought before the criminal courts after the expiry of the limitation period for the prosecution.[154]

---

[152] Art. 65, Act of 29 July 1881 on the Freedom of the Press.
[153] Crim., 7 déc. 1966, *D.* 1967.201.
[154] '*Art. 10. L'action civile se prescrit selon les règles du Code civil. Toutefois, cette action ne peut plus être engagée devant la juridiction répressive après l'expiration du délai de prescription de l'action publique.*'

The limitation period that applies to punishments

If, after a person has been convicted, a sentence has not been executed, the sentence is extinguished after the limitation period that applies to punishments has passed. Article 133–1 of the Criminal Code provides that a limitation period applies to the execution of a punishment. This applies where a person has been convicted but the punishment has not been applied or only partially applied. This failure to execute the punishment may be for legitimate reasons or because the convict has escaped justice. While the sentence is extinguished, the conviction remains on the public records.

The duration of this limitation period depends on the gravity of the offence. For serious offences it is 20 years,[155] for major offences five years[156] and for minor offences it is only two years.[157] No limitation period applies to crimes against humanity[158] and an extended limitation period applies to terrorist offences and drug trafficking.[159] The limitation period is normally calculated from the day when the conviction became definitive, that is to say when it could not be subjected to any further appeal. It can be stopped by acts to execute the sentence, for example by the issuing of an order for the arrest and detention of the convicted person. The calculation of the limitation period then starts again from the date of the conclusion of this act and previously elapsed time is ignored.

---

[155] Art. 133–2 of the Criminal Code.
[156] Art. 133–3 of the Criminal Code.
[157] Art. 133–4 of the Criminal Code.
[158] Art. 213–5 of the Criminal Code.
[159] Art. 706–25–1 and 706–31 of the Code of Criminal Procedure.

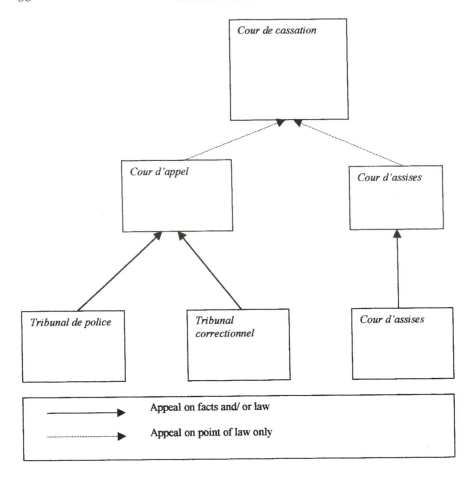

Figure 1.   The ordinary criminal courts

3

Actus reus

Introduction

Like English criminal law, the French analyse their offences as requiring both an *actus reus* (*l'élément matériel*) and a *mens rea* (*l'élément moral*). Some academic authors[1] also add a third requirement, that the offence must be laid down in a written source of law, known as the *principe de légalité*. This principle developed as a backlash to the perceived abuses of judicial discretion under the *Ancien Régime*. Royal *ordonnances* were drafted in vague terms, ordering punishment, for example, 'according to the requirements of the case, in such a way as will be an example to all others'.[2] This left considerable discretion to the judges to determine the precise punishment to impose. It caused considerable uncertainty which was particularly worrying as the punishments in vogue at the time could be extremely cruel. Montesquieu[3] developed the idea that offences and punishments should be fixed by the legislation and, after the Revolution, this principle was expressly included in articles 5 and 8 of the Declaration of the Rights of Man. While in England central offences such as murder are the creation of the judiciary under common law, and continue to be applied in the absence of any legislative provision, this is not possible in France. Article 111–3 of the Criminal Code provides:

No one can be punished for a serious crime or for a major offence whose elements are not defined by an Act or for a minor offence whose elements are not defined by a regulation.[4]

---

[1] See for example, Benoît Chabert and Pierre-Olivier Sur (1997) *Droit pénal général*, Paris: Dalloz.

[2] *'selon l'exigence du cas, en telle manière que ce soit exemple à tous autres.'*

[3] Montesquieu, *L'esprit des Lois*, livre XII, ch. IV.

[4] *'Nul ne peut être puni pour un crime ou pour un délit dont les éléments ne sont pas définis par la loi ou pour une contravention dont les éléments ne sont pas définis par le règlement.'*

Actus reus

As in England it has long been established that a person should not be punished for their thoughts alone, but that these thoughts must have crystalised into some material conduct. Though applied in practice, no direct reference was made to this principle by the 1810 Criminal Code. An exception to this general rule was that criminal conspiracy[5] made no mention of any requirement of an *actus reus*. The general principle is now expressly provided for in article 121–1 of the new Criminal Code which states that 'a person is only criminally responsible for his conduct'.[6] A conspiracy[7] now requires the existence of some 'material facts', though the Code does not specify what form these must take.

Omissions

In most cases the *actus reus* consists of a positive act, and it can only consist of an omission if that is expressly incriminated by a specific text. In all these cases it is the omission itself which constitutes the offence and which is punishable, whatever may be the consequences of the omission. Liability is analysed by the academic writers as being imposed for a failure to carry out a particular duty to act. For example, the offence of allowing a military secret to be divulged is based on the duty to protect the military interests of the State.[8]

In the nineteenth century there was no general duty to act in relation to one's neighbour, as it was considered that this fell within issues of moral responsibility rather than criminal responsibility, but this individualistic approach was gradually abandoned. First, offences for omissions were created to protect the vulnerable in society, such as minors and the disabled. Offences were therefore created of neglecting a child in 1898 and of abandoning the family in 1924. Then in the 1940s offences imposing obligations to act to protect a wider range of people were created, with offences such as failing to give evidence in favour of an innocent person and failing to prevent the commission of a crime against another. This development reached its height with the new Criminal Code which created the offence of failing to help a person in danger.[9] This offence is committed regardless of whether any harm has actually been caused and is an important tool for imposing liability for an omission – it was initially

---

5 *le complot.*
6 *'nul n'est responsable pénalement que de son propre fait.'*
7 Art. 412–1 and 450–1 of the Criminal Code.
8 413–10 of the Criminal Code.
9 Art. 223–6 of the Criminal Code. See E. N Monréal, *'L'infraction d'omission et responsabilité pénale par comission'*, *Rev. Int. dr. pén*. Rapport général XIII Congrès AIDP. 1984, p. 473.

raised as a possible ground for imposing liability on the paparazzi who were accused of failing to assist Princess Diana after the car accident in which she was killed.

But, where legislation does not expressly provide for liability by omission, there can be no liability by treating an omission as if it were an action.[10] This approach of the criminal law was highlighted by the case known as the 'hostage of Poitiers'.[11] In that case the court of Poitiers decided that the crime of intentionally injuring another[12] had not been committed by parents who had left without care, in a dark room, an old and frail person suffering from a mental illness to the point that her life was in danger. It was held that this omission could not be treated as equivalent to an act, and so fell outside the legal definition of the offence.

Comparison with the English law on omissions

The French law on omissions is very different to the English law in the field. It requires that the offence itself be expressly defined to include omissions for liability to be imposed. The academic writing merely analyses the duty owed in order to justify the approach taken by the law, but there is no requirement on the courts to find this duty. English law not only imposes liability for omissions where offences are expressly defined to include omissions, but also if the courts consider that a person owed a duty to the victim to act.

Causation

The problem of causation can arise where an offence is defined as requiring a certain result and it has to be determined whether the defendant caused that harm to the victim. French academics consider that there are three possible approaches that can be taken in determining the issue of causation. The first is that of the 'equivalence of conditions',[13] according to which all the events which have led to the realisation of the harm are treated as having equivalent weight, it being possible to treat each one of them in isolation as the cause of the harm. The second approach is that of the 'proximity of the causes', which means that the only factor that will be treated in law as the cause is the one that is the nearest in

---

[10] Crim. 29 January 1956, *D.* 1936.134; see however, Crim. 27 October 1971, *B.* no. 698, *Gaz. Pal*, 1972–I somm. 2, for the case where the defendant had the obligation to oppose what he had allowed to happen; Crim. 25 January 1982, *B.* no. 29 (omission of written statements falsifying the accounts).

[11] André Gide, *La sequestrée de Poitiers*, 1930; Poitiers, 20 November 1901, *D.P.* 1902.2.81, note Le Poittevin; *S.* 1902.2.305, note Hemard.

[12] *coups et blessures volontaires*: art. 309 and 311 old Criminal Code.

[13] *'la théorie de l'équivalence des conditions.'*

time to the harm caused – this significantly limits the chain of causation. The third analysis is that of 'the adequate cause', by virtue of which the factor that will be treated as the cause will be the one that was most likely in normal circumstances to have been the cause.

The criminal courts have rejected the proximity theory and favour the 'equivalence of conditions'. Thus, in the context of the fatal and non-fatal offences against the person that do not require intention, the courts regularly state that there need not exist between the fault and the damage 'a direct and immediate causal link',[14] nor that the wrongful conduct of the defendant be the 'exclusive cause' of the harm.[15] In the same way, in the context of intentional offences against the person, the *Cour de cassation* considers that all the consequences of the wrongful conduct must be taken into account 'be they indirect'.[16] In every case, however, the causal link must be "certain" and wherever there is doubt the person must be acquitted.[17]

The courts do, however, fall back on the doctrine of the 'adequate cause' where the imposition of liability for conduct that indirectly caused a harm would appear unfair. For example, where a motorcyclist chased after a driver shouting insults at him after he was knocked over, and then died of a heart-attack, the driver was not liable for involuntary manslaughter.[18]

Following the Act of 10 July 2000[19] the legislature now draws a distinction between direct and indirect causation for the purposes of non-intentional offences committed by natural persons. Where the harm was indirectly caused by the accused a higher level of fault will be required. Until this reform there was no legal significance of the distinction between direct and indirect causation, all that mattered was that the accused caused the result. It has been left to the courts to develop a clear dividing line between the two forms of causation.

Comparison with English law on causation

The French approach is very different to that taken under English law, where the courts have a fairly flexible approach to causation. There are a range of questions that the English courts will ask themselves in order to determine whether the chain of causation has been broken, including

---

[14] 'un lien de causalité directe ou immédiate,' Crim. 20 June 1989, Dr. pén. 1989, comm.no.60; Crim. 19 mai 1958, B. no. 395; Crim 19 mai 1978, D. 1978, Inf. Rap., 345, obs Roujou de Boubée, D. 1980, J. 3 note Mme Galiabeauchesne.

[15] 'la cause exclusive,' Crim. 7 February 1973, B.no. 72.

[16] 'fussent-elles indirectes,' Crim. 27 fév 1992, Dr.pén. 1992, comm. no. 199.

[17] Crim. 26 May 1992, Dr pén. 1992, comm. no. 4; Crim. 14 févr. 1996, B. no. 78; Crim. 20 mai 1980. D. 1981, I.R. 257 obs. Penneau; Crim. 10 janv. 1991, Dr pén. 1991, p. 69, Rev. sc. crim., 1992, p. 77, obs. G. Levasseur.

[18] Crim. 25 April 1967, G.P., 1967, I, 3413.

[19] Act no. 2000–647.

whether the intervening act was reasonably foreseeable and whether the original injury was an operative and significant cause of death. The test relied on depends on which is most suitable to the particular facts and where appropriate a combination of tests can be used. But in determining causation the real impact of the defendant's conduct will be considered and there is no concept of the 'equivalence of conditions'.

4

Mens rea

Introduction

Mens rea in French law is called *l'élément intellectuel*, *l'élément moral* or *l'élément psychologique*. A basic distinction is drawn in French law between those offences which require intention and those which do not. Where no intention is required, the *mens rea* requirement can be satisfied on proof of negligence, that a person was deliberately put in danger or that the conduct was voluntary. The serious crimes are always intentional, major offences are in principle intentional except contrary legislative provisions requiring a fault of negligence or of deliberately putting another in danger. Minor offences normally only require that the accused behaved voluntarily. Each of the different forms of *mens rea* will be considered in turn.

Intention

The first paragraph of article 121–3 of the Criminal Code states:

> There is no serious crime or major crime in the absence of an intention to commit it.[1]

The Ministry of Justice prepared a circular which provides an extensive commentary of the articles in the new Criminal Code.[2] This points out that while there was no equivalent article in the old criminal code, the general principle it contained had guided those who had drafted the original code

---

[1] '*Il n'y a point de crime ou de délit sans intention de le commettre.*' All translations are provided by the author.
[2] Crim. 93 9/F1, 14 mai 1993.

and had been recognised by the judges. Paragraph 1 of article 121–3 was therefore merely clarifying the existing position.

Article 121–3(1) provides that all offences categorised as serious or major crimes will always need a mental element of intention even if the Code or other form of legislation defining the offence does not make direct reference to this requirement; while minor offences will only require intention if specific reference to this is made in the definition of the offence. For example, the offence of violence causing less than eight days incapacity to work is a minor offence which the legislature has specified requires intention.[3] So, in French criminal law intention is the minimum mental element of the gravest offences.

An important restriction to the general principle laid down in the first paragraph of article 121–3 is provided by the second paragraph, which states:

> However, when the law so provides, a major offence can be committed by imprudence, negligence or by deliberately putting another in danger.[4]

Major crimes can therefore be committed without intention if the legislature provides that one of the three forms of non-intentional *mens rea* suffices. This is the case, for example, in relation to the offences concerning attacks causing death or injury committed without intention, contained in articles 221–6 and 222–19 of the new Criminal Code.

To satisfy the requirements of article 121–3, the few non-intentional serious crimes that existed before the passing of the new Criminal Code have been abolished. Thus the offence of negligently divulging a secret relating to a matter of national defence has been changed from that of a serious crime to a major crime;[5] the serious crime of flying over French territory without authority by a foreign airplane was abolished altogether.

While there is no equivalent legislative provision in English criminal law to the French article 121–3, in practice the most serious offences such as murder and s.18 of the Offences against the Person Act 1861 do require intention. But there are many grave offences in English law where either intention or recklessness will be sufficient.

Does this mean that the criminal threshold is set lower in England than in France? This really depends on whether the French and the English are giving the concept of intention the same definition. In considering the meaning of intention in the two legal systems, it is proposed to go one step further than is strictly necessary for a comparative approach, and try to critically evaluate these definitions. In order to do this the national

---

[3] Art. R. 625–1 of the Criminal Code.

[4] '*Toutefois, lorsque la loi le prévoit, il y a délit en cas d'imprudence, de négligence ou de mise en danger délibérée de la personne d'autrui.*'

[5] Art. 75 of the old Criminal Code, art. 413–10 of the new Criminal Code.

definitions will be judged against a hypothetical ideal. The crimes for which the *mens rea* requires intention are the most grave offences which constitute a breach of the fundamental moral rules of society, such as murder, rape and robbery. Given that intention is the fault element required for the most heinous offences, it should be given a strict, narrow, etymological meaning; this has the additional benefit of conforming with the meaning given to it in everyday language by those citizens to whom the criminal law ultimately applies. The hypothetical ideal definition of intention is therefore 'a desire directed towards a certain goal'. Where the offence requires a result, the goal would be that result, otherwise the goal would be a harm defined by the law pitched at a level appropriate to the gravity of the offence and the punishment imposed.

The old and new French Criminal Codes provide no definition of the concept of intention, and it has been left to academics to analyse its meaning. In French criminal law there are in fact two forms of intention, known as *dol général* and *dol spécial*, which will be translated respectively as 'general intention' and 'special intention'.

General intention

The classic definition of general intention is provided by the eminent nineteenth century French criminal lawyer, Emile Garçon:

> 'Intention, in its legal sense, is the desire to commit a crime as defined by the law; it is the accused's awareness that he is breaking the law.'[6]

Thus, according to its classic definition, there are two mental elements that make up general intention: desire and awareness. This definition of general intention has been accepted by the majority of subsequent authors on the subject, for example, Merle and Vitu write that general intention is 'criminal awareness and desire'.[7] The concept of awareness simply requires the accused to be aware that they are breaking the law. Because of the principle '*nemo censetur ignorare legem*' there is a presumption in French law (as in English law) that people know the law, so the existence of this element of general intention will normally be assumed. A legislative exception to this presumption was added by the new Criminal Code under article 122–3. This states that:

---

6 '*L'intention, dans son sens juridique, est la volonté de commettre le délit tel qu'il est déterminé par la loi; c'est la conscience, chez le coupable, d'enfeindre les prohibitions légales....*' Emile Garçon, *Code pénal annoté*, 1ère éd., art. 1, no. 77.

7 '*la conscience et la volonté infractionnelles*': R. Merle et A. Vitu, *Traité de droit pénal*, no. 542.

A person is not criminally liable if they prove that they believed, due to a mistake of law that they were not in a position to avoid, to be allowed to legally carry out the act.[8]

The scope of this provision will depend on the interpretation it is given by the courts, but the parliamentary debates that preceded the passing of the new Code suggest that it will be limited to where the mistake as to the law was induced by a misrepresentation emanating from the civil service.

As to the requirement of desire, this is traditionally interpreted as simply referring to a desire to commit the wrongful act and not a desire to commit the result of that act. Thus, if one takes the factual situation of a person throwing a stone at a victim and the victim dying as a result, to prove that the person has a general intention for the offence of murder it would merely need to be proved that they desired to throw the stone. For the purposes of general intention there would be no requirement to show the person desired the result of killing that person.[9]

It is only in exceptional situations that an accused, who carried out the *actus reus* of an offence, will be found not to have general intention. This will arise where the person made a mistake as to the true nature of their act and was therefore not aware that it broke the law, in other words a mistake as to the facts: a person is not guilty of theft if they mistakenly believe they are the owner of the goods which are the subject matter of the accusation.[10] In the same way, a person will not be guilty of sexually assaulting a minor under the age of 15[11] if they reasonably and honestly believed that the person was older.[12] Of course, an error of fact that was unrelated to the *actus reus* of the offence would not prevent the existence of general intention. For example, a thief who makes a mistake as to the object he is taking, believing it to be made of gold when it was in fact made of copper, would still have the general intention of theft. In addition, a person will be found not to have general intention if they are mentally deranged as a result of which they were not aware that they were carrying out the wrongful act.

In principle the burden of proving the *mens rea* of an offence lies with the prosecution. In practice, general intention is often implied from the nature of the *actus reus* and the *Cour de cassation*, the highest French court,

---

[8] 'N'est pas pénalement responsable la personne qui justifie avoir cru, par une erreur sur le droit qu'elle n'était pas en mesure d'éviter, pouvoir légitimement accomplir l'acte.'

[9] Note that the French offence of murder requires both general and specific intention.

[10] Crim. 16 nov. 1934: *D.H.* 1934, p. 183.

[11] Art. 227–25 of the new Criminal Code; Crim, 6 nov. 1963, *Rev. sc. crim.*, 1964, *obs.* Hugueney.

[12] Crim., 6 nov. 1963: *D.* 1965, p. 323, note Vouin; *JCP* 1964, éd. G, II, 13463.

is prepared to conclude that such an intention exists because of the very nature of the *actus reus*.[13]

Some academics have concluded that the concept of general intention is artificial and adds nothing to the legal definition of an offence, as it merely overlaps with pre-existing defences available to a defendant which apply to all offences.[14] It is clear that the classic definition of general intention falls far short of the hypothetical ideal. In the light of these criticisms, a dissenting view on the meaning of general intention has been developed, which is notably expressed by Professor Decocq.[15] According to this analysis, general intention would still contain two mental elements of desire and awareness. But, while awareness would be given the same meaning as discussed above, the accused would need to have the desire to commit the result of the crime, rather than simply the wrongful act, which would bring general intention within the meaning of the hypothetical ideal. This approach has not gained the support of the French courts or the majority of French academics.

Paragraph 1 of article 121–3 is actually only referring to general intention. As a result of this article, the Criminal Code no longer includes in its definition of serious or major crimes references to the need for general intention through terms such as *sciemment, intentionnellement, volontairement, de mauvaise foi* or *en connaissance de cause*. For example, the offences of violence causing either death (article 222–7), a mutilation or permanent infirmity (article 222–9) or more than eight days incapacity for work (article 222–11) do not state in their definition that the offences must have been carried out intentionally[16] unlike the previous equivalent provision of article 309 of the old Criminal Code.[17] Occasionally the legislator still chooses to refer to the requirement of general intention, for example article 432–5, penalising the failure to put an end to an arbitrary detention, makes express reference to the requirement for this to be intentional. Such references have either been kept to prevent any ambiguity on the matter, or are the product of careless drafting on the part of the legislator.

---

[13]   Crim. 25 mai 1994, *B.* no. 203; *J.C.P.* 1994 éd. G, IV, 1962; *D.* 1994, *inf. Rap.* p. 217; le 12 juillet 1994, *B.* no. 280; *Dr. pén.* 1994 , comm. 237, obs. J-H Robert: '*la seule constatation de la violation en connaissance de cause d'une prescription légale ou règlementaire impliqu[ait] de la part de son auteur, l'intention coupable exigée par l'article 121-3 du Code pénal.*'

[14]   See, for example, Legros, *L'élément moral dans les infractions*, 1952, p. 104 et s. and p. 331 et s.

[15]   Decocq, *Droit pénal général*, coll. U. Armand Colin, 1971, p. 207 s. See also, Griffon, *De l'intention en droit pénal*, th. Paris 1911, p. 91s.

[16]   *volontairement.*

[17]   Art. 309 of the old Criminal Code: '*Toute personne qui, volontairement, aura porté des coups ou commis des violences ou voies de fait … '*

Special intention

The second form of intention in French criminal law, special intention, requires an intention to cause a result forbidden by the law.[18] For example, the special intention required for murder is the intention to kill. If one takes the offence of theft, the general intention required is the desire to take property belonging to another and an awareness that such conduct breaks the law; while the special intention required is the intention to behave as the owner of the property belonging to another.[19] So a person who picks up an object that has been lost by its owner with the intention of returning it to him or her has not thereby committed a theft.

Depending on the definition of special intention for the particular offence, it may not be necessary to prove that the accused desired the result that constitutes the *actus reus*: intention as to some lesser result may be sufficient. This is the case where it is not possible for the defendant to know precisely what the result of their conduct will be and is known in French as a *dol indéterminé*.[20] Here the accused does an act seeking a result without being able to foresee what exactly the result will be. For example, if you hit someone on the nose, you are often unable to foresee what the exact result of that hit will be: a nose bleed, a broken nose, or unconsciousness. Thus the special intention required for a non-fatal offence against the person is an intention to injure. The punishment will reflect the harm imposed. For example, violence causing an incapacity to work of eight days or more amounts to a major crime[21] even if the accused did not want to cause such serious harm. On the other hand, violence causing an incapacity to work of less than eight days amounts to a minor crime,[22] even if the accused wanted to cause more serious injuries, but did not manage to because the victim was stronger than expected. The acceptance of *dol indéterminé* means that the concept of special intention falls below the hypothetical ideal.

As a result of article 121–3, general intention applies to all serious and major crimes. By contrast, special intention only applies to certain serious and major crimes, usually those which require a particular result. There are, therefore, some serious and major crimes for which only general intention is required. For example, the major crime of wrongly using signs which can only be used by the State[23] only requires a general intention.

---

18 According to Decocq's analysis, op. cit., special intention adds nothing to general intention as it merely duplicates the narrower definition he gives to general intention.
19 Crim., 30 janv. 1862: *D.P.* 1862, 1 p. 442. – 19 févr. 1959: *B.* no. 123; *D.* 1959, p. 331, note Roujou de Boubée; *J.C.P.* 1959, éd. G, II, 11178, note Chambon; *S.* 1959, p. 21, note MRMP; 21 mai 1963: *Gaz. Pal.* 1963, 2, p. 259.
20 Also known as *le dol imprécis*.
21 Art. 222–11 new Criminal Code.
22 Art. R. 625.1 new Criminal Code.
23 Art. 433–14 new Criminal Code.

Deciding whether a particular offence requires special intention can cause problems in practice. Sometimes the legislature expressly states in the definition of the offence that special intention is required. This is the case for the offence of providing intelligence information to a foreign power, which expressly states that the accused's acts must be carried out 'in order to incite hostilities or acts of aggression against France'.[24] But often the legislature does not make any express reference to the issue, and it is left to the judges to clarify the matter. As a general rule, all crimes defined to require the commission of a result need special intention.

genocide

The question is particularly delicate when the result is not part of the *actus reus* of the offence, for example the offence of poisoning[25] occurs even in the absence of the death of the victim. The nature of the special intention for this offence has given rise to considerable discussion because of the prosecutions undertaken against those responsible for the *Centre National de Transfusion Sanguine* (the National Blood Transfusion Centre). In 1985, unheated blood products infected by the AIDS virus were knowingly, and arguably for financial reasons, left on the market. As a result thousands of people, particularly haemophiliacs, were infected with AIDS. Employees of the *Centre National de Transfusion Sanguine* were prosecuted and convicted for the fraudulent offence of supplying goods under a false description in breach of the Consumer Code. In the light of the serious harm caused in this tragedy, this was considered to be too minor an offence by those who had been victims of the scandal; they described it as the 'grocer's offence'[26] because it is usually used against retailers who misrepresent the nature and quality of their goods. They have argued that those responsible, including the ministers concerned, should have been prosecuted for poisoning. This has raised the question of whether poisoning requires a special intention of intending to kill (which did not exist on the facts), or whether it was sufficient to prove a general intention that a defendant was aware that the products administered were of a nature to cause death. The traditional analysis by academics and judges is to require an intention to kill. However, in a judgement of 22 June 1994, the *Cour de cassation*, while accepting that the crime of fraud had on the facts been proven, did not exclude the possibility that the offence of poisoning might also have been committed. Though the Court stated that this offence required 'an essentially different guilty intention' than that of the offence of fraud, it did not specify that the offence required an intention to kill.[27]

---

[24] Art. 411–10 new Criminal Code: *'en vue de susciter des hostilités ou des actes d'agression contre la France'*.

[25] Art. 301 old Criminal Code; art. 221–5 new Criminal Code.

[26] *le délit d'épicier*.

[27] Crim., 22 juin 1994: *Bull. crim.*, no. 248. See also CA Paris, ch. acc. 13 juill. 1993, *Dr. pén.* 1994 comm. 12, par J- Robert.

Through the requirement or non-requirement of special intention the French legislation can graduate criminal responsibility according to the fault of the accused, even where the *actus reus* of the offence is the same. For example, violence causing the death of a victim will amount to murder if the accused had the intention of causing the death and is punished by a maximum of 30 years imprisonment.[28] If the accused merely had the intention to injure the victim they can only be liable for the offence of violence causing death without the intention of doing so, which is punished with a maximum of 15 years.[29]

Oblique intention

There is one major restriction on the meaning of intention for the purposes of French criminal law and that is in respect of indirect or oblique intention, which in French is called *le dol éventuel*. Here we are concerned with where a person foresees that they could possibly cause a result, but they do not desire it. In French law this does not amount to special intention.[30] It may now amount to a lesser fault recognised by the new Criminal Code and treated as an aggravating factor in relation to involuntary murder and non-fatal offences against the person.[31] It can also now constitute an offence in its own right under article 223–1 of the new Criminal Code where there was an immediate risk of death or serious injury.

Dol aggravé and *dol dépassé*

French academic writing on the meaning of intention is slightly deceptive, because as well as drawing a distinction between *dol spécial* and *dol général* it also draws distinctions between *dol aggravé* and *dol dépassé*.[32] These concepts have no direct translation in English criminal law. In fact, on closer examination, these are not different forms of intention, but instead raise separate issues with implications for the punishment incurred by the defendant. The *dol aggravé* refers to the situation where some additional *mens rea* is required beyond general or special intention. For example, the crime of *assassinat*[33] is more serious than 'ordinary' murder[34] because in addition to general and specific intention, it requires the *dol aggravé* of

---

[28] Art. 221–1 new Criminal Code.
[29] Art. 222–7 new Criminal Code.
[30] Crim. 27 mars 1902, *Bull*. no. 128.
[31] Art. 221–3, 222–19, 222–20 and 223–1 new Criminal Code.
[32] Also known as *le dol praeterintentionnel*.
[33] Art. 221–3 new Criminal Code.
[34] Art. 221–4 new Criminal Code.

premeditation.[35] It can therefore be punished by a maximum sentence of life imprisonment while murder can only be sentenced by a maximum of 30 years imprisonment.

The *dol aggravé* will often be the requirement for the crimes to have been carried out with a particular motive. While intention is essentially an abstract concept which remains the same for each offence, regardless of the defendant, the potential motives for a crime are infinite and dependent on the individual and their circumstances. Thus the offence of terrorism requires that one of a range of 'ordinary' criminal offences have been carried out; in addition to satisfying the intention requirement of that 'ordinary criminal offence', the acts must have been committed 'with the aim of causing serious disruption to public order through intimidation or terror'.[36] The existence of this *dol aggravé* will render the person convicted liable to a punishment which is one level higher on the sentencing scale than if the *dol aggravé* had not been present. Offences against the person and criminal damage are rendered more serious when they are committed against a witness or victim to stop them reporting the crime.[37] In this situation the accused must not only have the intention of injuring a person or property, but in addition of intimidating the victim. A further example is the offence of genocide: under article 211–1 of the new Criminal Code, certain serious crimes such as murder will amount to genocide when they have been committed as part of a systematic plan 'aimed at destroying completely or in part a national, ethnical, racial or religious group'. The presence of this motive justifies special procedural rules and a higher sentence.

Dol indéterminé and *dol dépassé* arise when the result desired is different to the result attained. *Dol dépassé* occurs where the result that is caused goes beyond the intention and foresight of the defendant, for example, where the defendant merely wanted to injure the victim but in fact the victim is killed. On these facts, the defendant lacks the special intention as regards the result caused. In principle, a *dol dépassé* is not sufficient to constitute a special intention. But the legislature sometimes takes into account both the intention and the result by punishing defendants more severely than would have been the case if they had been judged uniquely on the basis of their intention, but less severely than if they had been judged solely according to the result caused. Such is the case where a person commits acts of violence against their victim without intending to cause death, but death results. For example, the offence of article 222–7 in the French Criminal Code concerning voluntary acts of violence which involuntarily cause death incurs a maximum sentence of 15 years, which is

---

[35] Defined at art. 132–72 new Criminal Code.

[36] Art. 421.1 new Criminal Code: *'ayant pour but de troubler gravement l'ordre public par l'intimidation ou la terreur'*.

[37] Art. 222–3–5 and art. 322–3–4 new Criminal Code.

higher than that applicable to a person who caused serious but non-fatal injuries to the person which is punished by ten years imprisonment;[38] but less than that imposed for murder under article 221–1 which applies a maximum sentence of 30 years.

To conclude on the French law of intention, the concept of general intention is a low threshold for criminal liability which undermines the impact of paragraph 1 of article 123–1. The concept of special intention is very close to the hypothetical ideal, particularly as it refuses to allow indirect intention, but is slightly undermined by the recognition of *dol indéterminé* and the fact that it does not apply to all offences requiring intention.

Comparison with the English law on intention

Passing now to the law on intention in English criminal law, it is traditional to study the law of intention in England through the law of murder as this is where the case law has been developed. Unlike the French system, under English law there is legally only one concept of intention. While for the purposes of analysis and comprehension this can be divided for convenience between direct and oblique intention, this division has no significance as regards the definition of criminal offences requiring intention. A person has direct intention when they wish to cause a particular harm. This harm is not necessarily the result required as part of the *actus reus* of an offence. For example, with the offence of murder either an intention to kill or to cause grievous bodily harm will suffice; for section 20 of the Offences Against the Person Act 1861 an intention to cause some harm is sufficient, while the *actus reus* of the offence can require the causing of grievous bodily harm. This is also potentially the position in French law, through their concept of *dol indéterminé*, though in the context of murder only an intention to kill will suffice.

The French concept of special intention and the English concept of direct intention have the same meaning. Both, while close, do not reach the standards of the hypothetical ideal intention, as they do not always require a desire to achieve the result of the crime which is defined to include a result; instead a desire to commit some lesser harm can suffice. The offence of murder in English law, and the non-fatal offences against the person in French law, illustrate that this represents a significant weakening of the criminal threshold.

Indirect intention can arise in English law where the person does not wish the relevant harm to occur (be it the result of some lesser harm, depending on the definition of intention for the particular offence) but foresees that it is virtually certain to do so. In this case there is strong

---

[38] Art. 222–9 new Criminal Code.

evidence from which it can be concluded that the defendant had the requisite intention.[39] We have seen when considering the French concept of *dol éventuel* that this would not be sufficient to constitute special intention in French law, though such foresight can be used to aggravate a punishment under the doctrine of *dol indéterminé*. Indirect intention is a long way from satisfying the requirements of the hypothetical ideal.

For neither direct or oblique intention, unlike the French concept of *dol général*, are the English courts concerned with whether the person intended to carry out the act; this is considered as part of the *actus reus*, in analysing whether the act was voluntary and whether the defence of automatism is available. Nor does the issue of awareness of the law fall within the definition of intention; any defences put forward by the accused claiming that they were unaware of the law will be rejected on the basis of the principle *nemo censetur ignorare legem*.

This analysis shows that there are marked differences in the meaning of intention in the French and English legal systems, even though both have chosen to use this concept to refer to the mental element required of offenders accused of committing the most heinous offences.

Negligence

Originally article 121–3 simply stated that there was a major offence 'where there was carelessness [or] negligence ...'[40] and provided no definition of the terms. Traditionally academics consider that the existence of negligence is appreciated subjectively (*in concreto*) by the judge. This statement is, however, misleading as the judge does not take into account the psychology or the particular characteristics of the defendant, who cannot thus plead their inexperience or incompetence to escape liability.[41] The element of subjectivity simply stems from the fact that the courts will take into account the actual external circumstances of the defendant. The judge will compare the defendant's conduct with that of a normally prudent and careful individual and, taking into account the circumstances, determine whether the defendant has been negligent. It would thus be more accurate to describe negligence as an objective test. ⟶

The principle that the judge can look at the external circumstances had little impact on the outcome of criminal trials. In effect, under articles 221–6 and 222–19 of the Criminal Code (concerned with non-intentional offences against the person), the *mens rea* of these offences can consist in the single violation of a rule of security or of care laid down by the law.

---

[39] *R v Nedrick* [1986] 3 All ER 1, [1986] 1 WLR 1025.
[40] *'en cas d'imprudence [ou] de négligence'*.
[41] J. Dumont, *Atteintes involontaires à la vie, Jur. Class. Pén.* no. 49; Merle et Vitu, no. 577.

Once a violation of such a rule was shown the judges appeared to give little weight to the circumstances of the case. Some people, particularly elected representatives who felt vulnerable to such prosecutions, considered this to be excessively severe and contrary to the general principles of the new Criminal Code.[42]

Article 121–3 was therefore amended by the Act of 13 May 1996 to reassure the elected representatives and civil servants that they would not be the subject of an unjust prosecution. When originally presented to the Senate, the Bill only contained a single provision concerning locally elected individuals. Inspired by the principle of equality, the government introduced amendments to insert a general principle into the criminal law that the external circumstances of the individual should be taken into account, and made express provisions for civil servants as well as elected representatives to be introduced to legislation outside the Criminal Code. Barely two years after the coming into force of the new Criminal Code, paragraph 3 of article 121–3 was amended to state:

> There is also a major offence, when the law so provides, where there is carelessness, negligence or a failure to fulfil an obligation of care or of security laid down by Acts or regulations except if the author of the facts has exercised normal care taking into account, where appropriate, the nature of his mission, functions and competence as well as the power and the means at his disposal.[43]

Thus, the 1996 Act added an extended definition of the concepts of negligence and carelessness and included express reference to the fault of 'failing to fulfil an obligation of care or of security laid down by Acts or regulations'. This failure had previously been recognised by academic authors prior to the new Criminal Code but this was the first time that the legislator expressly referred to it. The driving of a car is today so tightly regulated that, when a person is injured, the slightest misdemeanour is likely to be analysed as a breach of a regulation giving rise to this form of fault. In particular, the failure to control a car[44] is treated as a minor offence with a broad application. As a result, any death in a road accident constitutes almost automatically involuntary manslaughter unless the defence of *force majeure* is proven.

With the last part of the paragraph ('except if the author …') the legislator was stating something that was obvious, but that the courts may on occasion have lost sight of. In essence, the provision sought to remind

---

[42] Pradel no. 474.

[43] '*Il y a également délit, lorsque la loi le prévoit, en cas d'imprudence, de négligence ou de manquement à une obligation de prudence ou de sécurité prévue par la loi ou les règlements sauf si l'auteur des faits a accompli les diligences normales compte tenu, le cas échéant, de la nature de ses missions ou de ses fonctions, de ses compétences ainsi que du pouvoir et des moyens dont il disposait.*'

[44] *le défaut de maîtrise de son véhicule*: art. R. 11–1 *Code de la Route*.

the court that a person cannot be found to have been at fault if they showed a normal level of care in the circumstances of the case. The circumstances to which the judge was invited to take into account are the nature of the missions or functions of the person, his or her competence, powers and means. But these are only examples which do not bind the judge. The term 'competence' has a narrow meaning equivalent to 'authority' and does not refer to the psychological or physical characteristics of the accused.[45]

The accompanying circular of the Ministry of Justice pointed out that the provisions would have little effect in the context of road traffic accidents. For example, a driver who has caused an accident will not be able to argue that he or she did not have the means to avoid it because their vehicle had faulty brakes: such an argument would only show their fault, which was to drive a vehicle in breach of the legislation regulating the safety of vehicles on the road. On the other hand, in other fields, when a person has, in good faith, done what was objectively in their power to assure the respect of the law, their acts will not be blameworthy and no fault will be attributed to them.

At the same time as making changes to article 121–3 of the Criminal Code, the legislator made amendments to the General Code on Local Authorities[46] and to the Act of 13 July 1983[47] concerning the rights and obligations of civil servants. These provisions specify that local and regional representatives and civil servants cannot be convicted on the basis of the third paragraph of article 121–3 of the Criminal Code for facts that were not intentionally committed in the exercise of their functions 'unless it is established that they did not exercise normal care taking into account their competence, the power and the means that they disposed of as well as the difficulties specific to the missions that the law confers on them.'[48] These provisions were highly controversial, but the arguments for making specific provision for elected representatives and civil servants were that they were in a different and more vulnerable position to, for example, heads of business. They did not always have a free choice as to the people they had to work with, and frequently had little control over their budget. They had a wide range of responsibilities, including public security, and due to their limited means they had to prioritise. It was thus felt to be vital that after a death or injury due to perhaps a fire or pollution within the constituency of a politician or civil servant, that the judge

---

[45] Circular of application of 27 August 1996.
[46] *Code général des collectivités territoriales.*
[47] inserting art. 11bis.
[48] *'que s'il est établi qu'elles n'ont pas accompli les diligences normales compte tenu de leurs compétences, du pouvoir et des moyens dont elles disposaient ainsi que des difficultés propres aux missions que la loi leur confie.'*

should consider whether they were personally at fault before imposing criminal liability.[49]

Further reform was made to the legislation on criminal liability for non-intentional offences by the Act of 10 July 2000.[50] There had been concern, particularly among politicians, that people in public office were continuing to be exposed to criminal liability where there was no real evidence of personal fault. Presenting the proposed legislation to the National Assembly on 29 June 2000, the Minister of Justice, Madame Guigou, cited two recent examples where she felt criminal liability had been inappropriately imposed. The first was where a mayor had been convicted for involuntary homicide when a child was electrocuted by a street light that had been installed by his predecessors over twenty years earlier, and he had never been alerted to the problem of maintaining these lights. The second was a conviction of a headmistress of a nursery school who had been convicted of causing non-intentional injuries to the person. A child had broken a leg when he fell from a slide that had been installed in the playground by the council. The headmistress was convicted despite the fact that she had never been warned that this piece of equipment might not conform to the latest regulations in force.

The third paragraph of article 121–3 was amended and a fourth paragraph was added as follows:

> There is also a major offence, when the law so provides, where there is carelessness, negligence or a failure to fulfil an obligation of care or of security laid down by legislation or regulation, if it is established that the person who carried out this conduct did not exercise normal care taking into account, where appropriate, the nature of his mission, functions and competence as well as the power and the means at his disposal.
>
> In the case foreseen by the preceding paragraph, physical people who had not directly caused the harm, but who have created or contributed to creating the situation which has permitted the realisation of the harm or who have not taken the measures permitting its avoidance, are criminally responsible if it is established that they have, either obviously deliberately breached a particular obligation of care or security laid down by legislation or regulation, or committed an established fault and who exposed another to a particularly serious risk of which they could not have been unaware.[51]

---

[49] For an extremely critical analysis of the Act see M-L Rassat, *Du code pénal en général et de l'article 121–3 en particulier, Dr pén.* juill. 1996, *Chr.* 28.

[50] Act no. 2000–647.

[51] '*Il y a également délit, lorsque la loi le prévoit, en cas de faute d'imprudence, de négligence ou de manquement à une obligation de prudence ou de sécurité prévue par la loi ou le règlement, s'il est établi que l'auteur des faits n'a pas accompli les diligences normales compte tenu, le cas échéant, de la nature de ses missions ou de ses fonctions, de ses compétences ainsi que du pouvoir et des moyens dont il disposait.*'

Thus, the Act of 10 July 2000 created a distinction for natural persons (as opposed to legal persons), between where the harm has been directly caused by the accused and where the harm has been indirectly caused by the accused. Where the harm has been directly caused by the accused the third paragraph of article 121–3 applies. Only minor changes have been made to this paragraph. Firstly, the legislation expressly refers to carelessness, negligence or the failure to follow an obligation of care or security as a form of 'fault', to emphasise the fact that fault is required. Secondly, the legislator refers to a breach of a 'regulation' in the singular rather than in the plural. This change means that when looking for a breach of a regulation, only a breach of a decree or an official order[52] is sufficient, breach of a circular or internal company rule is not sufficient. Thirdly, the change in drafting seeks to highlight the fact that it is for the prosecution to prove that the accused satisfies the requirement of fault, and the burden of proof is not on the accused to show that they lacked this element of fault.

Where the accused caused the harm indirectly, then a higher threshold of fault must be proven. This level of fault can take one of two forms: firstly, the accused may have obviously deliberately breached a particular obligation of care or security laid down by legislation or regulation; or secondly, they could have committed an established fault that exposed another to a particularly serious risk of which they could not have been unaware. Thus, where paragraph 4 applies, a conviction will only be justified where three conditions are satisfied:

- The accused's conduct constituted an established fault (which is defined in the third paragraph as carelessness, negligence or a failure to fulfil an obligation of care or of security);

- The person exposed another to a risk that he or she must have been aware of;

- The risk was particularly serious. According to the Minister of Justice this risk will frequently be a risk of death or of serious injury.[53]

Thus the distinction between direct and indirect causation is now fundamental to the law on liability for negligence. The legislator has only given very limited guidance on where a person will be treated as an in-

---

Dans le cas prévu par l'alinéa qui précède, les personnes physiques qui n'ont pas causé directement le dommage, mais qui ont créé ou contribué à créer la situation qui a permis la réalisation du dommage ou qui n'ont pas pris les mesures permettant de l'éviter, sont responsables pénalement s'il est établi qu'elles ont, soit violé de façon manifestement délibérée une obligation particulière de prudence ou de sécurité prévue par la loi ou le règlement, soit commis une faute caractérisée et qui exposait autrui à un risque d'une particulière gravité qu'elles ne pouvaient ignorer.'

[52] *un arrêté.*

[53] Speech of Madame Guigou, Minister of Justice, to the National Assembly on 29 June 2000.

direct cause of harm, and it will be left to the courts to develop this concept, which up to now has had no legal significance.

Paragraph 4 only applies to natural persons, so that the general principles laid down in paragraph 3 apply to legal persons regardless of whether the harm was caused directly or indirectly.

Offences that can be committed without intention include involuntary manslaughter,[54] negligent assaults on the integrity of the person[55] and the revelation by carelessness of a national defence secret.[56] There are only two offences against property that can be committed by negligence and these are the major offences of causing an explosion and of negligently causing a fire.[57]

A defendant with this *mens rea* will not usually have intended to breach the criminal law. The concept of negligence in civil law is contained in article 1383 of the Civil Code. For a long time the courts drew a distinction between civil and criminal negligence, but the *Cour de cassation* reversed this approach in 1912.[58] For almost a century the courts treated the two concepts as having the same meaning. An example of negligence is where a surgeon or anaesthetist does not take before, during or even after an operation, the precautions expected by established scientific opinion against the foreseeable risks of death to the patient.[59] With the reform introduced by the Act of 10 July 2000, a distinction has been reintroduced between civil negligence and criminal negligence where the harm has been caused indirectly by a natural person.

Comparison with English law

Until the Act of 10 July 2000 French law had not tried to draw a distinction between gross negligence for the purpose of manslaughter and negligence for the purpose of other offences. With the new Act a higher level of negligence is being created for all non-intentional offences where the harm was caused indirectly by a natural person. Gross negligence is being given quite specific requirements by the English courts (for example, that there must have been an obvious risk of death) which would not be imposed by French law. Under French law, negligence has the same meaning in both civil and criminal law where harm has been directly caused by a natural person, while in England following the long established case of *R v*

---

[54] Art. 221–6 Criminal Code.

[55] Art. 222–19 Criminal Code.

[56] Art. 413–10 para.3 Criminal Code.

[57] Art. 322–5 Criminal Code.

[58] Civ. 19 déc 1912, *S*. 1914.I.249, note Morel. This case law has been maintained after the Act of 8 July 1983: Crim. 18 nov. 1985, *B*. no. 343, obs. Levasseur, *Rev. sc. crim.*, 1987, p. 427.

[59] Trib. Montpellier 21 déc. 1970, *D*. 1971.637, note Chabas; Crim. 23 nov. 1994, *Dr. pén*. 1995, no. 88, obs. Véron.

Bateman[60] gross negligence only exists if the person's conduct goes beyond a 'mere matter of compensation'.

Deliberately putting someone in danger

The fault of deliberately putting someone in danger[61] is a creation of the new Criminal Code. Until then there had only been the *mens rea* of intention and negligence (and arguably that of voluntary conduct). It was felt that this failed to recognise the different degrees of fault that could exist, and in particular no express provision was made for the person who saw a risk and took it, but did not actually intend the result. This situation would be covered in English law by the concept of recklessness and has traditionally been described by French jurists as *dol éventuel*. Prior to the new Code it did not amount to a specific category of *mens rea*, instead the person would simply be treated as if they had been negligent. The person taking a risk knowingly and causing by this fact a harm was liable to the same punishment as that for causing a similar harm by negligence, despite the fact that this conduct was extremely dangerous and immoral. This type of situation would occur where, for example, a driver deliberately goes through a red light, or overtakes on a bend.

The new fault of deliberately putting another in danger aims to deal with this perceived weakness of the old law. Some clarification as to the scope of the concept is provided by the offences which rely on this *mens rea*.[62] These describe the fault of deliberately putting another in danger as being a 'deliberate failing in an obligation of security or care imposed by the law'.[63] This fault supposes thus, in the first place, the desire to breach an obligation of security or care. Such an intention will often be difficult to prove. Secondly, there must have been a breach of the law. In this context breaches of the health and safety regulations are likely to be important as this *mens rea* is intended to cover some accidents at work.

Offences which have the *mens rea* of deliberately putting another in danger[64] are treated as aggravated offences of negligence with a higher sentence. For example, for involuntary manslaughter the punishment increases from three to five years imprisonment,[65] and for a non-fatal offence leading to an incapacity to work for over three months committed

---

[60] *R v Bateman* [1925] 19 Cr App R 18; [1925] All ER Rep 45.

[61] *'mise en danger délibérée de la personne d'autrui'*.

[62] Art. 221–6 and 222–19, Criminal Code.

[63] *'manquement délibéré à une obligation de sécurité ou de prudence imposée par la loi ou les règlements'*.

[64] Art. 221–6, 222–19, 222–20, R.625–2 and 322–5 of the Criminal Code.

[65] Art. 221–6.

without intention from two to three years.[66] It has been argued that these increased sentences are still inadequate to reflect the gravity of the conduct, an argument that can be supported by the facts of the contaminated blood scandal.

In addition the fact of deliberately putting another in danger can constitute an offence in its own right under article 223–1 of the Criminal Code, which states that the offence is committed by:

> directly exposing another to an immediate risk of death or injury leading to a mutilation or permanent infirmity by the manifestly deliberate violation of a particular obligation of security or care imposed by the law.[67]

This offence arises whether or not any harm was actually caused by the deliberate risk taking. A sentence of one year's imprisonment or a FF100,000 fine can be imposed. This new offence gave rise to considerable controversy in parliament as it is the only offence punishable with imprisonment that does not require intention or a harm to be caused. In particular, the parliamentarians were concerned that it might be too lightly relied upon by prosecutors following a road accident. Concern at the prospect of over-zealous prosecutions led to the inclusion of the requirement that the conduct must have been 'manifestly' deliberate. This requirement does not exist where the fact of deliberately putting another in danger is simply used as an aggravating circumstance. It should also be noted that the provision only refers to '*le règlement*' instead of '*les règlements*' in order to limit this term to its narrow meaning of decrees and executive orders.[68] It would not cover, for example, the internal rules of a company. A year after the new Code came into force, there had been over a hundred convictions for this offence, the majority of which were against car drivers.

Comparison with English law

The nearest equivalent in English law is that of recklessness, which was a model for the French when they developed this form of *mens rea*. However, the French version is purely subjective whereas following the case of *Metropolitan Police Commissioner v Caldwell*,[69] recklessness can have an objective meaning. The French concept of deliberately putting another in danger can also be the foundation for an offence in its own right without proof of any harm, which is not the case for recklessness.

---

[66] Art. 222–19.
[67] '*le fait d'exposer directement autrui à un risque immédiat de mort ou de blessures de nature à entraîner une mutilation ou une infirmité permanente par la violation manifestement délibérée d'une obligation particulière de sécurité ou de prudence imposée par la loi ou les règlements*'.
[68] '*décrets*' and '*arrêtés*'.
[69] [1982] AC 341; [1981]2 WLR 509.

Voluntary conduct

Criminal liability can only be imposed for voluntary acts.[70] With special intention a person must have wanted the result of their conduct to occur, here they must simply want to carry out their act. This is the only *mens rea* requirement for the majority of minor offences, and in this context it is known as *la faute contraventionnelle*. It is recognised that this is a very low threshold of *mens rea*[71] which in the past applied not just to minor offences but also to a few major offences.[72] These were abolished by the new Criminal Code.

The prosecution do not have to provide any evidence of the existence of this *mens rea*. Liability will only be avoided if the defendant can prove the existence of *force majeure*[73] or insanity.[74] Proving good faith or the absence of negligence does not prevent liability being imposed. There is a debate among academics whether it should be said that, as the burden of proof is not on the prosecution, there is a presumption as to the existence of *mens rea*. But, as contrary proof of the absence of negligence or the existence of good faith does not prevent the existence of this fault element, a minority feel that it would be more accurate to state that it is the simple fact of committing the *actus reus* of the offence that amounts to the fault of these offences, under the principle of *res ipsa loquitur*.[75]

Comparison with English law

In English law the requirement that the conduct must be voluntary is seen as primarily an issue of *actus reus* rather than *mens rea*.[76] Where the conduct has not been willed due to an external factor, the defendant will benefit from the defence of automatism or, if it is due to an internal factor, from the defence of insanity. The French analysis that this is primarily an issue of *mens rea* that can be disproved when contrary evidence is supplied is more satisfactory as the focus should really be on the defendant's state of mind, the external conduct being the same whether or not an offence has been committed.

Offences which only require *la faute contraventionnelle* are known in French law as *infractions matérielles*. Since this fault is not considered in

---

[70] *'Toute infraction suppose que son auteur ait agi avec volonté'*: Crim. 13 *Décembre* 1956, D. 1957, 349, note M.R.M.P.

[71] Crim. 7 mars 1918, S. 1921.1.89, note Roux.

[72] known as *'délits matériels'*.

[73] The last paragraph of art. 121–3 specifies that *'il n'y a point de contravention en case de force majeure'*; see also Crim. 15 mai 1926, S.1928.I.33, note Roux.

[74] *aliénation mentale*.

[75] See, for example, Légros, *L'élément moral dans les infractions*.

[76] See, for example, Smith and Hogan (1999), *Criminal Law*, London: Butterworths p. 36.

English law to amount to a *mens rea*, but is primarily an issue of *actus reus*, the closest equivalent to an *infraction matérielle* in English law is a strict liability offence.

5

Secondary party liability

Article 121–1 of the Criminal Code lays down the fundamental rule that a person is only criminally responsible for their own acts.[1] The principal offender is known as *l'auteur matériel* and is defined in article 121–4:

> The principal offender is the person who:
> 1. Commits the criminal conduct;
> 2. Attempts to commit a serious offence or, in the cases provided for by the legislation, a major offence.[2]

Joint principals are known as *coauteurs*.[3] Exceptionally, the law will occasionally treat people who cause the commission of a principal offence, but do not actually personally carry out the *actus reus* of that offence, as the principal offender, known as *l'auteur intellectuel* or *l'auteur moral*[4] (though frequently they will be treated as accomplices). For example, if a child has been abducted, the law will treat not only the person who physically removed the child as a principal offender, but also the person who arranged for the child to be abducted.

As regards accomplices (*les complices*), the key legislative provisions can be found in articles 121–6 and 121–7. These state:

> *Art. 121–6.* The accomplice of the offence, as defined in article 121–7, will be punished as a principal offender.[5]

---

[1] Art. 121–1: *'Nul n'est responsable pénalement que de son propre fait.'*
[2] *'Est auteur de l'infraction la pesronne qui:*
    1. Commet les faits incriminés;
    2. Tente de commettre un crime ou, dans les case prévus par la loi, un délit.'
[3] See Dominique Alix, *Essai sur la coaction*, LGDJ 1976.
[4] Crim. 24 oct. 1972, *G.P.*, 1973.I.218; Crim. 4 déc. 1974, *G.P.*, 1974 I, som. 93; Laguier, *'La notion d'auteur moral'*, obs. *R.S.C.*, 1976, p. 409.
[5] *'Sera puni comme auteur le complice de l'infraction, au sens de l'article 121–7.'*

Art. 121–7. An accomplice to a serious or major offence is the person who knowingly, by help or assistance, facilitated its preparation or commission.

A person is also an accomplice who by gift, promise, threat, order, abuse of authority or power has provoked an offence or given instructions to commit it.[6]

In order to impose criminal liability on a secondary party a crime must have been committed by a principal offender. Secondly, there must have been an act of complicity and thirdly the accomplice must have the requisite *mens rea*.

Actus reus

A principal offence

A crime must have been committed by the principal offender in order for liability to be imposed on the accomplice. As suicide is not a crime, a person cannot be liable as an accomplice to a suicide. The crime must have been either a serious or major offence. As regards minor offences, the new Criminal Code distinguishes according to the form of complicity. Where the complicity took the form of the accomplice instigating the principal offence,[7] liability can be imposed.[8] By contrast, if the complicity simply takes the form of help or assistance, no liability can be imposed.[9] Occasionally, help or assistance given for the commission of a minor offence will be separately punished as an autonomous offence. For example, the new Code punishes those who help or assist the commission of a breach of the peace,[10] or a minor offence against the person.[11]

Liability can be imposed on the secondary party even though they could not themselves have committed the principal offence. Thus, a person who is not a director of a company can be liable as an accomplice to the offence of abuse of company property, even though the principal offender must be a company director.[12]

Accomplices will avoid liability where potential principal offenders have a defence that justifies their conduct. This includes the legitimate defence, an order of law and the order of a legitimate authority. They will also avoid liability where the potential principal offender benefits from an

---

6 *'Est complice d'un crime ou d'un délit la personne qui sciemment, par aide ou assistance, en a facilité la préparation ou la consommation.*

Est également complice la personne qui par don, promesse, menace, ordre, abus d'autorité ou de pouvoir aura provoqué à une infraction ou donné des instructions pour la commettre.'

7 *Complicité par instigation.*

8 Art. 121–7 para. 2 and R. 610–2.

9 Art. 121–7 para. 1.

10 Art. R. 623–2.

11 Art. R.625–1.

12 Crim. 20 mars 1997, *Dr. pén.,* 1997, comm. 131.

immunity, for example the provisions of Article 311–12 offer an immunity between spouses for the offence of theft. Complicity is not punishable where the acts of the principal offender can no longer be punished due to the expiry of the limitation period,[13] or due to a general amnesty on offences of that type (as opposed to an amnesty for the principal offender personally).

The principal offence can be an attempt, though a person cannot be liable for attempting to be an accomplice.[14] When the potential principal offender has started to carry out the principal offence but has voluntarily chosen to desist and thus avoided liability for an attempt, the accomplices will also avoid liability even though they were not party to this voluntary decision. The *Cour de cassation* has therefore decided that a defendant was not liable as an accomplice where he had hired a hit man to assassinate a designated person, but the hit man failed to carry out the offence.[15]

The case law has partly got round this potential gap in criminal liability by imposing instead liability for conspiracy.[16] In one case a man was found in possession of notes concerning the movements of a woman described at the trial as 'blond and attractive'. He admitted to the police that he had been contacted by a third party who had been abandoned by the woman and wanted to get revenge against her. The third party had paid him money to attack her and driven him to the place where he was to carry out the attack. He had taken the money and spent it, but had subsequently changed his mind and not carried out the attack. The two men were both convicted of conspiracy.[17]

There must exist a sufficiently clear causal link between the conduct of the supposed accomplice and the commission (or the attempted commission) of the principal offence.[18]

The principal offence need not have been the subject of a conviction. The absence of a conviction may be due to the fact that, for example, the principal offender has escaped detection or died, or it may be due to the existence of a defence such as insanity, being a minor or having received a personal amnesty.[19] In the same way, the accomplice can be punished, even

---

[13] See p. 54.

[14] Crim. 4 janv. 1975, *G.P.*, 1975–I343, note J.-P.D., obs. Larguier, *R.S.C.*, 1976, p. 707.

[15] Crim., 25 oct. 1962, *affaires Lacour et Schieb-Benamar*, *J.C.P.*, 1963.II.12985, note R. Vouin, *D.*, 1963.221, note P. Bouzat; *R.S.C.*, 1963.553, obs. Légal.

[16] *une association de malfaiteurs.*

[17] Crim., 30 avril 1996, *B.*, no. 176, *R.S.C.*, 1977.100 et obs. B. Bouloc, 113 et obs. J.P. Delmas Saint-Hilaire.

[18] Salvage, '*Le lien de causalité en matière de complicité*', *R.S.C.*, 1981, p. 25; Crim. 3 nov. 1981, *B.* no. 289, *Gaz. Pal.*, 1982.1, somm. 66, note J.P. Doucet, obs. Larguier, *R.S.C.*, 1984, p. 489.

[19] Crim., 12 mai 1970, *B.* no. 158, where the accomplice was convicted even though the principal offender remained unidentified; 18 nov. 1976, *B.* no. 332; 28 mai 1990, *B.* no. 214, obs. Levasseur, *R.S.C.*, 1991, 346.

though the principal offender has been acquitted for subjective reasons of non-responsibility (such as the existence of the defence of constraint or madness) or has benefited from an exemption from punishment.[20] In other words, the accomplice can be punished, even if the principal offender escapes punishment. It suffices that the decision concerning the principal offender does not exclude the existence of a criminal act.

If the principal offence has been committed in France, it does not matter that the act of complicity has been committed in another country, it is punishable in France. In the reverse hypothesis of an offence committed outside France, the person who has been the accomplice in France can be convicted by the French courts, even if the principal offender has not been convicted by a foreign court, as long as a foreign court has confirmed that the offence was committed.[21]

An act of complicity

Article 121–7 lists the type of conduct that can give rise to liability as an accomplice, and conduct falling outside this widely drawn list cannot give rise to liability.

A positive act is usually required. Generally mere presence at the scene of a crime is not sufficient to constitute complicity.[22] Thus, in an old case a defendant was not liable for complicity where he had found several individuals in the process of committing a crime and had agreed to remain silent on the payment of a sum of money.[23] However, liability as an accomplice will be imposed on an individual who did not carry out a positive act when this abstention was blameworthy. It might be blameworthy because their mere presence encouraged the principal offender, which was the case when a woman's lover was present at the scene of her illegal abortion.[24] Alternatively, it may be that there was a prior agreement with the principal offender. This was the position in a case where an inspector of taxes had agreed to turn a blind eye to dishonest acts of the principal offender.[25] Or the accused may have had an obligation to act due to his or her profession. Thus, a club owner was liable as an accomplice when he failed to stop his clientele from causing excessive noise at night which prevented his neighbours from sleeping.[26] Another example arose

---

[20] Crim., 21 mai 1990, *B.* no 205.
[21] Art. 113–5.
[22] Crim., 30 nov. 1810, *B.* no. 154; 27 mars 1846, *B.* no. 82; 26 oct. 1912, *.S*, 1914.I.225, note J.A. Roux.
[23] Crim. 15 janv. 1948, *S.*, 1949.I.81, note A. Légal; ; Cass. Ass. pl. 20 janv. 1964, *J.C.P.* 1965-II-13.983, note Bouzat.
[24] Crim. 5 nov. 1941, *S.*, 1942.I.89, note Bouzat.
[25] Crim. 27 oct. 1971, *B.* no. 284, *R.S.C.*, 1972.376, obs. J. Larguier.
[26] Crim. 8 juill. 1949, *J.C.P.*, 1949.II.5128, note Colombini; 17 février 1988, *B.* no. 80.

when a police officer was found to be a secondary party to a theft when he failed to stop his colleague from committing the theft while they were on duty together.[27]

Indirect complicity is punishable.[28] This occurs where the defendant assists the accomplice and not the principal offender, for example, where a housekeeper gives information to an acquaintance about the layout of her employer's house, and her acquaintance then passes this information on to a burglar.

Complicity can consist of helping or assisting the commission of the principal offence or instigating its commission.

Help or assistance

The old Criminal Code had expressly included as a form of complicity 'the provision of means'[29] for the commission of the principal offence. The drafters of the new Code decided that this was merely a specific form of help or assistance and therefore did not need to be expressly included in the Code.

A classic example of providing help or assistance is where a bugle was played to hide the victim's cries while the principal offender raped her. Other examples are providing duplicate keys for the commission of a burglary,[30] or loaning a car to be used to commit a theft.[31] In one case the director of a driving school was found to be an accomplice when he allowed a person who lacked the requisite professional qualification[32] to give driving lessons.

It does not matter that the principal offender did not actually take advantage of the help or assistance provided.[33]

Complicity by instigation

A person will be treated as an accomplice where they have instigated the commission of the principal offence (Article 121–7 para. 2). This instigation can take the form of either provocation or the giving of instructions.

In order for there to be a provocation two conditions must be satisfied. Firstly, the provocation must be directed at a specific individual, rather than being addressed to the world at large. Secondly, the provocation must have been accompanied by one of the circumstances listed in Article 121–7,

---

[27] Trib. corr., Aix, 14 janv. 1947, *J.C.P.*, 1947.II.3465, note Béraud.

[28] Crim. 1er sept. 1987, *B*. no. 308; 10 oct. 1988 *G.P.*, 1989.1.189, note Doucet; 30 mai 1989, *B*. no. 222; obs. Vitu, *R.S.C.*, 1990, p. 325.

[29] *la fourniture de moyens.*

[30] Crim. 13 juin 1811, *S., chr.*, 1809–1811.I.360.

[31] Crim. 6 déc. 1967, *B*. no. 311.

[32] Montbéliard, 22 nov. 1963, *D.* 1964, 78, note Pelier.

[33] Crim. 17 mai 1962, *D.*, 1962.473, *R.S.C.*, 1964.134, obs. A. Légal; 31 janv. 1974, *J.C.P.*, 1975.II.17984, note Mayer-Jack.

that is to say it must have been committed through a gift, promise, threat, order, abuse of authority or of power. An example of a promise constituting a provocation is where the owner of a restaurant promised to pay FF35 to a woman if she agreed to play table tennis in a topless swimsuit.[34] An example of a threat occurred where an employer obtained false statements from some of his employees by threatening to sack them.[35] If an individual merely gives advice, even if it is forceful advice, this is not sufficient to constitute a provocation.[36] Where these two conditions are not satisfied, there are sometimes autonomous offences for which liability can be imposed on the individual as a principal offender. For example, there are offences of provoking a person to use drugs in the Code for Public Health,[37] of provoking racial discrimination in the Act of 29 July 1881[38] and of provoking a person to commit suicide under article 223–13 of the new Criminal Code.

As regards the giving of instructions, there is no need for these to be accompanied by one of the circumstances listed for provocation. The instructions must be precise as the provision of vague information is not sufficient. Giving the address of an abortionist has been found to be sufficient, as has the provision of details of the future victim's movements.[39] By contrast, when a man simply advised his mistress that she could have an illegal abortion by means of injections, he was not liable as an accomplice.[40] The instructions may be given directly or through the intermediary of a third person.[41] Liability will still be imposed even if the principal offender did not carry out the offence according to the instructions given by the accomplice.[42]

Timing

The instigation, help or assistance must have been provided prior to or at the time of the principal offence.[43] An exception exists where assistance was provided after the commission of the offence, but had been promised beforehand. In one case an individual was found guilty as an accomplice

---

[34] Trib. corr., Grasse, 23 sept. 1964, *J.C.P.*, 1965.II.13974, note A. Rieg.
[35] Crim. 24 juill. 1958, *B.*, 573.
[36] Crim. 24 déc. 1942, *J.C.P.*, 1944.II.2651.
[37] Art. L.630.
[38] Art. 24 para. 6.
[39] Crim. 21 juillet 1943, *S.*, 1943.I.115.
[40] Crim. 24 déc. 1942, *S.*, 1944.I.7.
[41] Crim. 30 mai 1989, *B.* no. 222.
[42] Crim. 31 janv. 1974, *J.C.P.*, 1975.II.17984, note Mayer-Jack, *R.S.C.*, 1975.679, obs. J. Larguier.
[43] Crim. 23 juillet 1927, *S.*, 1929.I.73, note J.A. Roux.

where he had been paid by two women to wait at the wheel of a car ready for them to make their escape, while they went into a shop to steal.[44]

Mens rea

Accomplices must have knowingly participated in the principal offence. They need to have known the criminal intention of the principal offender, though they need not have shared this intention. Thus, in the case of Maurice Papon, the *Cour de cassation* found that he had been an accomplice to a crime against humanity and it was not necessary that he personally shared the same political ideology as the principal offenders.[45]

Problems can arise where the principal offence differs from that which had been foreseen by the potential accomplice. If the offence committed has a different *actus reus* or *mens rea* than that foreseen by the potential accomplice, the latter is not liable. For example, where a person lent another a gun so that the other person could go hunting, but that person actually used the gun to kill someone else, the owner of the gun could not be treated as an accomplice to the murder.[46] The creditor who gave a third party two revolvers to intimidate a debtor into paying back the money owed could not be convicted as an accomplice to the murder of the caretaker of the building by the third party following an argument.[47]

If, on the other hand, the only difference between the offence foreseen and the offence committed is a secondary circumstance then this will not prevent the accomplice from being liable, provided he caused the offence to be committed. Thus, where a person provided information to help the commission of an ordinary theft, and the principal offender committed this offence at night with a group of people, the person will be liable as an accomplice to the aggravated form of theft. The courts take the view that 'he should have foreseen all these forms of the offence which the conduct was susceptible of giving rise to'.[48] In a case known as *l'affaire du SAC*, the instigator of the principal offence had wanted members of the *Service d'Action Civique* (SAC) to take back compromising documents from a rival member. Five people were killed in the process and he was found to be an accomplice to these killings.[49] By contrast, in another case the potential accomplice was not liable when he gave instructions for the killing of one

---

44　Crim. 30 avr. 1963, *B.* no. 157, *R.S.C.*, 1964.134, obs. A.Légal; Crim. 8 nov. 1972, *B.* no. 329, *D.* 1973, somm. 17.

45　Crim. 23 janv. 1997, *D.*, 1997.147, note J. Pradel.

46　Orléans, 28 janv. 1896, *D.*, 97.2.5.

47　Crim. 13 janv. 1955, *D.*, 1955.291, note Chavanne, obs. Légal, *R.S.C.*, 1955, p. 513.

48　'*il devait prévoir toutes les qualifications dont le fait était susceptible*': Crim. 31 déc. 1947, *B.* no. 270; 21 mai 1996, *B.* no. 206, *Dr pén.*, 1996, comm. 213 et obs. M. Véron.

49　Crim. 19 juin 1984, *B.* no. 231.

individual, but the principal offender decided not to kill this person but killed another instead.[50]

Sometimes, the secondary party has not foreseen the commission of a specific type of offence, instead he or she has given an open hand to the principal offender. For example where people are seeking revenge they might simply give some money to a person with a bad reputation and tell them to take revenge. In such circumstances the courts take the view that the accomplice accepts all the risks and is liable as a secondary party to whatever offence is subsequently committed.[51]

An individual can be found liable as a secondary party to an offence of carelessness. This could be committed, for example, where a passenger encourages a driver to speed and this causes an accident.[52] In one case a bobsleigh was launched at excessive speed down a slope and killed a child. The driver was convicted as the principal offender, and the other occupants were convicted as his accomplices because 'bobsleighing constitutes a team sport in which all the participants have a role to play in driving the device'.[53]

Defence of withdrawal

Where accomplices, having instigated, helped or assisted in the commission of a principal offence, subsequently change their mind and wish to abandon the criminal enterprise, they can avoid liability if they take positive action to prevent the commission of the offence. So, if a potential accomplice lends a weapon to an individual to commit a robbery, he or she might avoid criminal liability by informing the police, taking back the weapon or warning the potential victim. Merely refusing to provide further assistance to the principal offender is not sufficient.[54]

Sentencing

The old Criminal Code stated that the accomplice was liable to the same punishment as the principal offender. This approach was abandoned by the new Code because it introduced liability to moral people such as companies who could only be subjected to a limited range of punishments, most of which would not be suitable for imposition on their human

---

[50] Crim. 10 mars 1977, *D.* 1977, I.R. 237, obs. Larguier, *Rev. sc. crim.,* 1979, p. 75.

[51] Crim. 28 oct. 1965, *J.C.P.,* 1966. II. 14524.

[52] Crim. 17 nov. 1887, *B.* no. 392; 15 févr. 1982, *D.,* 1983.275, note D. Mayer et J.P. Pizzio.

[53] '*la pratique du bobsleigh constitue un sport d'équipe dans lequel tous les participants ont un rôle à remplir dans la conduite de l'engin*': Chambéry, 8 mars 1956, *J.C.P.* 1956.II.9224, note Vouin, observ. Légal; *R.S.C.,* 1956, p. 531.

[54] Crim. 6 févr. 1812, *S.,* chr.

accomplices (for example the dissolution of a company).[55] Thus the new Code states that the accomplice will be punished 'as a principal offender'.[56] This change in wording is unlikely to make any real change. In practice, the courts tend to impose lighter sentences on accomplices than on principal offenders.

Where principal offenders are liable to have their sentence increased due to the existence of aggravating circumstances, the imposition of the aggravated sentence on the accomplices will depend on whether these circumstances are categorised as personal, impersonal[57] or mixed. Aggravating circumstances which are personal to the principal offender do not affect the accomplice. Such is the case of the repeat offender. But, for the same reason, the secondary party cannot benefit from reductions in the sentence due to the personal characteristics of the principal offender, such as that he or she is a minor.

Where the aggravating circumstances are impersonal, that is to say they relate to the offence rather than the individual, they can be applied to the accomplice. For example, the offence of theft is aggravated where it was committed in a group, involved breaking into a building or the use of a weapon. The increased sentence will be imposed on accomplices even if they did not know or approve of this mode of committing the offence.[58]

Aggravating circumstances which are linked both to the offender and to the offence (because they affect the way it was carried out) are known as *les circonstances aggravées mixtes*. An example is premeditation. Under the old Code these were treated like impersonal aggravated circumstances and were therefore applied to the accomplice as well as the principal offender. Thus the accomplice of the son who killed his father incurred the aggravated sentence for parricide.[59] Following the passing of the new Code there has been some debate as to whether this approach should still be followed, since article 121–6 now states that the accomplice should be punished 'as principal offender'. The issue was not considered by the legislator and there is not yet any case law on the issue.

Overlap between accomplices and principal offenders

Occasionally, the courts treat secondary parties as joint principals. They have stated that 'the person who helps the principal offender in committing the offence necessarily co-operates in the perpetration of the

55 J.O. Sénat, 12 mai 1989, pp. 647 et s.
56 Art. 121–6.
57 *réel.*
58 Crim. 26 janv. 1957, *B.* no. 32; 21 mai 1996, *B.* no. 206, *Dr pén.*, 1996, comm. 216, obs. Véron.
59 Crim. 24 mars 1853, *D.*, 1853.I.115.

offence as a joint principal'.[60] The courts are inclined to treat a potential accomplice as a joint principal where this will enable them to impose liability for a particular aggravating circumstance. They will also do so where otherwise the potential accomplice would avoid liability due to the absence of an adequate principal offence, for example, where the potential accomplice had only assisted the commission of a minor offence. Thus, in one case the *Cour de cassation* declared as joint principals individuals who had accompanied a person carrying a flag judged to be subversive and forbidden by a local bye-law.[61] In the same way, in order to punish people who had helped to prepare the commission of an offence, which was not punishable because the potential principal offender voluntarily stopped before the full offence was committed, the Criminal Division decided that they were joint principals to the attempt.[62] An accomplice was labelled as a joint principal to an offence of negligence (involuntary homicide), where he had lent his car to a friend who did not have a driving licence, and who almost immediately afterwards caused a fatal accident.[63]

Sometimes joint principals are treated as accomplices. Thus, in an old judgement of 1848 it was stated that 'the joint principal of an offence necessarily helps the other guilty person in the commission of the offence and thereby automatically becomes his accomplice'.[64] This analysis is known as *complicité corespective* and it enables the court to sentence a person as an accomplice where this means that they will get a higher sentence. Thus under the old Criminal Code there was a separate offence of parricide[65] and until 1981 this bore the death penalty while the ordinary offence of murder incurred life imprisonment. Where two individuals killed the father of one of them, the son committed parricide. By treating the second individual as an accomplice he too could be subjected to the death penalty.

The concept of *complicité corespective* is sometimes applied where a group of people violently attack and kill their victim. When it is clear that all the members of the group hit the victim but it is not clear which one gave the fatal blow, the court can impose liability as joint principals on all the participants for the homicide offence, as they are treated as secondary parties to the fatal attack.

---

[60] *celui qui assiste l'auteur dans les faits de consommation coopère nécessairement à la perpétration de l'infraction en qualité de coauteur*: Crim. 24 août 1827, *B.* no. 224.

[61] Crim. 24 juin 1922, *S.* 1923.1.41, note Roux.

[62] Crim. 19 avr. 1945, *S.* 1945–1–82, concerning an abortion.

[63] Crim. 12 avril 1930, *G.P.*, 1930.II.95.

[64] that *'le coauteur d'un crime aide nécessairement l'auteur coupable dans les faits qui consomment l'action et devient, par la force des choses, son complice'*: Crim. 9 juill 1848, *S.*, 1848.1.527.

[65] Art. 299 and 302 para. 1 of the old Criminal Code.

Comparison with English law

There are marked similarities between the approach of the French and English law to the position of accomplices. Both require the existence of a principal offence but not a conviction. While the terminology is different, the law in both systems essentially covers help or encouragement provided before or at the time of the principal offence. This has been extended slightly by the French law to include conduct that was carried out after the offence where it had been agreed on prior to its commission. In English law the prior agreement might be found to constitute encouragement and fall within complicity on this basis. The French law has taken a more robust approach to the problem of where the principal offender went beyond the criminal acts foreseen by the accomplice.

The notion of *l'auteur intellectuel* has similarities with that of the concept of innocent agents in English law, though the French law will impose liability as a principal offender even where the person who carried out the *actus reus* of the principal offence had the *mens rea*.

6

Inchoate offences

Introduction

There are two inchoate offences in French criminal law: attempts (*la tentative*) and conspiracy (*une association de malfaiteurs*). French academics treat conspiracy as an ordinary autonomous offence, rather than expressly categorising it as an inchoate offence.

Attempts

There are three key elements to the existence of an attempt. For the *actus reus* the defendant must have started to execute the full offence (*le commencement d'exécution*). The *mens rea* requires that the defendant intended to commit the full offence, and the full offence was not committed due to circumstances independent of the will of the defendant (*l'absence de désistement volontaire*). In the words of article 121–5:

> An attempt is constituted when the defendant has started to execute the full offence, which was only suspended or failed to achieve its result because of circumstances independent of the will of the defendant.[1]

This is identical to the definition found in the old Criminal Code. There can be two reasons why the full offence was not committed: either the defendant stopped before completing the full offence (known as an 'interrupted attempt'[2]), or the defendant did everything necessary for the

---

[1] *'La tentative est constituée dès lors que, manifestée par un commencement d'exécution, elle n'a été suspendue ou n'a manqué son effet qu'en raison de circonstances indépendantes de la volonté de son auteur.'*

[2] *une tentative interrompue.*

commission of the full offence but the result was not attained (known as a 'failed attempt'[3]).

Actus reus

The defendant must have started to carry out the full offence,[4] mere preparatory acts are insufficient. The *Cour de cassation* treats this as a question of law which is subject to its control.[5] No element of the *actus reus* of the full offence need have been committed. The Criminal Division uses various formulae to identify the point when the *actus reus* has been committed:

- 'acts directly aimed at the commission of the offence;'[6]

- 'acts having for direct and immediate consequence the completion of the offence;'[7]

- 'any act directly aimed at the commission of the offence when it has been carried out with the intention of committing it;'[8]

- 'acts that should have for direct and immediate consequence the completion of the offence, having entered into the stage of executing the offence.'[9]

Sometimes the *Cour de cassation* avoids using any formula, simply confirming the existence of the attempt.[10] The approach of the *Cour de cassation* has lacked consistency but it would appear that it requires a sufficiently close and direct link between the conduct of the defendant and the full offence (an objective element).

---

[3] *une tentative achevée/une tentative stérile.*
[4] *le commencement d'exécution.*
[5] Crim. 1er mai 1879, *S..*, 1880.I.233; 3 janv. 1913, *affaire dite du faubourg Saint-Honoré, D.*, 1914.I.41, note H. Donnedieu de Vabres; *S.*, 1913.I.281, note J.A. Roux.
[6] *'les actes tendant directement à l'accomplissement du délit'*: Crim. 3 mai 1974, *B.* no. 157; 5 juin 1984, *B.* no. 212.
[7] *'les actes ayant pour conséquence directe et immédiate de consommer le délit'*: Crim. 4 juin 1920, *B.* no. 257; 3 nov. 1927, *S.*, 1929.I.119.
[8] *'constitue un commencement d'exécution tout acte qui tend directement au délit lorsqu'il a été accompli avec l'intention de le commettre'.*
[9] *'les actes devant avoir pour conséquence directe at immédiate de consommer le crime, celui-ci étant entré dans la période d'exécution'.* Crim. 25 oct. 1962, *D.* 1963.221, note Bouzat, *J.C.P.* 1963.II.12985, note Vouin; 29 déc. 1970, *J.C.P.* 1971.II.16770, note Bouzat, *R.S.C.* 1972.99 obs. Ligal; 5 juin 1984, *B.* no. 212.
[10] Crim. 14 juin 1977, *B.* no. 215, *R.S.C.*, 1979.539, obs. J. Larguier; 4 janv. 1978, *B.* no. 5; 5 mai 1997, *B.* no. 167; 25 oct. 1995, *Dt pén.* 1995.63; 10 janvier 1996, *Dt pén.* 1996.97, *R.S.C.* 1996.846, obs. Bouloc.

Thus the case law has found an attempt where the defendant carried equipment to commit a burglary, followed a bank messenger on his circuit and positioned himself ready for an ambush in a stairway where the messenger was due to pass.[11] Convictions were upheld where the defendants were in a car with guns, scarves, glasses and false noses to conceal their identity, waiting for the arrival of a security van.[12] Three individuals were found to have committed an attempt when they were arrested at night equipped with a jemmy heading towards a shop which they intended to burgle.[13] A person who broke into a parked car and sat at the steering wheel but was stopped before they were able to turn on the engine was guilty of attempted theft,[14] as was the person who went to a place where there was a safe to verify the layout of the place and to test the strength of the bars in the windows.[15]

On the other hand, hiring a hit man to kill a designated person was merely preparation and insufficient to constitute an attempt when the hit man backed out of the plan.[16] The owner of a lorry, insured against fire, who voluntarily set light to his vehicle to receive insurance payouts, had not committed an attempted fraud when he was stopped before having submitted a declaration of the fire to his insurer.[17]

Sometimes, for policy reasons, the courts appear to distinguish between different types of offences, so that the same acts might be sufficient for one offence to amount to an attempt, but for another will be treated as merely preparatory acts. Thus the courts take a severe approach to sexual offences. They have therefore found an attempted rape where a man pretended to be a doctor and invited a young woman who was looking for employment to his flat. He had temporarily transformed the flat to make it look like a surgery, and had instructed her to undress in order to undergo a medical examination before she could be interviewed for a job. Suspicious, the woman ran away and the man was found liable for attempted rape despite the fact that it was not clear whether the man intended to rape or sexually assault the woman.[18]

The courts are also more likely to find an attempt where the defendant is a repeat offender.

---

[11] Crim. 3 janv. 1913, *affaire dite du faubourg Saint-Honoré, D.*, 1914.I.41, note H. Donnedieu de Vabres; *S.*, 1913.I.281, note J.A.Roux.
[12] Crim. 29 déc. 1970, *J.C.P.*, 1971.II.16770, note P. Bouzat.
[13] Trib. enf., Nanterre, 6 juillet 1971, *R.S.C.*, 1972.100, obs. A. Ligal.
[14] Crim. 28 oct. 1959, *D.*, 1960.314 note. A. Chavanne; *J.C.P.* 1959. II. 11343, note Chambon; 29 juin 1960, *D.* 1960.617.
[15] Crim. 5 juillet 1951, *B.* 198, *R.S.C.* 1952.439, obs. Ligal.
[16] Crim. 25 oct. 1962 , Lacour and Schieb-Benamar, 2 judgements, *B.*, no. 292 and 293, *D.*, 1963.221, note P. Bouzat, *J.C.P.*, 1963.II.12985, note R. Vouin.
[17] Crim. 27 mai 1959, *B.* no. 282.
[18] Crim. 14 juin 1995, *B.* no. 222, *Dr pén.* 1995. 22, *R.S.C.* 1996. 365, obs. Mayaud.

There are certain complete offences which do not require a result, known in French as *les infractions formelles*. An example of such an offence is poisoning where article 221–5 states that the offence is committed on the simple administration of the toxic substance, there is no need for the victim to have actually been killed. It is possible to be liable for attempting such offences, and the *actus reus* will occur at a relatively early stage. For example, a person was convicted of an attempted poisoning where he threw poison into the victim's well.[19]

Mens rea

The defendant must have an irrevocable intention to commit the full offence. The courts will only find an attempt if the full offence was not committed because of circumstances independent of the will of the defendant. The failure to commit the full offence will be voluntary where defendants freely decide not to proceed with their criminal enterprise. This decision might have been reached due to pity for the victim or to the fear of being caught. The failure to carry out the full offence will be involuntary where it is solely due to an external factor, for example, if they are prevented from proceeding because the police arrive at the scene[20] or because they are unable to open the safe.

It is more difficult to determine this issue in intermediate situations where an external factor intervened but the defendant had a choice whether or not to proceed. For example, where the defendant hears a noise and runs away. It will be a question of fact in each case whether or not the courts will find an attempt in such circumstances. In one case the defendants were digging in a cemetery with the intention of removing a body when they became frightened and ran away. On these facts, the court found that there was no attempt.[21]

The impossible offence

Where the full offence was impossible the legislation gives no general guidance as to the appropriate approach. In the specific case of poisoning article 221–5 requires the administration of substances 'of a type to lead to death,'[22] thus if a non-toxic substance had been given by mistake the

---

[19] Crim. 5 févr. 1958, *B.* no. 126.
[20] Crim. 5 juillet 1951, *B.* no. 198; 19 juin 1979, *B.* no. 219; *R.S.C.*, 1980, 969, obs. J. Larguier.
[21] Fort-de-France, 22 sept. 1967, *J.C.P.*, 1968.II.15583, note M. Biswang; *R.S.C.* 1969.130, obs. Ligal.
[22] *'de nature à entraîner la mort'*.

offence would not be committed. In the absence of any general provision on the subject, the courts' approach has changed over the years. The development of the case law can be divided into three stages. Until 1860 the courts excluded liability for attempting the impossible, on the ground that 'where there is a physical impossibility in the commission of an offence, there is an equivalent impossibility in fact and in law for the existence of an attempt'.[23]

Later the *Cour de cassation* appeared to support a distinction between absolute impossibility and relative impossibility. There is an absolute impossibility where the object of the offence does not exist (for example, the potential murder victim is dead), or where the means used are by their nature ineffective (for example, there were only blank bullets in the gun). Criminal liability would not be imposed for such cases. By contrast, there is relative impossibility when the object of the offence is only momentarily unattainable, and criminal liability would be imposed. The *Cour de cassation* therefore ruled that looking inside an empty church collection box was merely a case of relative impossibility[24] as was shooting in a room which the intended victim had just left;[25] and putting one's hand into an empty pocket.[26]

Following a judgment of 9 November 1928,[27] the *Cour de cassation* appears to have accepted that all attempts to commit impossible offences can give rise to criminal liability. In this decision the *Cour de cassation* upheld the conviction for abortion where there was an absolute impossibility of committing the full offence due to the method used.

Thus, there is an attempted theft when a person gets into a car but takes nothing because it is empty or if a house is entered but there is nothing of value to remove.[28] Attempted fraud was committed when a person made a false declaration about a fire to an insurance company in order to receive insurance payouts, despite the fact that the terms of the insurance policy excluded liability of the insurance company.[29] A *chambre d'accusation*[30] has sent back to the *Cour d'assises* an individual who had set light to their victim, who had actually been killed shortly before by a bullet shot by another.[31] Soon afterwards, the *Cour de cassation* approved the conviction

---

[23] '*là où se rencontre une impossibilité matérielle à la perpétration du crime même, il se rencontre une impossibilité de même nature pour l'existence en fait et la qualification en droit de la tentative*'. Crim. 6 janvier 1859, S., 1859.I.362 (concerning the use of abortive practices on a woman who was not pregnant); Montpellier, 26 févr. 1852, S. 1852.2.464.

[24] Crim. 4 nov. 1876, S., 1877.I.48.

[25] Crim. 12 avril 1977, S., 1877.I.329.

[26] Crim. 4 janv. 1895, D., 1896.I.21, note R. Garraud.

[27] Crim. 9 nov. 1928, Fleury, D., 1929.I.97, note A. Henry, J. Pradel and A Varinard.

[28] Crim. 15 mars 1994, *Dr pén*, 1994, comm. 153.

[29] Crim. 7 janv. 1980, B. no. 8, D., 1980, I.R. 521, obs. M. Puech.

[30] Now known as '*la chambre de l'instruction*'.

[31] Paris, 9 avril 1946, R.S.C., 1948.147, obs. Gulphe.

for murder by a *Cour d'assises* of two individuals who had acted together, but one of them must have shot the victim after he had already been killed by the bullet of the other.[32] Most recently, the *Cour de cassation* has approved the conviction for attempted murder of a victim who was already dead at the time of the attack.[33] In that case a brawl had broken out in a café and the victim was mortally wounded but had managed to return to their home to die. The next day the defendant had gone to the victim's home and used violence which would have been fatal but for the fact that the victim had already died from his earlier injuries.

Which offences can be attempted?

Following article 121–4–2, all serious offences can be the subject of an attempt. Major offences can be the subject of a criminal attempt if the legislator has expressly provided for this. In most cases there is such express provision. The main exceptions are where it would not be practicable to categorise an incident as an attempt. This might be because the label would depend on the result attained which, by definition, has not been attained, or where it would not be logical to have an attempt, for example, with involuntary homicide (as an attempt requires intention) or offences committed by omission. Minor offences can never be the subject of a criminal attempt.

Sentencing

Under article 121–4 the person who attempts an offence is treated as if they committed the full offence, and is potentially liable to the same sentence. In practice, the courts show greater leniency towards those convicted of an attempt.

Conspiracy

The offence of conspiracy is defined in article 450–1 which states:

> *Art. 450–1.* A conspiracy consists of any group formed or understanding established with a view to the preparation, evidenced by one or more physical facts, of one or more serious offences or one or more major offences punishable by ten years imprisonment.

---

[32] Crim. 5 oct. 1972, *G.P.*, 1973.I.25, *R.S.C.*, 1973.880, obs. J. Larguier.
[33] Crim. 16 janv. 1986, *D.*, 1986.265, note D. Mayer and C. Gazounaud; *J.C.P.* 1987.II.20774, note G. Roujou de Boubie, *R.S.C.*, 1986.839, obs. A. Vitu.

Participation in a conspiracy is punishable by ten years imprisonment and a FF1,000,000 fine.[34]

A similar definition can be found in article 132–71 which defines an organised gang,[35] but that article does not create an autonomous offence, instead it establishes an aggravating circumstance for offences such as theft[36] and rape.[37]

Following the Act of 17 June 1998, inserting article 450–4 into the Code, the offence was extended to apply to moral persons.

Under the original drafting of the 1810 Code a conspiracy only arose where there was a clear hierarchical structure to the criminal organisation,[38] of a type associated with the Italian Mafia. This proved ineffective faced with anarchic movements in the late 1800s. The Code was therefore amended to cover more loosely organised groups and it was subsequently used during the Algerian crisis.

The offence was again reformed by the Act 'Security and Liberty' of 2 February 1981. This sought to broaden the offence, by not requiring more than one crime to have been the subject of the group's activities, despite criticism that this would reduce the distinction with liability for complicity. Its status was also reduced from a serious offence to a major offence in order to facilitate the prosecution process. Further legislation of 10 June 1983 reversed some of these reforms, but following several terrorist attacks the wider definition of the offence was reinstated by the Act of 9 September 1986. The new Criminal Code has further widened the scope of the offence.

In order to establish the existence of a conspiracy three elements must exist:

- An understanding
- Aim to prepare certain offences
- Intention

---

[34] 'Art. 450–1. *Constitue une association de malfaiteurs tout groupement formé ou entente établie en vue de la préparation, caractérisée par un ou plusieurs faits matériels, d'un ou plusieurs crimes ou d'un ou plusieurs délits punis de dix ans d'emprisonnement.*

La participation à une association de malfaiteurs est punie de dix ans d'emprisonnement et de 1 000 000 F d'amende.'

[35] 'Art. 132–71. *Constitue une bande organisée au sens de la loi tout groupement formé ou toute entente établie en vue de la préparation, caractérisée par un ou plusieurs faits matériels, d'une ou de plusieurs infractions.'*

[36] Art. 311–4 para 1.

[37] Art. 222–24 para. 6.

[38] Art. 265–268 old Criminal Code.

Actus reus

An understanding

The legislation states that either a 'group' must have been formed or an 'understanding' established between wrongdoers. In fact, the emphasis of the case law is on the existence of an understanding. The understanding can be very informal, and the offence will be committed where one individual simply recruits another to assist him in the commission of an offence.[39]

The existence of this understanding must be supported by physical evidence, in order to avoid a potential miscarriage of justice. This evidence could consist of, for example, a vehicle containing weapons, balaclavas, surgical gloves, registration documents and documents relating to the reconnoitring of the premises[40] or the fact that the defendants purchased weapons and explosives.[41]

Aim to prepare certain offences

In order for there to be a conspiracy, the defendants must have reached an understanding relating to the preparation of one or more offences. The planned offences must either be serious offences or major offences punishable with a maximum sentence of at least ten years imprisonment. It is not necessary for the prosecution to identify the precise nature of the offence, provided it is clear that the planned offence would fall within one of the two categories specified. Thus in a case in 1993, the *Cour de cassation* upheld a conviction of a man for his involvement in a conspiracy where he supported the activities of terrorist organisations.[42]

It is not sufficient that the group simply shares the same ideas, they must have resolved to act together in a criminal enterprise. It does not matter where the proposed offences would be carried out, whether in France or abroad, provided the conspiracy itself occurred in France.[43]

The offence is committed even before there is an attempt, as it occurs at the point when preparatory acts are undertaken.[44] In one case[45] the person recruited and paid to commit an offence against another person had decided not to go ahead with the planned offence, but was still liable as a party to the conspiracy. In another case,[46] the defendants had driven to the

---

[39] Crim. 30 avr. 1996, *B.* no. 176; *R.S.C.*. 1997.113, obs. Delmas-Saint-Hilaire.
[40] Crim. 6 sept. 1990, *Dr. pén.* 1991, no. 3.
[41] Crim. 15 déc. 1993, *Dr. pén.* 1994, comm. 131.
[42] Crim. 15 déc. 1993.
[43] Crim. 20 févr. 1990: *B.* no. 84; *D.* 1991, p. 395, note A. Fournier.
[44] Crim. 29 déc 1970, *B.* no. 356; *JCP* 1971.II.16770, note P. Bouzat; *R.S.C.* 1971. 675, obs. A. Vitu.
[45] Crim. 30 avr. 1996.
[46] Crim. 22 janv. 1986: *B.* no. 29.

proposed scene of the crime equipped with weapons and then decided against carrying out the offence due to the high risks involved and returned to their car. The offence of conspiracy had been committed.

Where the full offence or offences have been committed, liability can still be imposed for the defendants' involvement in the conspiracy.[47]

Mens rea

Intention

This offence requires intention. Each participant in the conspiracy can only be liable if he or she joined the criminal group knowingly and with the intention to provide the other members of the group with effective help in the pursuit of the criminal enterprise. The members of the group do not need to intend to commit a specific crime,[48] though a fairly precise plan is required.[49]

Sentencing

The maximum sentence for this offence is ten years and a FF1,000,000 fine, regardless of whether the planned crime was a serious or major offence. Moral persons can only be subjected to a fine.

Following article 450–2, conspirators can avoid punishment where they have helped the police detect the existence of the conspiracy. This article states:

> *Art. 450–2.* Any person having participated in a group or an understanding defined by article 450-1 is exempt from punishment if he has, before any prosecution, revealed the group or understanding to the competent authorities and enabled the identification of the other participants.[50]

Comparison with English law

The *actus reus* of an attempt is defined as occurring at a very similar stage in the two systems. In English law the Criminal Attempts Act 1981 requires an act that is 'more than merely preparatory' and this is often described in the case law as occurring where the defendant had 'embarked on the crime proper'. In the same way French law excludes mere preparation from the scope of the offence. The *mens rea* puts a different emphasis, allowing in

---

[47] Crim. 22 janv. 1986, *B.* no. 29; 3 juill. 1991, *B.* no. 288.

[48] Crim. 7 déc. 1966, *B.* no. 281.

[49] Crim. 5 mai 1999, pourvoi no. 97-83117: *Juris-Data* no. 002091.

[50] '*Art. 450-2. Toute personne ayant participé au groupement ou à l'entente définis par l'article 450-1 est exempte de peine si elle a, avant toute poursuite, révélé le groupement ou l'entente aux autorités compétentes et permis l'identification des autres participants.*'

French law indirectly a defence at any stage prior to the commission of the full offence that the defendant had changed their mind. While in English law, once defendants have the intention to commit the result of the full offence, the attempt can be committed regardless of whether they later change their mind. Under both systems minor offences cannot be the subject of criminal attempts.

Though there is no separate inchoate offence of incitement in French law, factors that would constitute an incitement or a conspiracy in English law are treated in French law as aggravating circumstances of other offences or within the framework of secondary party liability.

7

Defences

Introduction

In the new Criminal Code the defences are laid down in articles 122–1 to 122–8. French academic writers draw a distinction between objective defences (sometimes called justifications) and subjective defences (sometimes called excuses), though this distinction is not expressly referred to by the Code. Objective defences are concerned with the surrounding circumstances in which the offence was committed rather than the defendant him or herself. They provide a justification for the criminal conduct which ceases to be viewed as anti social.[1] Under the old Code, articles 327 and 328[2] went as far as to say that when such a defence applied, no offence existed at all. The new Code does not go this far, simply stating that the accused will not be liable for the offence. There are four objective defences: order of law, order of a legitimate authority, legitimate defence and necessity. Subjective defences are those which are directly linked to the defendant. There are four subjective defences which remove the liability of the individual:[3] mental illness, the defence of being a minor, constraint and mistake of law. The objective defences will be considered, followed by the subjective defences.

Objective defences

Order of law

Where a person appears to have committed an offence, they may have a defence if their conduct was authorised by another piece of legislation. The Criminal Code states in the first paragraph of article 122-4:

[1] *faits justificatifs.*
[2] *'il n'y a ni crime ni délit'.*
[3] *causes de non-imputabilité.*

A person is not criminally liable who carries out an act ordered or authorised by legislative or regulatory provisions.[4]

This is clearer than article 372 of the old Code and gives express approval to the case law on the subject. The old article had referred to there being neither a serious or major crime when the conduct was authorised by the law, but made no reference to minor offences. The case law had accepted that the defence also applied to minor offences, an approach which has been followed by the new Code as it broadly states that no criminal liability will be incurred. The old Code referred to acts ordered by the law, but made no reference to the situation where the act was simply permitted by the law. Again, the case law had taken the view that this was also covered by the defence and this approach is adopted by the new Code, which refers both to the conduct being ordered and authorised by the law.

An example of where the defence applies is in the context of police powers. Legislation allows the police to arrest and detain suspects. As long as the arrest and detention is carried out in accordance with this legislation, the police have a defence to a charge of unlawfully detaining a person against their will. A classic French illustration of this point is that the state executioner[5] could, until 1981, lawfully execute people sentenced to the death penalty and had a defence to any charge of murder that he was carrying out an order of law.

When considering whether the defence applies, the courts will take account of the hierarchy of the sources of law as laid down in the French Constitution. Thus an Act can always lay down an exception to the provisions of another Act or regulation, but a regulation cannot normally form the basis of an exception to an Act and in such circumstances the defence could not be relied on.

A situation can arise where legislative provisions conflict, with legislation laying down an offence for failure to do something, while other legislative provisions state that an offence will be committed if that conduct is carried out. Such a conflict arose in the Act on the Freedom of the Press of 29 July 1881. Article 13 of that Act imposed an obligation on newspaper editors to publish a statement provided by a wronged party, with the failure to publish being an offence, while the Act also lays down an offence of defamation. The courts have taken the approach that the editor can refuse to publish the statement if it contains a defamation.[6] In a comparable situation, the editor of the *Journal Officiel* was found not liable for a defamation resulting from declarations of association which he was bound to publish by virtue of the law.[7]

[4] '*N'est pas pénalement responsable la personne qui accomplit un acte prescrit ou autorisé par des dispositions législatives ou règlementaires.*'

[5] *le bourreau.*

[6] Crim. 19 déc. 1989, *B.* no. 493.

[7] Crim. 17 fév. 1981, *B.* no. 63.

The courts are sometimes reluctant to allow defendants to rely on a civil law as a defence to the commission of a criminal offence. For example, the Civil Code lays down in article 215 an obligation for spouses to cohabit. This implies the existence of sexual relations and in the past it was relied on as a basis for ruling that a husband could not rape his wife. This interpretation of the law was rejected by the *Cour de cassation* in 1990.[8]

While article 122–4 makes no express reference to customs, the courts do sometimes allow the defence to be based on a custom rather than a piece of legislation. Thus, custom is relied on as a defence to offences against the person committed during sports, including those involving fighting such as boxing.[9] It is also used to defend doctors carrying out their profession and to parents who commit minor offences against the person to discipline their children.[10] This defence is not available to teachers since the judgement of 21 February 1967.[11] In the context of bullfights and cock fights, the criminal law expressly allows these practices to fall outside the offences concerning acts of cruelty and bad treatment of animals where a local custom for their practice exists.[12]

Generally, the defence will cease to be available if a person has gone beyond what was necessary to satisfy the legal imperatives. In one case,[13] a child had a stone in his hand and had threatened to throw it at his companion. The defendant had seen the danger and seized and twisted the child's arm so brutally that he caused a fracture. He was charged with intentionally inflicting violence on another and in his defence he relied on the existence of the offence of failing to give assistance to a person in danger (now article 223–5 of the new Criminal Code). The defence succeeded in relation to the offence of intentionally inflicting violence on another, but not for the non-intentional offence as excessive force had been used.

Superior orders

The defence of an order of law is contained in the first paragraph of article 122–4 C.C. The second paragraph contains the defence of superior orders, which states:

> A person who carries out an act ordered by a legitimate authority is not criminally liable, except if this act is obviously illegal.[14]

[8] Crim. 5 sept. 1990, *B.* no. 313; *D.* 191. 13, note Angevin; *J.C.P.* 1991. II. 21629, note Rassat; *G.P.* 1991, 1. 58, note Doucet.

[9] Crim. 8 juin 1994, *Dr. pén.* 1994, comm. no. 230.

[10] Crim. 21 fév. 1990, *Dr. pén.* 1990, 216.

[11] Crim. 21 fév. 1967, *B.* no. 73.

[12] Art. 521–1, R. 654–1 and R. 655–1 Criminal Code.

[13] Alger, 9 nov. 1953, *D*, 1954, 369, note Pageaud.

[14] '*N'est pas pénalement responsable la personne qui accomplit un acte commandé par l'autorité légitime, sauf si cet acte est manifestement illégal.*'

These two defences are actually closely linked, as frequently the order of a law is put into practice by a superior authority ordering a subordinate to carry out the law. For example, a policeman who carries out an arrest and is subsequently accused of unlawfully detaining an individual against their will, can usually rely both on the defence of an order of law (discussed above) and on the defence of superior orders, as the mandate for the arrest may have been issued by an investigating judge. Where the order was illegal (but not manifestly so) then the defence of superior orders will be available where the defence of an order of law will not.

In determining whether the defence applies, the courts need to consider whether the order came from a legitimate authority and whether the order was obviously illegal.

A legitimate authority

The authority must be a public authority (either civil or military), but cannot be a private authority. Thus the authority cannot be the head of a family ordering his children,[15] a husband ordering his wife,[16] or an employer ordering his employee.[17] The authority must have had the competence to issue the order, which is particularly problematic where a person has, in good faith, carried out orders from an incompetent authority which appeared to be competent. This is what happened on a grand scale under the Vichy régime, between 1940 and 1944. At the time of the liberation of France, an *ordonnance* of 9 August 1944 was issued which re-established the French Republic and ruled that the Vichy government had not been recognised in law. This meant that the civil servants who had been carrying out the orders of this government could have no defence of superior orders for any criminal offences they committed at the time under the régime, for example by carrying out arrests and searching property. To avoid further social difficulties, an *ordonnance* of 28 November 1944 was passed to provide a defence to civil servants who had obeyed superior orders between 1940 and 1944, except where they had voluntarily participated in anti-national acts destined to favour the occupiers.

The person obeying the order must have been the subordinate of the authority issuing it.

Obviously illegal orders

French academic theory distinguishes three possible approaches to illegal orders. The first is known as 'passive obedience'[18] where the law insists that the subordinate must always obey orders of a superior without

---

[15] Crim. 4 mai 1837, *B.*, 143 (*délit forestier* committed by a son on the order of his father).
[16] Crim. 25 sept. 1818, *Ancien Rép. Dalloz*, Vo. *Peine*, no 418 (theft).
[17] Crim. 20 nov. 1834, *B.* 380 (tax offence).
[18] *l'obéissance passive.*

questioning their legality and as a counterbalance the subordinate will never be liable for his acts. The second is known as the 'intelligent bayonets'[19] and requires subordinates to ensure the legality of the order before executing it, and imposes criminal liability where illegal orders are carried out. The third is a pragmatic compromise where liability for carrying out an illegal order is only imposed if the order was obviously illegal. It is this third approach that has been adopted by the new Criminal Code. Thus, under French law, where an order was obviously illegal the person who carried it out has no defence on the grounds of superior orders, though they may be able to argue that they acted under a constraint (discussed on p. 116). Thus a police officer who carries out an arrest under a mandate issued by an investigating judge, which is subsequently declared to be illegal, would have a defence if the illegality was not obvious.

In determining whether the illegality was obvious the courts will take into account the nature of the conduct carried out. The more serious the conduct the more likely that a court will conclude that it was obviously illegal. For example, an order for soldiers to kill a prisoner or for police officers to torture a suspect are likely to be treated as obviously illegal. Article 213–4 of the Criminal Code expressly states that a person who commits a crime against humanity cannot rely on this defence, such an argument only being available as a cause of mitigation when the court is determining what sentence to impose.

The judges will also take into account the nature of the subordinate – a senior civil servant or a member of the armed forces being treated more severely than private citizens. This is the approach taken by the *Cour de cassation* in a case where a senior civil servant was convicted of a criminal offence when, on the order of the local Prefect, he interfered with private correspondence.[20]

If it can be shown that the subordinate knew the order was illegal, even though this illegality was not obvious, then the courts are not likely to allow this defence.

In the past, where a person violently resisted the execution of an illegal order they could be prosecuted for the commission of an offence of violence.[21] However, a recent appeal recognised the right to resist if the agent's actions were obviously illegal.[22]

Legitimate defence

Article 122–5 of the Criminal Code lays down the parameters of the legitimate defence. This states:

---

[19] *les baïonettes intelligentes.*
[20] Crim. 22 mai 1959, *J.C.P.* 1959, II, 11–162.
[21] Crim. 5 janvier 1821, *S.*, 1821.I.358; 27 aôut 1908, *D.*, 1909.I.79.
[22] Reims, 18 mars 1984, A.P., 1984. II.715, *R.S.C.*, 1985.69, obs. J.P. Delmas Saint-Hilaire.

A person who, faced with an unjustified attack against themselves or another, carries out at that time an act required by the necessity of the legitimate defence of themselves or another is not criminally liable, except if there is a disproportion between the means of defence used and the gravity of the attack.

A person who, in order to prevent the commission of a serious or major offence against property, carries out an act of defence, other than voluntary homicide, when this act is strictly necessary for the goal sought is not criminally liable when the means used are proportionate to the gravity of the offence.[23]

The traditional concept of self-defence thus falls within this defence, though its parameters are obviously wider than this. There are a range of conditions that need to be satisfied before the defence can be applied.

An unjustified attack

The attack that gave rise to the response must be in breach of the law, though it need not pose a threat to a person's life.[24] An attack on a person's honour will not ground the defence,[25] though an attack on a person's morals can be sufficient, particularly where the morals of a minor are concerned. In one case, a mother hit a young girl with loose morals who was corrupting her sixteen-year-old son.[26]

Actual or imminent attack

In order for the legitimate defence to apply there must be an actual or imminent attack. For example, if a person is threatened, but the aggressor is held back by others on the scene, the person threatened cannot lash out violently at their aggressor and then rely on their legitimate defence, as the attack was no longer actual or imminent.[27] Where the threat is not actual or imminent the law takes the view that the individual could seek the protection of the authorities, so that a direct response would be unnecessary. If there is a time lapse between the attack and the response, the latter amounts to revenge and falls outside the defence.[28]

---

[23] 'N'est pas pénalement responsable la personne qui, devant une atteinte injustifiée envers elle-même ou autrui, accomplit dans le même temps, un acte commandé par la nécessité de la légitime défense d'elle-même ou d'autrui, sauf s'il y a disproportion entre les moyens de défense employés et la gravité de l'attteinte.

N'est pas pénalement responsable la personne qui, pour interrompre l'exécution d'un crime ou d'un délit contre un bien, accomplit un acte de défense, autre qu'un homicide volontaire, lorsque cet acte est strictement nécessaire au but poursuivi dès lors que les moyens sont proportionnés à la gravité de l'infraction.'

[24] Crim. 14 avr. 1956, *Rec. dr. pén.*, 1956.191.

[25] Crim. 24 nov. 1899, *D.* 1901, I, 373.

[26] Trib. Pol. Valence, 19 mai 1960, *S.*, 1960.271, note L. Hugueney; obs. Légal, *R.S.C.*, 1962.321.

[27] Crim. 28 mai 1937, *G.P.*, 1937.2. 336.

[28] Crim. 4 juill. 1907, *B.*, 243; Crim. 28 mai 1937, *G.P.* 1937.2.336; Crim. 16 oct. 1979, *D.*, 1980, I.R., 522.

The defence will cease to exist where the threat has come to an end, such as where an aggressor has seen the defendant's gun and put his hands up in the air.[29] Nor can the defence be relied on where, in order to prevent a possible future attack, a person has attacked first.[30] On the other hand, while a person cannot attack first, they can take precautions to prevent a possible attack. But the means of defence prepared in advance must not be susceptible to produce a disproportionate response compared with the actual attack eventually suffered. This problem has arisen in relation to property owners who, in an attempt to protect their property, leave booby traps which explode automatically on contact.[31] The approach of the courts to such devices will depend on the facts of each particular case. In one case, a farmer had suffered several thefts, and had installed a trap gun in his chicken shed which had injured a thief. The farmer was convicted of an intentional offence against the person.[32] In another case, after several earlier burglaries, the victim had placed a trap in a transistor radio placed in a locked cupboard. A thief had been injured by the device, and the owner was convicted of an intentional offence against the person.[33]

A proportionate response

The response must bear some relation to the intensity of the attack. Thus, the legitimate defence ceases to be available when a person responds to a slap with a revolver.[34] In one case, some people had just climbed over a boundary wall and the property owner had tried to frighten them away by shooting without visibility into the darkness. One of the intruders was hit and injured. The defence was not available to the property owner as he had carelessly used excessive force.[35] In another prosecution the defendant had been grabbed by her collar and, in response, she had hit her aggressor with her high heeled shoe causing a lesion to the optic nerve of their left eye.[36] This response was considered to be disproportionate by the *Cour de cassation.*

Involuntary crimes

By definition the defendant will have responded to the attack by the commission of a crime. One area of debate has been whether this crime can be an involuntary offence. The respected academic Garçon considered that

[29] Crim. 20 oct. 1993, *Dr. pén.* 1993, 34.
[30] Crim. 27 juin 1927, S., 1929.I. 356.
[31] Levasseur, *Les pièges à feux*, R.S.C., 1979, p. 329; Romerio, *Les pièges à voleurs et le droit*, *J.C.P.*, 1979.I.2939; Pradel, *La défense automatique des biens*, Mélanges Bouzat, 1980, p. 217.
[32] T. Corr. Toulouse, 8 oct. 1969, D., 1970. 315, note Cédié.
[33] Reims, 9 nov. 1978, D., 1979.92, note Pradel; *J.C.P.*, 1979.II.19046.
[34] Crim. 4 aôut 1949, R.S.C., 1950, 47, obs. Magnoil.
[35] T. Corr. Mayenne, 6 mars 1957, D., 1957.458, note Pageaud.
[36] Crim. 6 déc. 1995, *Dr. pén.*, 1996, comm. 98.

such offences could fall within the defence.[37] But the *Cour de cassation* has taken the opposite view, on the basis that the defence requires a deliberate response to the attack.[38]

Mistake

Where the defendant mistakenly believes they are about to be attacked they will be able to rely on the defence if that mistake was reasonable.[39] For example, a prosecution was brought when an incident occurred after a police officer had surprised two individuals trying to steal some property in the middle of the night.[40] He was hit by one of them while the other, armed with a crowbar, had disappeared. He mistakenly believed that this person might return at any moment and as this belief was reasonable he could therefore rely on his legitimate defence when he shot the remaining suspect to defend himself.

Where there are no good reasons for the defendant to make the mistake, the defence will not be available, though the defendant may lack *mens rea*.

Defence of property

This form of the defence was not expressly mentioned by the old Criminal Code but had been developed by the courts since 1902. In that year, a defence had been allowed in civil proceedings where a poacher stealing fish had lost a leg after being injured by a trap placed in a pond by the property owner, M Fraville.[41] The National Assembly hesitated about including this form of the defence in the new Code as it was worried about encouraging vigilante activity but, having reached a compromise with the Senate, it is now expressly provided for in the second paragraph of article 122–5. It is therefore possible to use force against a thief. The criteria for the defence of property are more rigorous than those for the defence of the person. Article 122–5 states that the response must have been 'strictly' necessary to prevent the attack, an adverb that is not used in relation to the prevention of an offence against the person. So the defendant should normally have given the victim a warning before using violence. On the issue of proportionality, a voluntary homicide cannot be committed in order to protect property. The defence can only be exercised in relation to serious and major offences against property and not minor offences (such as minor damage to property under article R. 635–1).

---

[37] Garçon, no. 105.

[38] Crim. 16 fév. 1967, *J.C.P.*, 1967.II.15034, note Combaldieu. This decision has been strongly criticised by some authors, see for example: Légal, *R.S.C.*, 1967.854; Levasseu, *R.S.C.*, 1967.659.

[39] *'raisonnablement croire'*: Crim. 21 fév. 1996, *B.*, 84, obs. Bouloc, *R.S.C.*, 1996, p. 849.

[40] Paris, 9 oct. 1979, *J.C.P.*, 1979.II.19232, note Bouzat.

[41] Req., 25 mars 1902, *S.*, 1903.I.5, note Lyon-Caen, *D.*, 1902.I.356, *affaire de Fraville*.

Burden of proof

Normally the defendant has to prove that the conditions of the defence have been satisfied. On the issue of proportionality, where the threat was to the person the burden of proof is on the prosecution to show that the response was disproportionate, while with threats to property it is on the defendant.

More significantly, the legislator has sought to strengthen the protection of individuals in particularly dangerous situtations by reversing this burden of proof. Article 122–6 of the Criminal Code states:

> A person is presumed to have acted in a state of legitimate defence when they carry out the act:
> 1. To repel, at night, an entrance by force, violence or fraud into inhabited premises;
> 2. To defend themselves against the authors of theft or looting executed with force.[42]

In such circumstances it would be up to the prosecution to prove that the individual was not acting in a state of legitimate defence. For a long time this presumption was thought to be irrebuttable. Thus, on several occasions an individual had entered a house for an amorous rendezvous with a woman inside. Her husband was aware of his intentions and, having armed himself for his arrival, killed or injured him with a gun. In such cases, the conditions of legitimate defence were not satisfied, but the prosecution could not rebut the presumption that the defence applied.[43] In 1959 the *Cour de cassation* reversed its position on the matter, ruling that the presumption was rebuttable[44] and this is the approach adopted by the new Code.

Civil liability

The existence of this defence removes not only criminal liability, but civil liability as well.[45]

Defence of necessity

The old Criminal Code did not lay down a general defence of necessity, but there were certain offences which could not be committed where the

[42] '*Est présumé avoir agi en état de légitime défense celui qui accomplit l'acte:*
    1. *Pour repousser, de nuit, l'entrée par effraction, violence ou ruse dans un lieu habité;*
    2. *Pour se défendre contre les auteurs de vols ou de pillages exécutés avec violence.*'
[43] Crim. 11 juil. 1844, S. 1844, I, 777.
[44] Crim. 19 fév. 1959, D., 1959.161, note M.R.M.P., J.C.P., 1959.II.11112, note Bouzat.
[45] Crim. 13 déc. 1989, B. no. 478; Civ. 2e, Dr. pén. 1992, 226, note Viron.

person acted through necessity, such as obstructing the highway[46] or having an abortion.[47] During the 19th century, the courts were reluctant to recognise openly a general defence of necessity, preferring to treat such cases as falling within the defence of constraint.[48] Thus, in the famous case of Ménard[49] the mother of a family who had stolen some bread to feed her children was acquitted. In another trial, some Jews were acquitted of using false administrative documents which they had used to escape a police search under German occupation, by relying on the defence of constraint.[50] Alternatively the courts would avoid imposing liability on the grounds that the defendant lacked the requisite intention to commit the offence.[51] But both approaches were artificial, as the defence of constraint suggests the defendant could not make a free choice, but actually the defendant acting under necessity has made a positive choice. This is also why they really do have the *mens rea* of the offence and to pretend otherwise is to confuse *mens rea* with motive. It was in the 1950s that a court of first instance recognised the defence of necessity. The court acquitted the accused of the charge of building without a permit as he was trying to provide decent living conditions for his family who had been living in slum accommodation.[52] Soon afterwards the *Cour de cassation* formally recognised the defence of necessity.[53] The defence is now expressly provided for in article 122–7 of the Criminal Code which states:

> A person is not criminally liable who, faced with an existing or imminent danger which threatens themselves, another or property, carries out a necessary act to safeguard the person or property, except if there is disproportion between the means used and the gravity of the threat.[54]

The defence of necessity is available to all types of offences, but three conditions must be satisfied in order for it to be applied: there must be an existing or imminent danger, this danger must have necessitated the commission of the offence, and the offence must have been proportionate to the danger. These conditions are very similar to those for the legitimate defence because the latter is really just a special form of the former, always requiring that the danger to which the defendant was responding be a criminal offence.

---

[46] *'encombrement de la voie publique'*: art. R. 38, old Criminal Code.
[47] Act of 17 January 1975.
[48] Crim. 15 nov. 1856, *B.*, no. 358; 14 aôut 1863, *D.P.*, 64.I.399.
[49] Amiens, 22 avr. 1898, *S.*, 1899.2.1, note Roux.
[50] Paris, 6 oct. 1944 and 5 janv. 1945, *S.* 1945.2, 81.
[51] Amiens, 22 avr. 1898, *S.*, 1899.2.1, note Roux; Crim. 27 janv. 1933, *G.P.*, 1933.I.489.
[52] Trib. corr., Colmar, 27 avril 1956, *D.*, 1956.500.
[53] Crim. 25 juin 1958, Lesage, *J.C.P.*, 1959.II.10941, note J. Larguier, *D.*, 1958.693, note M.R.M.P.
[54] *'N'est pas pénalement responsable la personne qui, face à un danger actuel ou imminent qui menace elle-même, autrui ou un bien, accomplit un acte nécessaire à la sauvegarde de la personne ou du bien, sauf s'il y a disproportion entre les moyens employés et la gravité de la menace.'*

An existing or imminent danger

As with legitimate defence, the defence of necessity is only available when there is an existing or imminent danger. The danger can be to the defendant, a third party or to property and the nature of the danger does not matter. In one case the defence was allowed where the danger was to a family's wellbeing. A tenant had destroyed a fence which had been built by the landlord to stop the tenant's family from having access to the water, gas and electricity meters and to the toilet facilities.[55] Where squatters have broken into property and argued that it was in order to have shelter during a housing crisis the courts have not been prepared to accept that the danger existed or was imminent.[56]

The danger must not be imposed by the law. For example, a soldier cannot flee combat as he has an obligation to fight when ordered to do so.

The defence is also not available if the defendant had themselves created the danger through their own fault, though this condition has been criticised by some academic writers.[57] Thus, a lorry driver could not rely on the defence when he had been forced to knock down the barrier of a level crossing, onto which he had unwisely driven, to avoid being crushed by a train.[58]

Necessity of the offence

The danger must have truly necessitated the offence – if the offender had other means of safeguarding the threatened interests, they will be convicted,[59] unless this was the best course of action.[60] In recent proceedings a defendant had taken some meat from a shop to improve the diet of his children. But his bank account was in credit and he had stolen more than £100 worth of meat so the defence of necessity was rejected.[61]

The offence must be proportionate to the danger

The offence will only be justified if it protected an interest of superior or equivalent value to the one sacrificed. Thus the hungry vagabond cannot kill the baker who refuses to give him food. In practice comparing the relative values of different interests can often prove difficult. The burden of proof is on the prosecution to show that the offence was not proportionate to the original danger.

[55] Crim. 4 janv. 1956, *D.*, 1956, *S.*, 130; obs. Légal, *R.S.C.*, 1956, p. 831.
[56] T. Corr. Nantes, 12 nov. 1956, *D.*, 1957.30; T.Corr. Brest, 20 déc. 1956, *D.*, 1957.348; T. corr. Avesnes-sur-Helpe, 19 nov. 1958, *J.C.P.* 59, II, 366; Angers 11 juil. 1957 D. 1958, 357.
[57] Cf. Bouzat, note in *S.*, 1954.2.185.
[58] Rennes, 12 avril 1954 S. 1954, II, 185.
[59] Crim. 25 juin 1958, *D.*, 1958.693, note M.R.M.P.; *J.C.P.*, 1959.II.10941, note Larguier.
[60] Paris, 6 oct. 1944 and 5 janv. 1945, *S.*, 1945.2.81.
[61] Poitiers, 11 avril 1997, *D.*, 1997. 512, note A. Waxin, *J.C.P.*, 1997.II.22933, note A. Olive.

Civil liability

The defence of necessity leaves intact any liability under civil law.

Subjective defences

Subjective defences do not generally abolish the existence of the offence, they simply remove liability for its commission from the individual. This means that secondary parties can be liable for the offence even where the principal offender has avoided liability by relying on the defence.

Constraint

Criminal liability will only be imposed if the defendant acted of their own free will. The defence of constraint applies when the defendant had no choice but to commit the offence. While this is treated as a subjective defence because the defendant was not acting with free will, this state is often brought about by external circumstances. Article 122–2 of the new Criminal Code states:

> A person is not criminally liable who acted under the influence of a force or a constraint which they could not resist.[62]

While the legislation appears to draw a distinction between 'force' and 'constraint' that distinction was not drawn by the old Code, and force is really just a specific example of a constraint.

The nature of the constraint

The types of constraint can be distinguished according to their form (physical or psychological) or according to their origin (external or internal). Looking first at physical constraints of an external origin, these can be due to the forces of nature such as a storm, an earthquake, a flood, or a fire, or due to the acts of third parties such as wars, riots and strikes. Thus, where torrential rain caused a wall to collapse, the defendant had a defence to a charge of obstructing the highway,[63] and a theatre owner had a defence where his customers had prevented him from being able to close his establishment at the time required by his licence.[64]

---

[62] 'N'est pas pénalement responsable la personne qui a agi sous l'empire d'une force ou d'une contrainte à laquelle elle n'a pas pu résister.'
[63] Crim. 6 mai 1887, D., 88.I.332.
[64] Crim. 8 août 1840, S., 1841.I.549.

Internal physical constraints take the form of illnesses. So, the *Cour de cassation* has ruled that a prostitute was not liable for failing to attend a compulsory health visit,[65] a defendant was not liable for abandoning his family when he was unable to work due to a serious heart problem,[66] and a passenger was not liable for travelling without a valid ticket when he fell asleep on a train and went past his station.[67]

Psychological constraint acts on the mind rather than the body of the defendant. An external psychological constraint exists, for example, when the offence is committed through fear induced by a threat made by a third party. There are only a few case law examples of this form of constraint.[68] One concerned an Algerian who, under a death threat, had lodged 40 armed rebels during the War for Independence of 1956.[69] This form of the defence can overlap with the defence of necessity.

The law does not recognise internal psychological constraints as a defence. Thus, parents whose child died when they failed to seek medical treatment due to their beliefs in the doctrine of a religious sect were successfully prosecuted for not assisting a person in danger.[70]

The constraint must have been irresistible

It must have been absolutely impossible for the defendant to resist the constraint.[71] This condition is logical as if the defender had the possibility of following another conduct and failed to do so, their acts are the expression of their own will, and there is then no reason why they should not answer for this before a criminal court. The courts have taken a strict approach to this matter. For example, the defence was not allowed where a lorry carrying fresh produce had broken down and its load had been added to that of a second lorry so that the produce would not perish while the vehicle was repaired. The offence of taking a vehicle on a road in excess of the permitted weight was committed.[72]

It is not sufficient that the defendant would have found it very difficult to abide by the law, it must have been impossible to abide by the law. Thus where passengers on a boat were carrying contraband products in their luggage, the boat's owner could not avoid liability for smuggling on the basis that he could not have checked everybody's luggage.[73]

---

[65] Crim. 3 mars 1865, *D.*, 66.5.394.

[66] Crim. 24 avr. 1937, *D. H.*, 1937.429.

[67] Crim. 29 oct. 1922, *D.P.*, 1922.I.233.

[68] T. Corr. Versailles, 27 fév. 1963, *D.*, 1963, *S.*, 110.

[69] Crim. 26 fév. 1959, *D.*, 1959.301, *B.*, 139.

[70] Crim. 29 juillet 1967, *J.C.P.*, 1968.II.15377, note J. Pradel.

[71] '*l'impossibilité absolue de se conformer à la loi*': Crim. 8 fév. 1936, *D.P.*, 1936.I.44, note Donnedieu de Vabres; Crim. 28 déc. 1900, *D.P.*, 1901.I.81, note Le Poittevin.

[72] Crim. 10 fév. 1960, *B.*, 79.

[73] Crim. 30 déc.1953, *B.*,360, obs. Légal, *R.S.C.*, 1954, p. 753.

In applying this provision the courts first apply an objective test and determine whether an ordinary person would have been able to resist committing the offence. The circumstances of the individual are not taken into account. Thus the *Cour de cassation* considered that the defence could not be applied to individuals who had failed to leave the country after they had been ordered to do so. The stateless people had argued that they had been turned away by all the neighbouring countries of France, and so were unable to leave the French territory. But the Court took the view that they could have tried to enter countries that did not share a border with France, without looking at whether the defendants could have afforded to fly or sail to these more distant destinations.[74] Many academic writers would prefer the courts to take a subjective approach, considering whether the particular defendant could have resisted.

The constraint was unforeseeable

The defendant will be treated as having been at fault if he fails to foresee a foreseeable constraint which he or she could have then acted to prevent. The classic example is the sailor who was found guilty of desertion when he was unable to regain his ship at the required time, because he got himself drunk on land and was arrested for being found drunk and disorderly in a public place.[75] The courts have also considered that a break-down does not excuse the parking of a vehicle in a no-parking zone, because the driver should have foreseen it by a preliminary verification of the condition of the vehicle before commencing their journey.[76] Again, this approach has been heavily criticised by academics as it is essentially imposing criminal liability for a prior state of mind. This condition has not been expressly mentioned by the new Code (nor the old Code) and some academics hope that future case law will consider that it no longer applies.

Mental illness

Article 64 of the 1810 Criminal Code stated:

> There is neither a serious nor major crime when the suspect was in a state of dementia at the time of his actions.[77]

There were significant weaknesses in the drafting of the old Criminal Code. The notion of dementia was too narrow, as in medicine it refers to a

[74] Crim. 28 fév. 1936, *D.P.*, 1936.I.44, note Donnedieu de Vabres; Crim. 21 mai 1941, *G.P.*, 1941.2.132.

[75] Crim. 29 janv. 1921, *S.*, 1922.I.185, note Roux; Crim. 15 nov. 1934, *D.P.*, 1935.I.11, note Donnedieu de Vabres.

[76] Crim. 4 déc. 1958, *D.*, 1959.36.

[77] '*Il n'y a ni crime ni délit lorsque le prévenu était en état de démence au temps de l'action.*'

particular type of mental illness taking the form of a progressive and irreversible deterioration in the mental faculties. This often affects old people (senile dementia) but it can also affect young people (precocious dementia). In law the courts gave the concept a much wider meaning to include any person suffering from mental delusions. The definition was also misleading in suggesting that no offence was committed, while in fact the defence simply removed the individual's personal responsibility, but their accomplices could still be liable. It also suggested that the defence was only applicable to serious and major offences, while the case law had recognised that the defence was also applicable to minor offences.

Some of these problems have been removed by the new Criminal Code, which states at article 122–1:

> A person is not criminally liable who was affected at the time of the facts, by a psychological or neuro-psychological illness which had removed his discernment or his control over his acts.[78]

While at the time of its introduction the media described this as a legal revolution, the new provision merely adopts much of the earlier case law and clarifies the legislation on the subject, rather than making any radical changes.

The courts start with a presumption that the person is sane and the burden of proof is on the defendant to prove that they fall within the defence. Three conditions must be satisfied: the defendant must have been suffering from a mental illness, this must have removed their discernment or their control over their acts and, lastly, the illness must have existed at the time of the commission of the offence. Each of these conditions will be considered in turn.

The mental illness

The new Code has replaced the concept of dementia by 'psychological or neuro-psychological illness' as this reflects more closely existing medical knowledge. The circular of the Minister of Justice dated 14 May 1993, which provides a commentary to the Code, states that:

> The new provisions, by abolishing the notion of dementia, highlight that the criminal defence flows from the loss of free will, whatever the nature of the mental illness that has caused this.[79]

---

[78] 'N'est pas pénalement responsable la personne qui était atteinte au moment des faits, d'un trouble psychique ou neuropsychique ayant aboli son discernement ou le contrôle de ses actes.'

[79] 'Les dispositions nouvelles, en supprimant la notion de démence, mettent en évidence que l'irresponsabilité pénale découle de la perte du libre arbitre, quelle que soit la nature du trouble mental qui en est à l'origine.'

Thus, these terms seek to cover all forms of mental illness, whatever their origin or nature. Sleepwalking and epilepsy[80] can both be treated as a mental illness. Intoxication through the consumption of drink or drugs can fall within the defence. Until 1957 the *Cour de cassation* took the view that intoxication could never give rise to a defence. In 1957 the Court abandoned this dogmatic approach and decided that the influence of drink on criminal responsibility was a question of fact that could only be resolved on the facts of each case.[81]

Absence of discernment or control

The central issue for the courts is whether the defendant has been deprived of their discernment or control over their acts due to a mental illness. Such a condition really means that they were not acting as a free agent. The absence of discernment means that the person has lost the capacity to understand the nature of their acts. This could be the case if a person was suffering from hallucinations or had become delirious. For instance, schizophrenics and alcoholics sometimes suffer from delirium tremens. An example of where a person has lost control of their acts is if they are suffering from an epileptic fit.

Time of the mental illness

The mental illness must exist at the time of the commission of the offence. Prior mental illness will only be taken into account when determining the appropriate sentence. This condition also implies a causal link between the mental illness and the commission of the offence. If the mental illness existed at the time of the commission of the offence and this is recognised during the judicial investigation then an order must be issued that there is no case to answer. If the mental illness is only established during the actual trial the defendant will be acquitted. With the termination of the criminal process, the administrative authorities rather than the criminal system are then responsible for providing treatment and protecting the public.

Later mental illness will lead to the suspension of the prosecution. The judicial investigation will, however, continue. While acts directly linked to the mentally ill person (such as questioning the suspect) cannot take place, other aspects of the investigation will proceed, including the gathering of witness statements, questioning accomplices and collecting expert evidence. If the suspect recovers from the mental illness the prosecution can recommence.

---

[80] Orléans, 22 juin 1886, *D.*, 1887.V.213; Crim. 14 déc. 1982, *G.P.*, 1983.I. doctr. 178.
[81] Crim. 5 fév. 1957, *B.*, 112, obs. Légal, *R.S.C.*, 1958, p. 93.

The partially responsible

Those people who are mentally ill but who are at least partially capable of discerning their wrongdoing or of controlling their conduct fall outside the defence. Kleptomaniacs or sexual perverts who find it extremely difficult to resist certain impulses could fall into this category of people. A famous ministerial circular of 12 December 1905 – the Chaumié circular – regulated the approach of the courts to such individuals. This circular invited psychiatric experts to look into how far these mentally abnormal people could have their criminal responsibility reduced. In the light of this circular it became established practice for this category of offender to benefit from mitigating circumstances at the time of sentencing in proportion to the gravity of their mental illness. The circular filled a legislative gap but was criticised as encouraging an artificial mathematical approach which took little account of medical knowledge or common sense, since a person suffering from such a mental illness was in many ways more dangerous but received less punishment than a person with no mental illness. Despite these criticisms, this approach continued to be followed even after the circular was repealed by article C. 345 of the Code of Criminal Procedure of 1959.

The partially responsible are now covered by article 122–1 paragraph 2 of the Criminal Code, which keeps the earlier approach. It states that:

> A person suffering, at the time of the facts, from a psychological or neuro-psychological illness which altered his discernment or impeded his control over his acts remains punishable; however, the case law takes account of this circumstance when it determines the length and mode of punishment.[82]

While this essentially continues the previous practice, technically it leaves a wide discretion to the judges, since the courts are told that they can take this mental illness into account when determining the sentence, but it is not stated that the sentence must be reduced, nor by how much.

Defence of being a minor

Evolution of the law since 1810

The Criminal Code of 1810 fixed the age of majority for the purposes of the criminal law at 16. This was subsequently increased to 18 by an Act of 12 April 1906. The age of the minor is appreciated at the time of the criminal conduct and not the time of the trial.[83] Criminal liability could only be

---

[82] *'La personne atteinte, au moment des faits, d'un trouble psychique ou neuropsychique ayant altéré son discernement ou entravé le contrôle de ses actes demeure punissable; toutefois, la jurisprudence tient compte de cette circonstance lorsqu'elle détermine la peine et en fixe le régime.'*

[83] Crim. 11 juin 1969 G.P. 1969, II, 140.

imposed on a minor if they had 'discernment', that is to say that they knew right from wrong. If the minor acted with discernment they could be convicted but would benefit from a reduction of sentence to the mitigation of their junior years. Otherwise they would be acquitted and could either be sent back to their parents or taken to a reform school.

Unfortunately, the delicate question of discernment was deformed by the courts, who declared minors to have discernment who they considered impossible to re-educate and wished thus to sanction, or stated that a minor had no discernment when they strictly did but the judge felt they could benefit from educative measures. Another weakness of the system was that convicted children were sent to the same reform schools as those who had been acquitted so that the distinction between those who benefited from the defence and those who did not was undermined.

An initial reform was made in 1912, but the major reform came in 1945.

Reform of 1945

An *ordonnance* of 2 February 1945 substantially reformed this area of the law. While the age of majority for the purposes of the criminal law remained 18, the question of discernment was abolished. In principle, all young offenders were taken out of the criminal system and subjected instead to measures of protection, assistance, supervision and education,[84] which will be described together as educative measures.

It was initially thought that the court simply had to note the commission of the *actus reus* of the offence in order to make an order of educative measures. This was the approach taken by the youth court in Meaux.[85] But in an important decision of 13 December 1956,[86] known as the Laboube case, the *Cour de cassation* rejected this interpretation of the law. The case concerned a six-year-old boy who had injured his playmate. The Court of Appeal had ordered that the minor be handed back to his parents, after it had concluded that the child had committed the *actus reus* of the offence of injuring through carelessness, without having looked at his state of mind. The *Cour de cassation* quashed this ruling and commented:

> … if articles 1 and 2 of the *Ordonnance* of 2 February 1945 lay down the principle of the criminal irresponsibility of minors, disregarding the discernment of the interested party, and determine the court's competence … to take the appropriate measures of reform with respect to minors … it is still necessary, in conformity with the general principles of law, that the minor whose participation in the *actus reus* has been established, should have understood and

---

[84] *'mesures de protection, d'assistance, de surveillance et d'éducation'*: art. 2, para 1 of the *Ordonnance* 2 February 1945.
[85] T. Enf. Meaux 28 mai 1948, *G.P.*, 1948.2.177.
[86] Crim. 13 déc. 1956, *D.*, 1957.349, note Patin.

willed this act; every offence, even non-intentional ones, suppose in effect that its author has acted with intelligence and will.[87]

The *ordonnance* draws a distinction between those young offenders who are under 13 and those who are between 13 and 18.

Minors under 13

Young offenders under 13 can never receive a criminal sanction. They can, instead, be subjected in appropriate cases to educative measures. This can include them being ordered to receive professional training, being removed from their parents into the care of the social services, or being placed under supervision.

Minors aged 13 to 18

Minors aged 13 to 18 can be subjected to educative measures or, where the circumstances and the personality of the young offender so require, be convicted and punished.[88] Their sentence may be reduced due to their junior years, and in the case of 13 to 16 year olds, must be reduced.[89]

The Criminal Code of 1994

The new Criminal Code preserves the law under the 1945 *Ordonnance*. Article 122–8 of the Code states:

> Minors found guilty of criminal offences are the subject of measures of protection, assistance, supervision and education according to the conditions fixed by a special law.
>
> This law also determines the conditions in which punishment can be imposed on minors over 13.[90]

The government had intended to present to Parliament a separate law which would have focused on young offenders and would have constituted a major reform of the 1945 *Ordonnance*. As this Act was never

---

[87] 'si les articles 1er et 2 de l'Ordonnance 2 février 1945 posent le principe de l'irresponsabilité pénale du mineur, abstraction faite du discernement de l'intéressé, et déterminent les juridictions compétentes ... pour prendre à l'égard des mineurs les measures de redressements appropriée ... encore faut-il, conformément aux principes généraux du droit, que le mineur dont la participation à l'acte matériel à lui reproché est établi, ait compris et voulu cet acte; toute infraction, même non intentionnelle, suppose en effet que son auteur ait agi avec intelligence et volonté.'

[88] Ord. 2 February 1945, art. 2 para. 3.

[89] Art. 20–2 and 20–3 of the *ordonnance* of 1945.

[90] 'Les mineurs reconnus coupables d'infractions pénales font l'objet de measures de protection, d'assistance, de surveillance et d'éducation dans les conditions fixées par une loi particulière.
  Cette loi détermine également les conditions dans lesquelles des peines peuvent être prononcées à l'encontre des mineurs de plus de 13 ans.'

passed, the 'special law' to which article 122–8 refers is the 1945 *Ordonnance*, to which certain minor reforms of the substantive law and procedure were made by the Acts of 16 December 1992 and 1 July 1996.

Mistake of law

Article 122–3 of the Criminal Code states:

> A person is not criminally liable who proves that he believed, because of a mistake of law which he was not in a position to avoid, that he could legitimately carry out the act.[91]

There was no equivalent defence under the old Code[92] and the new defence was considered to be one of the major changes introduced by the new Code. But the defence is very narrowly defined and so is of only limited application. Everyone is still presumed to know the law[93] and the burden of proof to displace this presumption lies on the defendant. The defence of mistake of law will only reverse this presumption in very limited circumstances. The presumption has been justified on the basis that it is necessary in order to maintain social discipline, but the presumption is a legal fiction as in reality it is impossible to know all the laws in force.

When the old law applied a case arose where a horticulturist had asked the town hall on several occasions whether he needed planning permission to build some greenhouses. He was told that he did not and went ahead with the building. He was subsequently convicted of building without the necessary building permit.[94] If the same facts occurred today the horticulturalist would be able to avail himself of the new defence of mistake of law. The *Cour de cassation* does, however, seem to be taking a strict view of this defence. In one of its first decisions on the subject,[95] it quashed a decision of the Court of Appeal that had allowed the defence, because the suspects had not themselves sought to rely on the provisions of article 122–3, instead the issue had been raised on the initiative of the judge. According to the Criminal Division 'only the person prosecuted has the capacity to invoke a mistake of law within the terms of this text'.[96]

---

[91] '*N'est pas pénalement responsable la personne qui justifie avoir cru, par une erreur sur le droit qu'elle n'était pas en mesure d'éviter, pouvoir légitimement accomplir l'acte.*'
[92] Crim. 24 juil.1903, *D*. 1903, I, 490; 16 mars 1972, *B*. no. 110.
[93] '*nul n'est censé ignoré la loi*'; Crim. 24 fév. 1820, *B*. no. 33.
[94] Crim. 26 fév. 1964, *B*. no. 71.
[95] Crim. 15 nov. 1995, *Dr. pén*. 1996, comm. 56; *J.C.P*. 1996, *éd. G*, IV, 440; *J.C.P*. 1996, *éd. G*, I, 3950, M. Véron.
[96] '*seule la personne poursuivie est fondée à invoquer une erreur de droit au sens de ce texte*'.

Three conditions must be satisfied for the defence to succeed: the mistake must have been one of law and not fact, the defendant must not have been in a position to avoid the mistake and he or she must have thought their conduct was legal. Each of these will be considered in turn:

Mistake of law

There are no limits on the type of law that can be the subject of the mistake; it can thus be criminal or civil, a regulation or an Act of Parliament. The defence will normally be invoked in the more technical areas of the law, such as environmental law and company law.

Mistakes of fact may mean that the *mens rea* of an intentional offence is absent. Thus, the person who takes an object belonging to another thinking that they are the owner does not commit a theft. For the same reason, the head of a business who irregularly employs a foreign worker because he believes that he is French is not liable.[97] If the intention remains because the mistake related to a secondary element of the offence, then the defendant will still be liable. For example, if a person takes jewels thinking they were made with precious stones when in fact they were made of plastic they will still be liable for theft; or if the defendant kills one person thinking that they are killing another they have no defence.[98]

Mistakes of fact for non-intentional offences will not constitute a defence, and may actually amount to carelessness sufficient to form the *mens rea* of the offence. Thus, a person will be liable for involuntary homicide when they kill a friend while cleaning a gun which they believed to be unloaded.

An unavoidable mistake

Only two examples were given during the course of the parliamentary debates on article 122–3 of the type of mistake that would justify the defence: wrong information provided by the administration inducing the mistake and the failure of the administration to publicise a normative text. The latter situation is of very limited practical importance as Acts and regulations only come into force once they have been published in the *Journal Officiel*. Following the parliamentary debates during the passing of the relevant legislation, it seemed that false information emanating from a private person, including professionals (for example, a *notaire* or an *avocat*) could not constitute an unavoidable mistake. However, one of the first decisions of the *Cour de cassation* on article 122–3 appeared to accept the possibility that the mistake could be induced by the advice of a lawyer (*un*

---

[97] Crim. 1er oct. 1987 *B*. no. 327.
[98] Crim. 31 janv. 1835 *S*. 1835, I, 564.

avoué) though on the facts the mistake had not been unavoidable.[99] A couple had been going through a divorce and a court order had awarded the family home to the wife. The husband had sought professional advice from a lawyer on the meaning of the court order. It seems that the lawyer had advised the husband in writing that he had the right to enter the family home. While the wife was on holiday he entered the house and changed the locks, so that the wife and his children were forced to stay in a hotel when they returned. The husband was prosecuted for entering the home without authority. The Court of Appeal in Versailles accepted the defence of mistake but this decision was quashed by the Criminal Division, which considered that the mistake was not unavoidable as a request to a court for the order to be interpreted could have been made.[100]

In another recent case a lorry driver from abroad had driven in excess of the speed limit. It was held that he could not rely on the defence of mistake of law as his intention had been drawn to the speed limit by signs along the roadside.[101]

Belief in the legality of the act

The mistake of law can only be allowed if it caused the defendant to believe that their conduct was legal.

Comparison with English law

There are significant differences in the structure of the defences available in French law compared to English law. Some defences are defined more widely than their English counterparts, others more narrowly, and some have no equivalent in the other system. One of the most noticeable differences is that French law allows a defence of superior orders. It does so for two main reasons. Firstly, the existence of the defence may encourage the good functioning of an organised society as it promotes obedience. Secondly, it acknowledges that a subordinate's free will is reduced when they receive an order from their superiors, particularly as a failure to obey sometimes gives rise to criminal or disciplinary sanctions.[102]

The new Criminal Code has introduced some significant improvements both in the field of necessity and insanity. The old Criminal Code had

---

[99] C. A. Versailles, 24 juin 1994; *Gaz. Pal.* 26/30 août 1994, p. 6; Crim. 11 oct. 1995, *Dr. pén.* 1996, *comm.* 56; *J.C.P.* 1996, *éd. G*, I, 3950, *commentaires critiques* de M. Véron; *D.* 1996, p. 469, note M. Muller.

[100] Under art. 461 of the Code of Civil Procedure.

[101] Douai, 26 oct. 1994, *G.P.* 8 déc. 1994.

[102] For example, art. 447 of the Code of Military Justice punishes with two years imprisonment the soldier who refuses to obey his superiors, and art. R. 642–1 of the Criminal Code punishes with a FF1000 fine citizens who refuse to respond to a requisition of a legal or administrative authority.

made no mention of a general defence of necessity, but the French judges had been prepared to develop this defence, while relying on fairly weak legislative provisions. The new Criminal Code has taken the opportunity to modernise this area of the law, and now expressly provides for a general defence of necessity. Unlike the French judiciary, the English judges have remained stubbornly opposed to the idea of a general defence of necessity, justifying their position primarily on the basis of the 'floodgates' argument. It is interesting to see that there are no signs that the defence is being overused in France, but nor are there any signs that the English are going to be inspired by the activities on the continent to modernise their law on this matter.

The definition in the old Criminal Code of the defence of insanity dated from the same era as the *M'Naghten* rules and suffered from similar problems. It is refreshing to see that the French have managed to update the definition of their defence to take into account developments in understanding of mental illnesses, and it would be nice to think that the English might one day get round to doing the same.

By contrast, French law does not recognise a separate defence of intoxication, though the existence of intoxication could be taken into account in the application of some other defences. In particular, it could be a ground for the defence of mental illness.

The legitimate defence under French law has a similar scope to the private defence under English law, but there is no direct equivalent to the English public defence in so far as it applies to the prevention of the commission of an offence.

Somewhat strangely, the French do not really recognise a defence of consent,[103] and there is no general provision for the defence in the Criminal Code. The reasoning is that generally criminal sanctions are not imposed purely in the interests of a single victim, but in the interests of society as a whole, and therefore it is not in the hands of one individual to permit the commission of such criminal conduct. As with English law, a distinction is drawn between active and passive euthanasia, the latter sometimes avoiding criminal liability.[104] Some French academics suggest that in exceptional circumstances consent will act as a defence. They draw a distinction between where offences protect values which an individual can dispose of and others which protect values which an individual cannot dispose of (such as life or health). In the former situation they suggest the defence of consent applies, while in the latter it does not. Under this analysis the consent does not make the offence disappear, it never existed in the first place. Thus, the offences of rape and theft are not committed if the potential victim consents to sexual intercourse or the taking of their

---

[103] Crim. 23 juin 1838, S., 1838.I.626, concl. proc.gén. Dupin, commentary by Puech, I, p. 308 et s.

[104] Crim. 3 janv. 1973 B. no. 2.

property. In such cases the potential victim must have had the capacity to give their consent, and the consent must have been given freely, which is not the case where it has been obtained by fraud. Some French academics consider that violent sports and medical treatment fall under this heading, but the majority consider that these fall within the defence of an implicit order of law. But the situations dealing with disposable values are best treated as situations where the elements of the offence have not been proven rather than as situations where a defence of consent applies.

Many of the situations which are covered by the defence of consent under English law are analysed as falling within one of the other French defences. For example, a person injured during a boxing match under English law would be treated as having impliedly consented to their injuries; under French law the case would be analysed as falling within the defence of order of law, the law being a custom. While the case of *R v Brown*[105]/*Laskey v United Kingdom*[106] highlighted the obvious weaknesses and tensions in the English law on consent, the position seems to be a step ahead of the French.

There are clear similarities between the defence of duress and the defence of constraint, particularly now the English defence of duress has been extended to include duress of circumstances as well as duress of threats. However, the French defence remains more broadly defined, as there is no requirement that there be a threat of death or serious personal injury – other types of threat can suffice.

[105] [1993] 2 WLR 556.
[106] *The Times*, 20 February 1997.

8

Genocide and other crimes against humanity

Introduction

Until the passing of the new Criminal Code, no legislation in France provided for crimes against humanity. Instead the national courts were forced to rely on a range of international texts, and in particular the Statute of the International Military Tribunal of Nuremberg, in order to convict for these offences.

The first clear provision for a crime against humanity appeared in international law in the Nuremberg Charter of 1945. This provided the basis for the prosecution of senior German Nazis who had been active during the Second World War. Article 6 of this Charter states:

> The Tribunal established by the Agreement referred to in Article 1 hereof, for the trial and punishment of the major war criminals of the European Axis countries shall have the power to try and punish persons who, acting in the interests of the European Axis countries, whether as individuals or as members of organisations, committed any of the following crimes. The following acts, or any of them are crimes coming within the jurisdiction of the Tribunal for which there shall be individual responsibility:
>
> (a) Crimes against peace: namely, planning, preparation, initiation or waging of a war of aggression, or a war in violation of international treaties, agreements or assurances, or participation in a common plan or conspiracy for the accomplishment of any of the foregoing;
> (b) War crimes: namely, violations of the laws or customs of war. Such violations shall include, but not be limited to murder, ill-treatment or deportation to slave labour or for any other purpose of any civilian population, or in occupied territory, murder or ill-treatment of prisoners of war or persons on the seas, killing of hostages, plunder of public or private property, wanton destruction of cities, towns or villages, or devastation not justified by military necessity;

(c) Crimes against humanity: namely, murder, extermination, enslavement, deportation, and other inhumane acts committed against any civilian population, before or during the war; or persecutions on political, racial or religious grounds in execution of or in connection with any crime within the jurisdiction of the Tribunal, whether or not in violation of the domestic law of the country where perpetrated.

Leaders, organisers, instigators and accomplices participating in the formulation or execution of a common plan or conspiracy to commit any of the foregoing crimes are responsible for all acts performed by any persons in execution of such plan.

The Nuremberg Tribunal handed down its judgement on 1 October 1946 and then ceased to exist.

A large number of trials of less senior individuals involved in the atrocities of the Second World War were prosecuted by the national courts. In France, the prosecutions in the national courts, including those against the German military commanders Oberg and Knochen, were not for the offence of crimes against humanity, but for other less serious offences. Many people who had been involved in criminal activity during the war managed to avoid arrest and trial in the confusion of the post-war period. In France, most criminal offences are subject to a limitation period, according to which no criminal proceedings can be brought after a certain time limit has expired from the date of the commission of the offence[1] (no such limitation period exists in English criminal law). An exception was introduced into French law by the Act of 26 December 1964[2] which simply 'noted the inapplicability of the limitation period'[3] to crimes against humanity. Thus, crimes against humanity have particular significance in France for recent prosecutions against offenders from the time of the Second World War, because the other offences, including war crimes, are time barred.

Following the 'ethnic cleansing' that occurred in the former Yugoslavia, the United Nations established in 1993 the *ad hoc* International Criminal Tribunal for the Former Yugoslavia.[4] Faced with the genocide of Tutsis in Rwanda, an International Criminal Tribunal for Rwanda was established by the United Nations in 1994.[5] The Statutes for these courts were heavily influenced by the Statute for the Nuremberg Tribunal.

Progressively the international law on crimes against humanity has been incorporated into French national law, first by the courts relying on the principle of monism, and then by the legislator. In 1994 crimes against humanity were introduced for the first time into the French Criminal

---

[1] See p. 54.
[2] Act no. 64–1326 of 26 December 1964.
[3] *'constate l'imprescriptibilité'*.
[4] Resolution 808 of 22 February 1993 and 827 of 3 May 1993 of the Security Council.
[5] Resolution 955 of the Security Council.

Code. Crimes against humanity committed before 1 March 1994 remain subject to the law that existed prior to codification. The high profile trial of Maurice Papon highlighted that this area of law could still be of significance and will therefore be considered first, before examining the new codified provisions.

Consideration will first be given to offences committed on French territory, and then to offences committed outside French territory.

Offences committed on French territory

Offences committed before 1 March 1994

Until the passing of the new Criminal Code there was no national legislation defining crimes against humanity. The Act of 26 December 1964 recognising that the limitation period did not apply to such offences simply referred to crimes against humanity 'as they are defined by the resolution of the United Nations on 13 February 1946, taking into account the definition of crimes against humanity as they figured in the Charter of the International Tribunal of the 8 August 1945'.[6]

In the case of Paul Touvier, the *Cour de cassation* accepted that crimes against humanity were offences that could be heard by the ordinary courts. Touvier had argued that the offence had to be heard by the special court[7] that had been established after the Second World War to try war criminals. As this court had subsequently been shut down after these cases had been heard he had hoped through this argument to avoid the trial. Initially his analysis was accepted by the investigating judge who announced on 13 February 1974 that he did not therefore have jurisdiction to investigate the case. This decision was approved by the *Chambre d'accusation* of the court of appeal of Lyon,[8] but rejected by the *Cour de cassation*.[9]

The Klaus Barbie case

With the trial of Klaus Barbie in 1989, France had its first trial for crimes against humanity. Barbie was a German Nazi who had worked in Lyon during the French occupation. At the end of the Second World War, he had

---

[6] *'tels qu'ils sont définis par la résolution des Nations unies du 13 février 1946, prenant acte de la définition des crimes de l'humanité, telle qu'elle figure dans la charte du Tribunal international du 8 août 1945'.*

[7] *la Cour de sûreté de l'Etat* and *la Haute Cour de la Libération.*

[8] 30 May 1974.

[9] Crim. 6 févr. 1975: *B.* no. 42; *D.* 1975, 386, rapp. Chapar et note Coste-Floret; this approach was confirmed in Crim. 31 janv. 1991, *Bousquet: B.* no. 54; *D.* 1991 259, note Braunschweig.

been sentenced to death in his absence, and had fled to South America. He was 'removed' from his refuge after more than 40 years in hiding.

As only crimes against humanity avoid the limitation period the *Cour de cassation* had to draw a distinction between crimes against humanity and war crimes. While the judges at Nuremberg had tried to limit the role of crimes against humanity for fear of accusations of imposing retrospective legislation, the French courts were keen to give crimes against humanity a wide remit.

The court of appeal of Lyon drew a distinction between war crimes and crimes against humanity on the basis of the type of victim. War crimes protected soldiers and resistance fighters while crimes against humanity protected civilians who had been executed because of their religion or race. On appeal the *Cour de cassation* gave an important judgement[10] which rejected the distinction between resistance fighters and civilians executed on religious or racial grounds. It rejected the quality of the victims as a determinant element of the offence. On the other hand, the systematic extermination of the mentally ill, who do not constitute a racial or religious group or adversaries of a policy of ideological hegemony, are not protected by this definition of the offence.

But the Court went on to define crimes against humanity as including not only the core principles of the offence, but also the factual background in which the Nuremberg Statute was passed. The *Cour de cassation* declared:

> Given that inhuman acts and persecutions which have been committed in a systematic way, in the name of a State practising a policy of ideological hegemony, not only against people due to their race or religion, but also against political adversaries, whatever the form of their opposition, constitute crimes against humanity (falling outside the limitation period), within the meaning of article 6c of the Statute of the International Tribunal of Nuremberg annexed to the London Accords of 8 August 1945 – even though they would also amount to war crimes under article 6(b) of that text;[11]

Thus, in French national law, the *Cour de cassation* defined the offence of crimes against humanity as requiring an *actus reus* of inhuman acts and persecutions carried out in a systematic way in the name of a State

---

[10]   Crim. 20 déc. 1985; *B.* no. 407.

[11]   '*Attendu que constituent des crimes imprescriptibles contre l'humanité, au sens de l'article 6c du statut du tribunal militaire international de Nuremberg annexé à l'accord de Londres du 8 août 1945 – alors même qu'ils seraient également qualifiables de crimes de guerre selon l'article 6(b) de ce texte – les actes inhumains et les persécutions qui, au nom d'un Etat pratiquant une politique d'hégémonie idéologique, ont été commis de façon systématique, non seulement contre les personnes en raison de leur appartenance à une collectivité raciale ou religieuse, mais aussi contre les adversaires de cette politique, quelle que soit la forme de leur opposition.*'

practising a policy of ideological hegemony. These last limitations have been strongly criticised since it limits crimes against humanity to the historical context of the Second World War. It is true that article 6 of the Statute of the International Military Tribunal of Nuremberg limits its competence to the judging of people who 'acted on behalf of the European Axis countries'.[12] But by including these conditions the *Cour de cassation* avoided the offence being applicable to acts committed after the Second World War and in particular in the former colonies during the struggle for independence.

The *mens rea* of the offence was the intentional participation in the state policy and the intention to harm a category of people selected for their race, religion or political opinions.

Klaus Barbie was sentenced to life imprisonment.

The case of Paul Touvier

Paul Touvier was the chief of the Militia for the Lyonnaise region during the German occupation of France. He had been sentenced to death in his absence and only arrested 30 years later when he was discovered to be still living in France. The first formal complaint against Touvier was submitted in Lyon on 9 November 1973 by Professor Claeser. The complaint was concerned with Touvier's role in the massacre of Rillieux-le-Pape. This massacre had taken place after the Resistance had assassinated Philippe Henriot, an important member of the Militia. As a reprisal, seven men, all Jewish (and one of whom was the father of Professor Claeser), were assassinated by the Militia at Rillieux-le-Pape. Touvier admitted that he had himself arrested the victims and taken them to the site of the massacre, whilst his men, on his orders, carried out the execution itself. A long legal battle followed.

In its first decision in the case on 6 February 1975, the *Cour de cassation* ruled that the ordinary courts had jurisdiction to hear cases concerning crimes against humanity. The case was referred back to the *Chambre d'accusation* of the court of appeal in Paris. In its decision of 27 October 1975,[13] it accepted that it had in principle the jurisdiction to hear the case. But it ruled that the Act of 26 December 1964, which concerned the in-applicability of the limitation period to crimes against humanity, did not apply where the limitation period had already run out before the passing of the Act. An appeal was made to the *Cour de cassation*. The *Cour de cassation* decided that the *Chambre d'accusation* would have to suspend the case while it made a referral to the Minister of Foreign Affairs. The Minister would be asked to interpret the relevant provisions of the Statute of the International Military Tribunal of Nuremberg and article 7 of the

---

[12] 'agissent pour le compte des pays européens de l'Axe'.
[13] CA. ch. d'acc. 27 octobre 1975.

European Convention on Human Rights. This referral was made on 17 December 1976. The Minister of Foreign Affairs only gave his opinion on 15 June 1979. He concluded that the principle that could be deduced from the Statute of Nuremberg was that crimes against humanity could not be subject to a limitation period. He also concluded that under article 7 of the European Convention on Human Rights, crimes against humanity were excluded from the principle of non-retroactivity of criminal law. The *Chambre d'accusation* therefore decided that the limitation period did not apply and referred the case back to the investigating judge.

On 13 April 1992 the *Chambre d'accusation* of Paris gave a very controversial decision.[14] Following the formula of the *Cour de cassation* of 20 December 1985 in the Barbie case, it rejected the classification of a crime against humanity on the ground that the Vichy government had not practised a policy of ideological hegemony. As a result, it handed down a decision that there was no case to answer. This decision was only partially overruled by the *Cour de cassation* on 27 November 1992.[15] It noted that the authors and accomplices of crimes against humanity could only be punished 'if they had acted on behalf of a European Axis country'. But the murder of the seven Jewish men had been carried out on the orders of a member of the Gestapo. Thus it had been carried out on behalf of the German State, a European Axis country that had practised a policy of ideological hegemony.[16] By linking the acts of Touvier to Nazi Germany and not to the French State, the *Cour de cassation* avoided the real debate as to the nature of the Vichy government during the Second World War.

The requirement that the defendant was acting for a State that was practising a policy of ideological hegemony figures nowhere in the Statute of Nuremberg. While it is true that the Nazi ideology goes against the moral values commonly accepted in civilised society, it does not represent the only threat to the dignity of humanity.

By deciding that crimes against humanity only existed where the author or their accomplice acted on behalf of a European Axis country, the court seems to have maintained the requirement of a link with a war crime or a crime against peace that is contained in the Statute of Nuremberg.[17] On the other hand, article 1 of the Convention of 9 December 1948 on genocide specifies that this crime is punishable whether it is committed at a time of peace or war.

A further appeal was issued by Touvier claiming that the *Cour d'assises* had failed to show he had the requisite special intention to be the agent of the Nazi policy of ideological hegemony. The appeal was rejected by the

---

[14] CA Paris, ch. d'acc. 13 avril 1992: *Gaz. Pal.* 1992, 1, p. 387.

[15] Crim. 27 nov. 1992, *B.* 1992 no. 394; *J.C.P.* 93 éd. G, II, 17977, note critique Dobkine.

[16] The same criteria were used to justify an order of no case to answer in the case of *Boudarel*: Crim. 1er avril 1993: *B.* no. 143; *Gaz. Pal.* 1993 1,270.

[17] Cass. crim. 27 nov. 1992, 3e arrêt Touvier, *B.* 1992 no. 394.

Criminal Division on 21 October 1993. The requisite intention had been shown by the fact that Touvier had selected his victims due to their Jewish religion and had chosen to be a member of the Militia, which included as one of its aims 'to fight against the Jewish leper'.[18]

The case of Maurice Papon

Maurice Papon had been a Minister of Finance in Raymond Barre's government. During the Second World War he had been the secretary general of the prefecture of Gironde under the Vichy government. In May 1981, between the two presidential elections, the newspaper *Canard enchaîné* published several articles raising serious questions about Maurice Papon's role in the deportation of Jews from the Bordeaux region. On 8 December 1981 the families of several deportees killed in Auschwitz submitted official complaints against Maurice Papon for crimes against humanity before the office of the investigating judges of Bordeaux.

On 15 December 1981 a special jury, known as a *jury d'honneur*, made up of senior figures from the Resistance, considered Maurice Papon's role during the Second World War and delivered an ambiguous verdict.

The prosecution office for Bordeaux decided to open a judicial investigation in 1982, and Maurice Papon was charged with crimes against humanity on 19 January 1983. After five years, the investigation led by the investigating judge Nicod was annulled by the *Cour de cassation* on 11 February 1987 for a procedural irregularity.

So, on 4 August 1987 the investigation had to recommence from zero. In 1988, Maurice Papon and Maurice Sabatier, the former chief of police in the area, were charged. On 3 February 1989 new complaints were placed, referring to René Bousquet, the former secretary general of police and his delegate in the occupied territories, Jean Leguay. René Bousquet was charged on 19 April 1992. But Maurice Sabatier died on 19 April 1989, Jean Leguay died on 3 July 1989 and on 8 June 1993 René Bousquet was assassinated.

Thus, after numerous years of criminal investigations and legal proceedings, only Maurice Papon was eventually sent for trial as a secondary party to crimes against humanity. He was accused of having participated in the arrest, internment and deportation of one thousand, five hundred and sixty people of Jewish origin, including many children. The deportations were carried out in eleven convoys from Bordeaux. The victims were usually gathered first in the Mérignac-Beaudésert camp, then taken to Drancy, and from there to Auschwitz, where the majority of the victims were killed.

The chief of police, Maurice Sabatier, had delegated considerable powers to Maurice Papon, including authority over the police, the

---

[18] '*lutter contre la lèpre juive*'.

management of the Mérignace-Beaudésert camp and the 'Jewish question'. According to the prosecution case, Maurice Papon had fully co-operated with the German authorities in carrying out the deportations, and specifically knew the anti-Jewish policy adopted by the Vichy government.

The trial of Maurice Papon commenced on 8 October 1997 at the *Cour d'assises* of Bordeaux. The civil parties were *B'nai B'rith, SOS racisme* and *la Ligue contre le racisme et l'antisémitisme*. During the course of the trial and at previous legal hearings Maurice Papon had raised a range of defences, all of which were rejected. He argued that he could rely on the defence of order of law (see p. 105) based on an order issued to civil servants in France on 8 January 1942 by the French authorities exiled in London. This order had instructed French civil servants to remain in their posts so that the French administration was not handed over to the Germans. At the same time they were to try and subvert the occupants' orders, and where this was not possible they were to carry out their instructions. The *Cour de cassation* considered that this order did not free Maurice Papon of liability, as it could not be used to justify the deportations.

He also attempted to rely on the defence of constraint. This was rejected on the basis that the pressure exerted on the French civil servants had not been irresistible so that he had still acted of his own free will. There was evidence that no reprisals had been carried out against French civil servants who had refused to carry out orders.

He was not able to rely on the defence of order of law or order of a legitimate authority, as the *Chambre d'accusation* ruled that 'the illegality of an order bearing on the commission of crimes against humanity was always obvious'[19] (see p. 106).

Nor did the fact that he had been a member of the Resistance preclude him from having participated in criminal acts against Jews.

He was convicted on 2 April 1998 for complicity in crimes against humanity. The *Cour d'assises* found that he had been a secondary party to the illegal arrests, detentions and deportations in July, August, and October 1942 and January 1944. It found that he was not a secondary party to the deportation in September 1942 because he was absent from Bordeaux at the time. He was also not liable for the deportations in November and December 1943 and May 1944 because the Germans had not used the services of the prefecture on these occasions, but had carried out the deportations themselves. He was thus convicted for his role in four of the eight convoys deporting Jews from Bordeaux to Drancy. It is particularly interesting to see that the court and the jurors did not find that he was a secondary party to the actual killing of the deportees. According to the court, Maurice Papon did not have the intention to kill.

[19] *'l'illégalité d'un ordre portant sur la commission de crimes contre l'humanité était toujours manifeste'.*

On Thursday 2 April 1998, he was sentenced to ten years imprisonment and the removal of his civil and family rights for that period. His subsequent appeal to the *Cour de cassation* was rejected.

The criminal trial was followed the next day by a civil hearing of the *Cour d'assises* aimed at fixing the amount of damages that Maurice Papon should pay to his victims.[20] M Marcel Rouxel, one of the lawyers of Maurice Papon, submitted that the court did not have jurisdiction to award damages. He based this argument on the fact that Maurice Papon's acts could not be separated from his function as secretary general of the prefecture. Therefore the question of damages had to be decided by an administrative court. M Alain Lévy, a lawyer for one of the civil parties, shared this view, though for obviously different reasons. He argued that Maurice Papon acted as a civil servant of a State that had in practice existed, even if the Vichy government had been illegitimate.

The Court rejected these arguments and ordered Maurice Papon to pay FF4.6 million of which 3 million was for the lawyers' costs and 1.6 million for the victims.

Maurice Papon's conviction received a mixed response. The first secretary of the Socialist Party, François Hollande, considered that 'the main thing is that the trial has taken place, and that it has provided a history lesson for the French people and in particular for the young'.[21] Arno Klarsfeld, a lawyer for one of the civil parties, commented:

> [T]he French people have given a double verdict. Firstly, a condemnation of the apparatus of the Vichy State which participated in the hunt of Jewish families by deciding to convict the whole apparatus of the Vichy State through Maurice Papon, who is its symbol. It is also a verdict which is written into the future... The administration of tomorrow must be an administration with a conscience and with a soul.[22]

But the decision has also been the subject of strong criticism. The value of the trial has been questioned when it took place so long after the event, when Maurice Papon was 87 years old and had enjoyed all the honours of a successful political career. The legal proceedings took over 17 years and the trial took six months, which was the longest trial in French post-war history. One former minister, Hervé de Charette, has commented that the

---

[20] *Le Monde*, 5 avril 1998.

[21] 'l'important c'est que le procès ait eu lieu, et qu'il ait permis une leçon d'histoire pour les Français et notamment pour les plus jeunes', *Le Monde*, 4 April 1998.

[22] 'c'est un double verdict qu'a rendu le peuple français. D'abord une condamnation de l'appareil de l'Etat de Vichy qui a participé a la chasse aux familles juives [en] décidant une condamnation dans son entier de l'appareil de l'Etat de Vichy à travers Maurice Papon, qui est le symbole. C'est aussi un verdict qui s'inscrit dans l'avenir... L'administration de demain doit être une administration avec une conscience et avec une âme.'

Papon trial left the impression of an unfinished debate, with no clear, strong message for the future generations. There was also a danger that the trial was the trial of the Vichy government, rather than the trial of the individual. The verdict which found him guilty as a secondary party to the deportations but not to the killings has been criticised as contradictory, as by 1944, if not before, he must have known of the fate of the deportees. The punishment also looks inadequate faced with a conviction for crimes against humanity. As for the order that he pay damages, it will be very difficult to recover the sum. It seems that even before the trial, Maurice Papon organised his insolvency by making donations to his children.

The danger of case law developed by the national courts with respect to crimes against humanity is that they can show an excessive indulgence towards nationals of their own country.[23]

Offences committed after 1 March 1994

The new Criminal Code introduced national legislation expressly providing for the offences of crimes against humanity. Unlike the Act of 26 December 1964, no reference is made to the international texts. From now on, the repression of crimes against humanity will be assured in France on the basis of provisions of pure national law. The Code lays down autonomous offences which are separate from international law. It facilitates the imposition of liability for these serious offences.

According to a circular of 14 May 1993:[24]

> To express the values of our time the new Criminal Code must be a humanist code, a code inspired by human rights.[25]

The introduction of crimes against humanity into the Code is a direct reflection of this goal. These offences figure symbolically at the front of the Code as the first provisions for the substantive offences.

The Senate favoured simply reproducing article 6(c) of the Nuremberg Statute, but the view of the National Assembly prevailed. While heavily influenced by the international law and prior case law of the *Cour de cassation*, the legislator did not simply replicate the earlier law. In particular, there is no longer any requirement that the defendant was carrying out a State policy of ideological hegemony. The Code, unlike the

---

[23] Mireille Delmas-Marty, *Les grands systèmes de politique criminelle*, Paris: Presses universitaires de France, 1992, p. 417.

[24] Crim. 93/a/F1, 14 mai 1993.

[25] *'Pour exprimer les valeurs de notre temps le nouveau Code pénal doit être un code humaniste, un code inspiré par les Droits de l'homme.'*

view of the Criminal Division in its decision of 20 December 1985, does not limit the scope of the offence to criminality of the State. While this means that they can be applied to the work of independent terrorists, the danger is that these offences will be reduced to regulating the simple internal affairs of the State. There is a risk that the introduction of genocide and other crimes against humanity into the French Criminal Code could lead to a trivialisation of these offences and reduce their symbolic weight.

The earlier national law only applied a single offence of crimes against humanity, while the provisions of the new Criminal Code contain three basic offences, distinguishing genocide from other crimes against humanity. The offence in article 211–1 is inspired by the Convention of 1948 on Genocide, that in article 212–1 by article 6(c) of the Nuremberg Statute and that of article 212–2 by the case law laid down by the *Cour de cassation* in the Klaus Barbie litigation.

All of these offences require the execution of a concerted plan, a general requirement that did not exist in international law. The notion of a concerted plan was first introduced by a government amendment into the offence of genocide. During the parliamentary procedure it was extended to apply to all the offences. The notion itself is not new. The Statute of Nuremberg mentions it expressly, article 6 providing at the end for the liability of those who had taken part in the elaboration or the execution of such a plan. But in international law this notion was only secondary to the principal offence itself. The *Cour de cassation* had drawn attention to the concept in the last Barbie judgment, by deciding that this circumstance of participation in the execution of a concerted plan of deportation or extermination constituted 'not a distinct offence nor an aggravating circumstance, but an essential element of the crime against humanity'.[26] Thus, while the concept of a concerted plan existed in international law, its central place in the definition of the offences was developed by the *Cour de cassation* and has been adopted by the legislator. The reason for this development is far from clear.[27] The circular of 14 May 1993 indicates that this concept was favoured because it was more objective than the emphasis on motive in international law. But there is a real danger that the prosecution may find it difficult in practice to prove the existence of a concerted plan. In the case of Touvier, the *Chambre d'accusation* originally rejected the label of a crime against humanity because it considered that the Rillieux massacre had not been carried out as part of a concerted plan:

---

[26] '*non une infraction distincte ou une circonstance aggravante, mais un élément essentiel du crime contre l'humanité*': Crim. 3 juin 1988; B. no. 246.

[27] C. Grynfogel, *Le concept de crime contre l'humanité, hier, aujourd'hui et demain*, Revue de droit pénal et de criminologie, 1994, 13–51.

... everything shows that [the Rillieux massacre] cannot be placed within a methodical plan of extermination coldly executed, but essentially constitutes a spectacular, ferocious and relatively improvised on the spot criminal reaction.[28]

Genocide

The definition of genocide is contained in article 211–1 which closely follows that found in article 2 of the Genocide Convention of 9 December 1948.

Genocide consists in the execution of a concerted plan aimed at the total or partial destruction of a national, ethnic, racial or religious group, or of a group determined by any other arbitrary criteria, to commit or to have committed, against members of this group, one of the following acts:

- A voluntary attack on life;
- A serious attack on their physical or psychological integrity;
- Submission to living conditions likely to lead to the total or partial destruction of the group;
- Measures aiming to prevent reproduction;
- Forced transfer of children... [29]

Most of the acts listed in the offence amount to ordinary criminal offences (murder, serious non-fatal offences against the person, abduction), which become crimes against humanity by reason of the existence of a concerted plan for the total or partial destruction of a particular group.

On the question of the concerted plan, article 211–1 is significantly different from the international texts. Article 2 of the 1948 Convention characterised genocide by the subjective criteria of the existence of an intention to destroy a group of people. Parliament preferred to substitute the more objective criteria relating to the existence of a concerted plan. This plan must tend to the total or partial destruction of a human group – thus it is not a plan to persecute but a plan to exterminate.

[28] *'tout montre que [le massacre de Rillieux] ne peut s'insérer dans un plan méthodique d'extermination froidement exécuté, mais constitue essentiellment une réaction criminelle 'à chaud' spectaculaire, féroce et relativement improvisée'* CA Paris, 13 avr. 1992, quashed by Crim. 27 nov. 1992; JCP 93, éd. G, II, 17977, note critique Dobkine.

[29] *'Constitue un génocide le fait, en exécution d'un plan concerté tendant à la destruction totale ou partielle d'un groupe national, ethnique, racial ou religieux, ou d'un groupe déterminé à partir de tout autre critère arbitraire, de commettre ou de faire commettre, à l'encontre de membres de ce groupe, l'un des actes suivants:*
- *Atteinte volontaire à la vie;*
- *Atteinte grave à l'intégrité physique ou psychique;*
- *Soumission à des conditions d'existence de nature à entrainer la destruction totale ou partielle du groupe;*
- *Mesures visant à entraver les naissance;*
- *Transfer forcé d'enfants ... '*

The nature of the group of victims constitutes a third characteristic of the new offence. The group can be selected by the accused according to 'any arbitrary criteria'. This formula is wider than that found in article 2 of the 1948 Convention which contains a limitative list of potential victims which did not include, for example, the mentally ill.

While genocide is associated with the massacre of entire populations, a minimum number of victims is not mentioned in the legal definition. This corresponds with the earlier case law, where in the Touvier case a conviction for a crime against humanity was upheld when seven Jewish men were killed.

A court has judged that the French law authorising abortions does not fall within the offence of genocide, due to the absence of a concerted plan.[30]

Other crimes against humanity

Article 212–1 is known[31] as the unnamed crime against humanity, and is inspired by article 6(c) of the Nuremberg Statute:

> Deportation, slavery or the massive and systematic practice of summary executions, the abduction of people followed by their disappearance, torture or inhuman acts, inspired by political, philosophical, racial or religious motives and organised in the execution of a concerted plan against a group of the civil population are punished by life imprisonment.[32]

The *actus reus* consists of violent attacks on the fundamental rights of civilians. Murder is excluded as this now falls within the *actus reus* of genocide. In general the new test tries to be more precise than the Nuremberg Statute. For example, it no longer refers to persecutions but to the 'massive and systematic practice' of particularly serious acts of violence; and it makes express reference to deportation and slavery.

A special intention is required: the acts must be inspired by political, philosophical, racial or religious motives and organised in execution of a concerted plan. Philosophical motives were not referred to by the Nuremberg Statute. For genocide the concerted plan had to be aimed at the total or partial destruction of a group of individuals. For this offence, the concerted plan aims to deprive the individual of their fundamental human rights.

The offence of aggravated war crimes is contained in article 212–2 which states:

---

[30] Trib. cor. Le Puy-en Velay, 14 mars 1995, *Gaz. Pal.* 1995, 2. 18 juill. p. 7 note Doucet.

[31] *le crime contre l'humanité innommé.*

[32] *'La déportation, la réduction en esclavage ou la pratique massive et systématique d'exécutions sommaires, d'enlèvements de personnes suivis de leur disparition, de la torture ou d'actes inhumains, inspirées par des motifs politiques, philosophiques, raciaux ou religieux et organisées en exécution d'un plan concerté à l'encontre d'un groupe de population civile sont punies de la réclusion criminelle à perpétuité…'*

The acts referred to in article 212–1 are punished by life imprisonment when committed in times of war in the execution of a concerted plan against those who are fighting against the ideological system in the name of which are perpetrated crimes against humanity... [33]

Thus this offence sanctions the same acts as those in the previous subsection but when they are committed during wartime against individuals fighting against an ideological system that perpetrates crimes against humanity. The legislator has therefore followed the solution laid down by the *Cour de cassation* on 20 December 1985 in the Klaus Barbie case: crimes against humanity can be committed against freedom fighters during wartime. It can be either a national or international conflict, though the victims must be fighting against a system perpetrating crimes against humanity.

Article 212–3 provides for the offence of conspiracy to perpetrate a crime against humanity.

Offences committed outside French territory

Universal jurisdiction

As well as being competent to judge offences committed on French territory,[34] French courts have jurisdiction to judge offences committed outside France where the doctrine of universal jurisdiction applies. International law does not automatically recognise universal jurisdiction[35] as it constitutes a significant violation of national sovereignty. Instead it needs to be granted by an international treaty and/or by national legislation. In France, article 70 of the Code of Military Justice grants universal jurisdiction under certain conditions to war crimes. The Geneva Conventions of 12 August 1949 and the New York Convention of 10 December 1984 contain provisions against torture and other cruel, inhuman or degrading treatments. The first imposes an obligation on each contracting party to find the people suspected of having committed or ordered the commission of one of these serious offences and refer them to an appropriate court, whatever their nationality. The second lays down that every signatory must take measures to establish the jurisdiction of its national courts where the offender is on their territory.

---

[33]   '*Lorsqu'ils sont commis en temps de guerre en exécution d'un plan concerté contre ceux qui combattent le système idéologique au nom duquel sont perpétrés des crimes contre l'humanité, les actes visés à l'article 212-1 sont punis de la réclusion criminelle à perpétuité...*'

[34]   Art. 689 of the Code of Criminal Procedure; art. 113–1 of the Criminal Code.

[35]   For a contrary view see David, *L'actualité juridique de Nuremberg* in *Le procès de Nuremberg, conséquences et actualisation*, proceedings of the international conference, Université libre of Brussels, 27 March 1988: Bruylant: Editions de l'Université de Bruxelles, p. 169 and 170.

Until the 1970s there was no specific legislation with regard to crimes against humanity. The London Accord of 8 August 1945 and the Genocide Convention of 9 December 1948 did not provide for universal jurisdiction. However, the resolution of the General Assembly of the United Nations of 3 December 1973 proclaims that:

> War crimes and crimes against humanity, wherever they may have been committed and whenever they have been committed, being the object of an investigation, and the individuals against whom there exists evidence establishing that they have committed such crimes must be sought, arrested, brought before the courts, and, if they are found guilty, punished.

Following the tragedies in the former Yugoslavia and Rwanda, the international community, and then the French legislature, felt obliged to react by introducing a limited universal jurisdiction for crimes against humanity. The United Nations resolutions[36] creating the two international tribunals provide that the international tribunals and the national courts are both concurrently competent to judge the offenders in Rwanda and the former Yugoslavia.[37] They provide that every State has to take the necessary measures in their national law to apply the provisions of the Resolutions.[38]

Interpretation by French case law

In France, several complaints have been laid against people suspected of having taken part in the genocide perpetrated in Rwanda. To date, none of these prosecutions has been successful.[39] While a Convention or international treaty can automatically have binding force in France, this is not the case for resolutions of the United Nations. These are viewed as having merely symbolic value. Conventions will only be binding on the national courts if they are clear and precise, otherwise a national text must bring it into force. The *Chambre d'accusation* of Paris has taken the view that the Geneva Convention of 12 August 1949 was not sufficiently precise to impose universal jurisdiction.[40] At the time of the judgement (1994), it found that only the Convention on torture of 10 December 1984, expressly referred to in article 689–2 of the Code of Criminal Procedure, imposed universal jurisdiction.

The potential defendant has to be in France, and the complainants have

---

[36] Number 827 of 1993 creating the International Tribunal for the former Yugoslavia and 955 of 1994 creating the International Tribunal for Rwanda.

[37] Art. 9 La Haye and art. 8 Arusha.

[38] Point 4 in 1993 and point 2 in 1994.

[39] Michel Massé, *Ex-Yougoslavie, Rwanda: Une compétence 'virtuelle' des juridictions françaises?* Revue de science criminelle et de droit pénal comparé, oct–déc. 1997, p. 893.

[40] Paris, 8 août 1994 (*l'association Reporters sans frontières (RSF) contre des dirigeants de la Radio Télévision Libre des Mille-Collines*); Paris, 7 juillet 1994 (*aff. Kalinda et autres*).

to have a sufficient personal interest in the case to commence the proceedings.[41] In the litigation known as the *Reporters sans frontières*[42] this last condition was not satisfied. *Reporters sans frontières* was an organisation established to promote human rights around the world and lacked sufficient *locus standi* to bring the proceedings. They had hoped to bring proceedings for complicity in torture committed through the press during the Rwandan tragedy. While this organisation lacked *locus standi*, the public prosecutor could have taken over the prosecution, but chose not to do so.

The problem of *locus standi* was also one of the reasons for the rejection of the action in the *Kalinda* case. One of the complainants was acting as legal representative of his young daughter of French nationality, the majority of the members of their family having been massacred during the course of events that occurred in Rwanda. The Court decided that the daughter had not directly suffered the harm and therefore could not commence the proceedings under article 113-7 of the Criminal Code.

Only the case of the priest Munyeshyaka, where the presence on the national territory of the person suspected was proven, did all the conditions appear to be satisfied. The investigating judge declared himself competent, but only for the offences strictly referred to in the only applicable text, that is to say the New York Convention of 10 December 1984 for torture.[43]

Legislative intervention

Since these cases, the French legislature has intervened to introduce universal jurisdiction. Two Acts of 1994 and 1995 allow the prosecution in France of any person on French territory who could be subjected to a prosecution before the international tribunals for the former Yugoslavia and Rwanda, whatever their nationality and the nationality of their victims.

The Act of 2 January 1995 amended the French law to take into account the 1993 Resolution of the United Nations establishing the International Tribunal for the former Yugoslavia. The Act of 22 May 1996 amended the earlier Act to remedy some difficulties that had subsequently appeared. In particular, it removed the reference to 'serious or major offences defined by the French law'[44] to avoid any difficulties arising from the absence of specific offences of crimes against humanity before 1 March 1994, at the time of the Yugoslavian conflict.

The Act of 1995 was applied in the *Javor case*,[45] which were proceedings

---

[41]   Art. 2 Code of Criminal Procedure.
[42]   Cited by Michel Massi, *op cit*.
[43]   Nîmes, 21 mars 1996, cited by Michel Massé, *op cit*.
[44]   *'crimes ou délits définis par la loi française'*.
[45]   Also known as *'l'affaire des Bosniaques'*.

brought in Paris by refugees living in France who had escaped from Serbian camps. The *Chambre d'accusation*, in a decision of 24 November 1994, had ruled that the investigating judge did not have jurisdiction in the matter. On appeal the *Cour de cassation* applied the new legislation, but the appeal was still rejected because the accused were not present in France.[46]

The Act of 22 May 1996[47] adapts the French legislation to take into account the United Nations Resolution creating the International Tribunal for Rwanda. The Act of 1996 contains a risk of confusion for the French judge confronted by different definitions of the offence of genocide depending on the time when the offence was committed. By virtue of the principle of non-retroactivity of criminal law, the new Criminal Code does not apply to facts before March 1994.

The introduction of crimes against humanity into the new Criminal Code seemed to only have symbolic value at the time when the Code came into force. But the establishment of universal jurisdiction for the crises in the former Yugoslavia and in Rwanda has given a real purpose to these provisions.

---

[46] Cass. crim. 26 March 1996 *B*. no. 132.
[47] La loi no. 96–432 du 22 mai 1996; *J.O.* 23 mai 1996, p. 7695.

9

Voluntary homicide offences

The analysis of the offences against the person will be divided between homicide offences and non-fatal offences and between voluntary offences and involuntary offences. First, two specific issues which are relevant to all these offences will be considered: the question of aggravated circumstances and the availability of supplementary sentences.

Aggravating circumstances

Alongside the basic offences, many of the homicide and non-fatal offences can be aggravated in the presence of one of ten aggravating circumstances, or a combination of them. For example, article 222–8 provides for an aggravated form of the offence of unintentional killing laid down in article 222–7. Article 222–8 provides:

> The offence defined in article 222–7 is punished by 20 years imprisonment when it is committed:
>
> 1. On a minor under fifteen;
> 2. On a person whose particular vulnerability, due to their age, illness, infirmity, physical or mental disability, or pregnancy, is known or apparent to the offender;
> 3. On the legitimate or illegitimate parent or on the adoptive mother or father;
> 4. On a judge, juror, *avocat*, *officier public* or *officier ministériel*, an officer of the *gendarmerie*, a police officer, a customs officer, a prison officer, or any other holder of public authority or person charged with carrying out the public service, in the exercise or during the exercise of his functions, when the quality of the victim is apparent or known to the offender;
> 5. On a witness, a victim or private claimant, either to stop the denouncing of the facts, or the reporting of an offence or the giving of evidence;

6. By the spouse or partner of the victim;
7. By a person holding public authority or charged with carrying out a public service in the exercise or during the exercise of their functions or of their mission;
8. By several people acting as principal offenders or as accomplices;
9. With premeditation;
10. With the use or threat of a weapon.[1]

These aggravating circumstances can be grouped into three types. Firstly, those relating to the nature of the victim (who is young or particularly vulnerable); secondly, those relating to the status of the offender (as a spouse or cohabitee of the victim or a person in public office); and finally, those relating to the way the offence was committed (with premeditation, with a weapon or in a group).

The fourth aggravating circumstance supposes that the guilty person knows the position of the victim and knows that they are acting in the context of their functions or of their mission.[2]

As regards the last aggravating circumstance, the concept of a weapon is defined in article 132–75. This provides that:

> A weapon is any object conceived to kill or injure.
>
> Any other object susceptible of presenting a danger to people is classed as a weapon when it is used to kill, injure or threaten or it is destined by the person carrying it, to kill, injure or threaten.
>
> Any object which resembles and can be confused with a weapon defined in the first paragraph, and that is used to threaten, kill or injure or is destined, by

---

[1] '*L'infraction définie à l'article 222–7 est punie de vingt ans de réclusion criminelle lorsqu'elle est commise:*
  1. *Sur un mineur de quinze ans;*
  2. *Sur une personne dont la particulière vulnérabilité, due à son âge, à une maladie, à une infirmité, à une déficience physique ou psychique ou à un état de grossesse, est apparente ou connue de leur auteur;*
  3. *Sur un ascendant légitime ou naturel ou sur les père ou mère adoptifs;*
  4. *Sur un magistrat, un juré, un avocat, un officier public ou ministériel, un militaire de la gendarmerie, un fonctionnaire de la police nationale, des douanes, de l'administration pénitentiaire ou toute autre personne dépositaire de l'autorité publique ou chargée d'une mission de service public, dans l'exercice ou à l'occasion de l'exercice de ses fonctions ou de sa mission, lorsque la qualité de la victime est apparente ou connue de l'auteur;*
  5. *Sur un témoin, une victime ou une partie civile, soit pour l'empêcher de dénoncer les faits, de porter plainte ou de déposer en justice, soit en raison de sa dénonciation, de sa plainte ou de sa déposition;*
  6. *Par le conjoint ou le concubin de la victimé;*
  7. *Par une personne dépositaire de l'autorité publique ou chargée d'une mission de service public dans l'exercice ou à l'occasion de l'exercice de ses fonctions ou de sa mission;*
  8. *Par plusieurs personnes agissant en qualité d'auteur ou de complice;*
  9. *Avec préméditation;*
  10. *Avec usage ou menace d'une arme.*'

[2] Crim. 3 déc. 1970, *B.*. 1970, no. 325.

the person carrying it, to threaten, kill or injure, is classed as a weapon.

The use of an animal to kill, injure or threaten is classed as using a weapon. Where the owner of the animal is convicted or if the owner is not known, the court can decide to hand over the animal to an animal refuge, which can dispose of it as they wish.[3]

Thus, a weapon has been given its widest possible meaning. It includes any object that is used to kill or injure, such as a vehicle,[4] the flag of a sports official,[5] and a traffic cone.[6]

Supplementary sentences

Along with the main sentences of imprisonment and fines that are mentioned in the relevant legislative provisions laying down the offences, there are also frequently a range of additional sentences that can be imposed by a court where they consider this to be appropriate.

Voluntary homicides

A voluntary homicide is committed where a person kills with the intent to kill. The law draws a distinction between murder, aggravated murder and certain specific categories of murder. One practical difference between aggravated murder and the specific categories of murder is that where there is an aggravated murder, liability for that offence will also be applied to joint principals whether or not they were aware of the aggravating circumstances. By contrast, for the specific categories of murder liability for the particular offence only extends to joint principals if they personally satisfy the criteria for that offence.

---

[3]   '*Est une arme tout objet conçu pour tuer ou blesser.*

Tout autre objet susceptible de présenter un danger pour les personnes est assimilé à une arme dès lors qu'il est utilisé pour tuer, blesser ou menacer ou qu'il est destiné, par celui qui en est porteur, à tuer, blesser ou menacer.

Est assimilé à une arme tout objet qui, présentant avec l'arme définie au premier alinéa une ressemblance de nature à créer une confusion, est utilisé pour menacer de tuer ou de blesser ou est destiné, par celui qui en est porteur, à menacer de tuer ou de blesser.

L'utilisation d'un animal pour tuer, blesser ou menacer est assimilée à l'usage d'une arme. En cas de condamnation du propriétaire de l'animal ou si le propriétaire est inconnu, le tribunal peut décider de remettre l'animal à une oeuvre de protection animale reconnue d'utilité publique ou déclarée, laquelle pourra librement en disposer.'

[4]   Crim. 19 déc 1991, *Dr. pén.* 1992, comm. 171.

[5]   Crim. 11 mai 1989, *Dr. pén.* 1989, comm. 57.

[6]   Crim. 7 juill. 1992. *Dr. pén.* 1993, comm. 104.

Murder

The offence of murder is committed where a person deliberately kills another. It is defined in section 221–1 of the Criminal Code which states that

> The fact of voluntarily killing another constitutes murder. It is punished by thirty years imprisonment.[7]

Actus reus

The victim must have been born, for murder does not extend to the killing of an unborn child. The offence of murder is not committed where a person takes their own life, as suicide has not been criminalised since the Revolution.

Until recently it was accepted that there could only be a murder if the victim was alive at the time of the defendant's acts. Thus a court[8] had referred back to the *Cour d'assises* a man convicted of having set light to a victim who was already dead from a gunshot wound fired immediately beforehand by another person at the scene of the crime.[9] However, the criminal division of the *Cour de cassation* ruled in 1986 that the life of the victim is not a pre-condition for the offence of murder.[10] A brawl had started in a café and a person was fatally injured during the fight, but had been able to return to his home where he later died. A different individual to the original attacker had gone round to his house and used force that would have been fatal if the victim had not already been dead. The *Cour de cassation* held that the second attack constituted an attempted murder. The impact of this decision is open to debate. In having decided to convict for attempted murder and not murder, it is arguable that the Court impliedly recognised that it is impossible to murder a dead person. This is supported by the fact that in the context of negligent manslaughter the *Cour de cassation* gave an incompatible decision in the same year. In that case it held that a person could not be convicted for negligent manslaughter where he was the second person to drive over the lifeless body of a victim who had already been run over.[11]

A positive act by the defendant is required for the *actus reus* of murder, and psychological torture cannot be sufficient even though a causal link

---

[7]   'Le fait de donner volontairement la mort à autrui constitue un meurtre. Il est puni de trente ans de réclusion criminelle.'

[8]   la chambre de mise en accusation.

[9]   Paris, 9 avr. 1946, *R.S.C.* 1948.147, obs. Gulphe.

[10] Crim. 16 janv. 1986, *D.* 1986.J.265, Mayer, Gazounaud and Pradel; *J.C.P.* 1987.II.21774, note Roujou de Boubée, *R.S.C.* 1986.839 and 850, obs.Vitu and Levasseur.

[11] Crim. 25 juill. 1986, *B.* 242, *R.S.C.* 1987.200, obs. Levasseur.

could be established. There is no liability for murder by omission, a position that was established in the famous case of the *hostage of Poitiers*.[12] An abstention giving rise to a death can only give rise to a lesser offence such as a failure to assist a person in danger[13] or placing a minor in danger.[14]

Mens rea

It is the *mens rea* of murder that distinguishes it from other homicides. The *mens rea* has two elements: firstly a general intention (*dol général*) and then a special intention (*dol spécial*) which is the desire to kill. If the defendant only had an intention to wound, there can only be liability for a non-fatal offence, even if death results.

Sentence

Murder carries a maximum sentence of 30 years imprisonment. This sentence was reduced from life by the new Code so that a distinction could be drawn with the aggravated forms of murder. The sentence can be reduced to two years, which can be suspended. In addition the new Code adds a range of additional punishments that can be added to, but cannot substitute, the principal sentence.[15] These punishments include a ban on exercising a profession in the course of which the offence was committed, and a ban on carrying a weapon for five years.

Aggravated murder

Aggravated murder is committed where the murder victim fell within one of five categories of people who are given special protection by the Code. These people are listed in article 221–4 of the Criminal Code. This states:

> Murder is punished with a life sentence when it is committed:
> 1. On a minor under fifteen;
> 2. On a legal or natural parent or on the adoptive mother or father;
> 3. On a person whose particular vulnerability, due to their age, to an illness, to an infirmity, to a physical or psychological deficiency or to a pregnancy, is apparent or known to its author;
> 4. On a judge, juror, an *avocat*, an *officier public* or an *officier ministériel*, an official of the *gendarmerie*, a member of the national police, customs, the prison

---

12 Poitiers 29 nov. 1901, *D*. 1902.2.81, note Le Poittevin, *S*. 1902.2.305, note Hémard.
13 Art. 223–6, para 2 of the Criminal Code.
14 Art. 227–16 of the Criminal Code.
15 Art. 221–8, 9 and 10 of the Criminal Code.

service or any other person having public authority or charged with a mission of public service, in the exercise or on the occasion of their exercise of their functions or of their mission, when the status of the victim is apparent or known to the author;

5. On a witness, a victim or a private claimant, either to prevent him from denouncing the facts, reporting an offence or giving evidence in court, or because of their denunciation, complaint or deposition.[16]

This list is an innovation of the new Code, for there had only been an equivalent list in the old Code for non-fatal offences against the person. However, the list brings together in one single article certain particular provisions scattered in the old Code. All these aggravating circumstances relate to particular characteristics of the victim and reflect a desire to protect the more vulnerable in society. The first aggravating circumstance is aimed at victims who are under fifteen. There was no equivalent aggravating circumstance laid down by the 1810 Criminal Code. The specific offence of infanticide, which concerned the killing of a new born child that was under three days old, no longer exists. This offence is now covered by this new form of aggravated murder.

The second aggravating circumstance refers to the murder of a person's natural or adoptive parents. This aggravated offence replaces the specific offence of parricide that was contained in the old Code.[17]

All the aggravated murders are punished with life imprisonment and can include a minimum time that must be spent in prison. This minimum period is usually eighteen years where a person is given a life sentence, but it can be reduced or increased to 22 years by a special decision of the *Cour d'assises*. The additional punishments available for ordinary murder are also available in this context.

---

[16] '*Le meurtre est puni de la réclusion criminelle à perpétuité lorsqu'il est commis:*

1. *Sur un mineur de quinze ans;*
2. *Sur un ascendant légitime ou naturel ou sur les père ou mère adoptifs:*
3. *Sur une personne dont la particulière vulnérabilité, due à son âge, à une maladie, à une infirmité, à une déficience physique ou psychique ou à un état de grossesse, est apparente ou connue de son auteur;*
4. *Sur un magistrat, un juré, un avocat, un officier public ou ministériel, un militaire de la gendarmerie, un fonctionnaire de la police nationale, des douanes, de l'administration pénitentiaire ou toute autre personne dépositaire de l'autorité publique ou chargée d'une mission de service public, dans l'exercice ou à l'occasion de l'exercice de ses fonctions ou de sa mission, lorsque la qualité de la victime est apparente ou connue de l'auteur;*
5. *Sur un témoin, une victime ou une partie civile, soit pour l'empêcher de dénoncer les faits, de porter plainte ou de déposer en justice, soit en raison de sa dénonciation de sa plainte ou de sa déposition.*'

[17] Art. 299 of the old Criminal Code.

Multiple aggravating circumstances

The new Code in the second part of article 221–4 gives the court a wider range of powers when a child under fifteen was murdered and the murder was preceded or accompanied by additional aggravating circumstances. These additional aggravating circumstances are that the victim was raped, tortured or subjected to inhumane acts. Where these criteria are satisfied the court can increase the minimum period that must normally be spent in prison from 22 years to 30 years.[18] Where a court orders life imprisonment, it can specify that the convicted person should not benefit from any leniency in their sentence. This effectively means that they will normally spend the rest of their life in prison and will not benefit from parole.[19]

Specific murders

Two specific forms of murder, infanticide and parricide, were abolished by the new Code. There are now four specific murders, three created by the new Code and one retained from the old Code.

Assassination

Assassination consists of murder where there has been premeditation. Article 221–3 states:

> Murder committed with premeditation constitutes an assassination. It is punished with life imprisonment.
>
> The two first paragraphs of article 132–23 relating to the minimum period to be spent in prison are applicable to the offence laid down by this article. However, when the victim is under fifteen-years-old and the assassination is preceded or accompanied by a rape, torture or inhumane acts the *Cour d'assises* can, by a special decision, either increase the minimum time to be spent in prison to thirty years, or, if it hands down a life sentence, decide that none of the measures listed in article 132–23 can be granted to the convicted person;... .[20]

---

[18] *la période de sûreté.*

[19] But note art. 720.4 of the Code of Criminal Procedure.

[20] '*Le meurtre commis avec préméditation constitue un assassinat. Il est puni de la réclusion criminelle à perpétuité.*

Les deux premiers alinéas de l'article 132–23 relatif à la période de sûreté sont applicables à l'infraction prévue par le présent article. Toutefois, lorsque la victime est un mineur de quinze ans et que l'assassinat est précédé ou accompagné d'un viol, de tortures ou d'actes de barbarie, la cour d'assises peut, par décision spéciale, soit porter la période de sûreté jusqu'à trente ans, soit, si elle prononce la réclusion criminelle à perpétuité, décider qu'aucune des mesures énumérées à l'article 132–23 ne pourra être accordée au condamné.

Premeditation is defined in article 132–72 which states:

> Premeditation is the plan formed before the action to commit a particular serious or major offence.[21]

Thus the intention to kill must not only exist at the time of the killing but must also have preceded it. As a result, the offence will frequently result from a decision taken after careful reflection and the killing will have taken place in cold blood. There is unlikely to be a finding of premeditation where the killing was one of passion or anger.[22]

Murder combined with another serious offence

In law, the general rule is that when two distinct offences are committed by the same person they will benefit from a reduction in their sentence. However, when one of the two offences is murder this general rule is not applied and the conduct is treated as a distinct offence.[23] The government had only intended to keep this offence where the two offences were both murders. However, the Senate favoured retaining this offence for all serious offences and this view prevailed. Paragraph 1 of art. 221–2 states:

> A murder which precedes, accompanies or follows another serious offence is punished by life imprisonment.[24]

The two offences need not take place at exactly the same moment but must have been committed in a single period of time. The second offence can precede, accompany or follow the murder.[25] The two offences need not occur in the same place but must be part of the same chain of events.[26] The second offence must result from a separate act from the one that caused the murder, which would not be the case if the same bullet killed one person and seriously injured another.[27] An example of this offence would be where a man raped a woman and then killed her.

Murder combined with a major offence

A specific murder offence is committed where murder is linked to another major offence. Paragraph 2 of article 221–2 states:

[21] *'La préméditation est le dessein formé avant l'action de commettre un crime ou un délit déterminé.'*
[22] Crim. 18 juin 1969, *B.* no. 485.
[23] Art. 221-2 para 1 para 1 of the Criminal Code.
[24] *'Le meurtre qui précède, accompagne ou suit un autre crime est puni de la réclusion criminelle à perpétuité.'*
[25] Crim. 12 juill. 1982, *B.* 1990, *R.S.C.* 1983.261, obs. Levasseur.
[26] Crim. 14 janv. 1954, *B.*14.
[27] Crim. 6 juin, 1878, *D.* 1879.1.482.

A murder that aims to prepare or facilitate a major offence, either to enable the escape or to assure the impunity of the author or the accomplice of a major offence, is punished by life imprisonment.[28]

There must be a close connection between the murder and the major offence making them part of a single plan. The motive of the murderer is relevant: the murder must have been either to prepare or to facilitate the major offence, to facilitate the escape or to assure the impunity of the offender or their accomplice. There need not be a link in time or place and it does not matter in what order the offences took place. Nor need there be a single author for the murder and the major offence.[29] Unlike serious offences, a plan must have been made in advance.

Poisoning

Poisoning has always been severely sanctioned because it is seen as a particularly dangerous offence for two reasons: it is easy to commit and it can be difficult to detect.

The original 1992 Bill for the Criminal Code would have abolished the offence altogether. This move may have been politically motivated in an attempt to shelter politicians from prosecution for their role in the contaminated blood scandal, when individuals were unnecessarily contaminated with the AIDS virus from contaminated blood transfusions. The Senate insisted that this specific offence remain, though it is less severely punished than it was in the past. Article 221–5 of the new Code now states:

> The fact of attacking the life of another through the use or administration of substances that cause death constitutes a poisoning....[30]

Actus reus

This is not a result offence (*une infraction matérielle*) and therefore the offence is committed simply by administering a poisonous substance even if no death results. Thus, the concept of an attempt is included in the definition of the full offence. However, in a first instance judgement a court refused to convict a man of poisoning who, knowing he was

---

[28] '*Le meurtre qui a pour objet soit de préparer ou de faciliter un délit, soit de favoriser la fuite ou d'assurer l'impunité de l'auteur ou du complice d'un délit est puni de la réclusion criminelle à perpétuité.*'

[29] Crim. 26 mai 1948, *B.* no. 141.

[30] '*Le fait d'attenter à la vie d'autrui par l'emploi ou l'administration de substances de nature à entraîner la mort constitue un empoisonnement.*'

suffering from AIDS, had bitten a person with the intention of contaminating them with the AIDS virus. Instead he was convicted of a non-fatal offence.[31]

The poisoning can consist of a single dose that takes immediate effect, or a series of doses of a poison of which a single dose is insufficient to cause death, but the accumulated doses could be fatal.[32]

Mens rea

The offence requires intention, but in the light of the contaminated blood scandal there has been considerable debate as to precisely what the defendant must intend. The offender must know the lethal nature of the product they are administering and have intended to administer it. What is disputed is whether the defendant must have intended to kill. In the contaminated blood scandal there has been no suggestion that the ministers concerned intended to kill, but rather that they acted for economic and political reasons. Therefore if an intention to kill was a requirement they could not have been liable. If such an intention was required this offence would be very similar to murder. Until recently the question had not really been posed as in the majority of cases the person who administers a toxic poison also wants to kill. The issue has not yet been resolved. In support of the argument that an intention to kill is required, it has been noted that poisoning is classed by the Code with murder among the 'voluntary' attacks on life. On the other hand, there is a potentially significant difference in the drafting of article 222–1 where the requirement of an intention to kill is expressly referred to for the offence of murder, and that of article 221–5 where no such express reference is made.

In the first judgement looking at this issue in the context of the contaminated blood scandal, the court of first instance favoured interpreting the offence as requiring an intention to kill.[33] This view was supported by the Paris Court of Appeal in its decision of 13 July 1993.[34] The *Cour de cassation* subsequently failed to tackle directly the issue of intention, but left the door open for further prosecutions for poisoning in this affair.[35]

---

[31] T.G.I. Mulhouse 6 fév. 1992, *D.* 1992, 301, note Prothais; *Rev sc. crim.* 1992, 750, obs. Levasseur.

[32] Crim. 5 fév. 1958, *B.* no. 126.

[33] TGI Paris, 16e Ch. 23 oct. 1992, *D.* 1993, 222, note Prothais et Delmas Saint-Hilaire, *Gaz.pal.* 1992, 2, doctr.673.

[34] Paris, 13e ch. A, *D.* 1994 118, note Prothais et Delmassaint-Hilaire, *Gaz. pal.* 1994, 25 janv. doctr. 2: *l'homicide assassiné – Sur le problème*. See also M. Danti-Juan, *Dr. pén.* 1993, chron 5.

[35] Crim. 22 juin 1994, *B.* no. 248; *J.C.P.* 1994, éd. G. II, 22310, note M.L. Rassat; Delmas-Saint-Hilaire, *Gaz. pal.* 1994, 2, doctr. P. 1135; *D.* 1995, p. 65, concl. Perfetti and p. 85 note Prothais; Y. Mayaud, *Rev. sc. crim.* 1995, p. 347.

Punishment

The offence has a maximum sentence of 30 years imprisonment, with a compulsory minimum sentence that must be spent in prison (*peine de sûreté*). The additional sentences that apply to murder also apply to this offence. Also, under the new Criminal Code the aggravating factors contained in articles 221–2, 3 and 4 apply to poisoning, raising the sentence to life imprisonment.

Habitual violence on a minor or vulnerable person causing death

Article 222–14 states:

> Habitual violence on a minor under fifteen or on a person whose particular vulnerability, due to their age, an illness, an infirmity, a physical or mental disability or a pregnancy, is apparent or known to their author is punished by:
>
> 1. Thirty years imprisonment when it has led to the death of the victim:… [36]

The case law that preceded the new code found that there could be a habit when the violence had occurred on two occasions. The victim is treated as a vulnerable person if they are under fifteen or because they are as a matter of fact vulnerable.

Comparative analysis

Of particular interest to an English lawyer is the fact that murder requires an intention to kill, a mere intention to cause grievous bodily harm is not sufficient. There is no equivalent to voluntary manslaughter in French criminal law.

---

[36] '*Les violences habituelles sur un mineur de quinze ans ou sur une personne dont la particulière vulnérabilité, due à son âge, à une maladie, à une infirmité, à une déficience physique ou psychique ou à un état de grossesse, est apparente ou connue de leur auteur sont punies:*

1. De trente ans de réclusion criminelle lorsqu'elles ont entraîné la mort de la victime … '

10

Involuntary homicide offences

Introduction

Involuntary offences are often committed in the context of road and work accidents. An involuntary offence occurs where a person has caused physical harm to another without having wanted to do so, and sometimes without even having foreseen that they might do so. Thus, for an involuntary homicide there will have been no intention to kill. These offences are described in French as *involontaire* despite the fact that the act itself was voluntary, though the result was not. For example, in a fatal road accident, the driver was often voluntarily driving at an excessive speed, though he had not wanted to kill.

In the absence of a requirement of intention, these offences can be analysed as only requiring an *actus reus* which includes the element of fault, or the fault can be treated as the *mens rea*.

This area of law was left mainly unchanged by the new Code, though an effort has been made to give a heavier sentence where there is greater fault.

Ordinary involuntary homicide

Article 221–6 states:

> The fact of causing, in the conditions and according to the distinctions laid down by article 121–3, by ineptitude, carelessness, inattention, negligence or a breach of an obligation of security or of care imposed by legislation or regulation, the death of another constitutes an involuntary homicide punishable by three years imprisonment and a FF300,000 fine.

In the case of an obviously deliberate breach of a particular obligation of security or of care imposed by legislation or regulation, the punishments incurred are increased to five years imprisonment and a FF500,000 fine.[1]

Actus reus

The careless conduct must have caused a harmful result. The defendant's act must have been the cause of the death and the wording of the new Code suggests a shift away from the case law that developed under the old Code, though this does not appear to have been the intention of the legislature.

In this context there is an ongoing debate as to the offence committed when wounds inflicted on a pregnant women lead to the loss of the child she was carrying. A Court of Appeal ruled that this constituted a homicide where the baby had reached the term of the pregnancy, but was killed in the mother's womb when she was the victim of a road accident.[2] It emphasised the fact that the baby was viable and could have lived outside the womb. Another Court of Appeal adopted the same approach where a baby was killed due to carelessness before the umbilical cord had been cut.[3] The *Cour de cassation* confirmed this approach in a case where a newly born child was seriously handicapped because the doctor delayed intervention despite the repeated calls of the midwife.[4]

The causal link under the old Code

For a discussion of causation generally see p. 61. The old article 319 of the Criminal Code favoured the principle of equivalence of conditions (discussed on p. 61). Thus criminal liability was imposed where a person's fault had allowed or facilitated the realisation of the harm and it was not necessary that this fault should have been the unique, direct, exclusive or immediate cause of the death or injury,[5] though more recent case law

---

[1] 'Le fait de causer, dans les conditions et selon les distinctions prévues à l'article 121–3, par maladresse, imprudence, inattention, négligence ou manquement à une obligation de sécurité ou de prudence imposée par la loi ou le règlement, la mort d'autrui constitue un homicide involontaire puni de trois ans d'emprisonnement et de 300 000 F d'amende.

En cas de violation manifestement délibérée d'une obligation particulière de sécurité ou de prudence imposée par la loi ou le règlement, les peine encourues sont portées à cinq ans d'emprisonnement et à 500 000F d'amende.'

[2] Douai, 2 juin 1987, *Gaz. pal.* 1989, 145, note Doucet; *J.C.P.* 1989. II. 21250, note X. Labbée and *Rev. sc. crim.* 1989. 319 and 740, obs. Levasseur.

[3] Amiens, 28 avril 1964, *Gaz. pal.* 1964.2.167.

[4] Crim. 9 janv. 1992, *Dr. pén.* 1992, comm. 172 and *Rev. sc. crim.* 193.328, 5. 1. obs. Levasseur.

[5] Crim. 18 nov. 1927 *D.H.* 1928.53; 10 oct.1956, *B.* 622; 14 jan. 1971, *D.* 1971. 164, rapport E. Robert; 30 mai 1972, *B.* 179; 21 mai 1974, *B.* 187.

seemed to impose on the first instance judges the need to take more care to specify the causal link between the action and the harm.[6]

As soon as a fault was established, it engaged the responsibility of its author. If several faults were proven none exonerated the authors of the others.[7] This was particularly true in practice in the context of accidents at work or accidents following a surgical intervention where several people necessarily intervened. The criminal division of the *Cour de cassation* even went as far as considering that the common participation in a dangerous activity constitutes a unique fault imputable to all the participants and which dispensed with the need to find which of them had caused the harm.[8]

The acts of a third party were never exoneratory. The acts of the victim were only exoneratory if they were the unique and exclusive cause of the harm but ceased to play this role when they were allowed to remain a fault on the burden of the author: the act of the suicide candidate throwing himself under the wheels of a car removed the liability of the irreproachable driver but not that of the driver who was driving too quickly and as a result had not been able to stop. In the same way the acceptance of risk by the ultimate victim only exonerated the guilty person if the risk voluntarily run was completely abnormal. This was not the case in particular when the harm caused by a third party had been aggravated by a predisposition of the victim[9] and homicide by carelessness was up-held following a suicide whose accident had only been the indirect and partial cause.[10]

The only way of escaping the imputation of criminal responsibility was to show that the harm was entirely due to a case of *force majeure* but this was very difficult to get admitted by the courts. It had to be the unique cause of the harm and was thus rejected when the slightest fault had been found on the part of the agent.

The causal link under the new Code

Following the passing of the new Criminal Code, the courts seem to be continuing to adopt the principle of 'equivalence of conditions'. When the harm results from a chain of faults which have all contributed to its occurrence the *Cour de cassation* considers that the offence is committed by all the people whose fault contributed to its realisation. Thus, where two drivers drove at an excessive speed and both hit the victim without it being

---

[6] Crim. 19 mars 1975, *D*. 1976.79, note Rabinovitch; 9 janv. 1979, *J.C.P*. 1980.II.19272, note Chabas; 7 janv. 1980 *B*. 10; 18 déc. 1984, *B* 410.

[7] Crim. 25 nov. 1875, *D*. 1876.1.461; 7 mai 1968, *B*. 81; 16 févr. et 24 mai 1977, *B*. 61 et 186.

[8] Crim. 19 mai 1978, *D*. 1979.3, note Galia-Beauchesne, *D*. 1980. I.R.345, obs. Roujou de Boubée, *R.S.C*. 1979.90, obs. Levasseur; 23 juill. 1986, *B*. 243; 23 mai 1994, *B*. 112.

[9] Crim. 25 oct. 1972, *B*, 309; 10 juin 1992, *Dt. Pén*. 1993, comm. 6.

[10] Crim. 14 janv. 1971, *D*. 1971.164, rapport E. Robert.

possible to determine their precise contribution to the death, the *Cour de cassation* took the view that:

> ... each one has committed a fault by participating together in a dangerous action and by creating through their carelessness a serious danger to the victim.[11]

Following a fatal tragedy at a dance in Laurent-du-Pont, the dance organisers, the heating installers, the provider of inflammable materials and the mayor who had authorised the opening of the establishment were all found liable.[12]

The fault of the accused need not be the exclusive cause of the harm, it suffices that it has created the conditions which made it possible and without which it would not have been produced[13] even if the victims have themselves been careless.[14] Only a fault of the victim presenting the character of a case of *force majeure* exonerates the defendant.[15] The same approach is taken where the harm caused is more serious due to the predisposition of the victim – the defendant can still be treated as the cause of the harm.

A situation where there is no direct link between the defendant's fault and the harm caused, but causation will still be found, is where an employer imposes on a driver an excessive time limit,[16] or the organisers of a sporting event fail to provide adequate protection for participants or spectators.[17]

A finding of causation cannot be based on probabilities. In one case no liability was imposed because it could not be stated with certainty that a failure by the head of a school to follow the guidelines laid down in the case of fire had caused the death of a pupil.[18] For this reason the criminal judge will not impose liability where a doctor's fault has merely meant that a patient has lost a chance of survival, as it cannot be said with certainty that the fault was the cause of death.[19]

Following the Act of 10 July 2000 a distinction has been established in article 121–3 between direct causation and indirect causation, the latter requiring a higher degree of fault.

---

[11] 'chacun a commis une faute en participant ensemble à une action dangereuse et en créant par leur imprudence un risque grave pour la victime': Crim. 23 juill. 1986, *Gaz. pal.* 1987. 1. 104, note Doucet and *Rev. sc. crim.* 1987. 199 obs. Levasseur; *B.* no. 243; *J.C.P.* 1987. II. 20897, note Borricand.

[12] Lyon, 13 juill. 1973, *Gaz. pal.* 1973. 2. 830 and *R.S.C.* 1974. 98, obs. Levasseur.

[13] Crim. 28 mars 1973, *B.* no. 157.

[14] Crim. 8 mars 1995, *Dr. pén.* 1995, comm. 139.

[15] Crim. 25 oct. 1972, *B.* no. 309.

[16] Senlis, 14 déc. 1962, *JCP* 1963.II.13091.

[17] Poitiers, 16 oct. 1981, *D.* 1982.644, note Daverat.

[18] Crim. 4 oct. 1990, *Dr. pén.* 1991 comm 9.

[19] Crim. 9 janv. 1979, *JCP* 1980. II. 19272, note Chabas and *R.S.C.* 1980. 433, obs. Levasseur.

Mens rea

A detailed analysis of the relevant concepts of fault can be found at p. 74. The element of fault is determined objectively by comparing the defendant's conduct with that to be expected of a reasonable person.[20] The Criminal Code lists five forms of fault that can give rise to criminal liability. These can be grouped together into four categories.

Ineptitude (la maladresse)

This form of fault covers people who fail to carry out their craft or profession satisfactorily, but without necessarily being aware of this. Ineptitude might be found where a man working on scaffolding drops a tool which falls on the head of a passer-by, a doctor who misdiagnoses a patient,[21] a surgeon who fails to carry out an operation according to the established practice of his profession leading to the death of his patient,[22] or a hunter who shoots a passer-by when aiming at some game.[23] Under the initial government proposals for the new Criminal Code this form of fault would have been omitted, leaving it to give rise to civil liability only, but the Senate required it to be re-introduced. However, following the Act of 13 May 1996[24] this form of fault is no longer included in the general part of the code in article 121–3. This is a recognition that while the act may have been voluntary it was the result of a mistake. A surgeon was acquitted where his intervention was regrettable but fell within the established practice of his profession.[25]

Carelessness, inattention or negligence

These three forms of criminal fault apply where someone does something they know to be bad but either do not think it will physically harm another, or decide to take that risk. For example, if the man on the scaffolding in the example mentioned above, chose to juggle with his tools and one of the tools fell on the head of a passer-by. Alternatively this form of fault could exist where medical staff chose not to provide sufficient supervision of a patient.

It has generally been accepted that this form of *mens rea* existed where the harm was foreseeable by a reasonable person.[26] A decision of the *Cour de cassation* has thrown some doubt on this approach as it approved the

---

[20] *le bon père de famille.*
[21] Crim. 14 juin 1957, *D.* 1957.512; 12 juin 1961, *B.* 335; 26 janv. 1977, *B.* 38; 20 févr. 1982, *D.* 1982. IR. 379, obs. Penneau.
[22] Crim. 17 oct. 1989, *Dr. pén.* 1990, no. 122.
[23] Crim. 13 nov. 1974, *G.P.* 1975.1.173.
[24] Act no. 93.396.
[25] Crim. 18 nov. 1992, *Dr. pén* 1993, comm. 129.
[26] Nimes, 28 mai, 1966, *J.C.P.* 1967.II.15311, note Chauveau.

conviction of the owner of a quarry which collapsed even though 'the extent of the collapse could not have been foreseen'.[27]

Inattention and negligence are most likely to be found where there has been an omission, for example where no security measures have been applied to a building site.[28]

Failure to follow rules

A person is at fault where they fail to follow a rule. According to the relevant article, the rule must have been laid down by an Act of Parliament or an executive regulation. The accompanying circular originally claimed that as 'regulations' was put in the plural, this fault also applied to breach of an internal regulation of a company by an employee. This fault would arise where following an accident at work it became clear that the employer failed to follow the Employment Code. This is a more precise form of fault than the preceding ones and so will be easier to prove. This form of fault was found where an employer had failed to follow the rules on checking lifting equipment.[29] However, following the reform of 10 July 2000, the reference to regulations was changed from the plural to the singular. Thus, violation of a decree or official order[30] will be sufficient, while breach of circulars and internal company regulations will not suffice.

Deliberate breach of an obligation of security or care

Following an innovation of the new Code, the punishment is increased when the attack on the person results from a deliberate failure in an obligation of security or of care imposed by legislation or regulations. This qualification could be used against a company director who ignores the formal warnings of a health and safety inspector following an inspection.

For a discussion of this form of *mens rea* see p. 80.

Gross negligence

This concept is developed by paragraph 4 of the Act of 10 July 2000. It applies where harm has been indirectly caused by a natural person and is discussed in detail at p. 78.

---

[27] *'l'ampleur de l'effondrement ne pouvait être prévue'.*
[28] Crim. 5 fév. 1974, *B.* no. 54.
[29] Crim. 21 nov. 1973, *B.* no. 431.
[30] *un arrêté.*

Unintentional killing

Article 222.7 provides:

> Violence leading to death without the intention of doing so is punished with fifteen years imprisonment.[31]

Thus, violence causing a death which was not intended gives rise to a maximum of fifteen years imprisonment. The code places this offence in the section on voluntary offences, but as there is no intention to kill, it seems more appropriate to treat it as an involuntary offence. For a discussion of the meaning of 'violence' see p. 165. Where one of the ten aggravating circumstances exist this is increased to 20 years imprisonment, and to 30 years imprisonment when the victim was under fifteen years old and the offender was in a position of authority over them.

Comparative analysis

The different forms of fault are interesting though the overlap between them is significant and the single concept of gross negligence in UK law would appear to be sufficient with one exception. When the French developed the idea of deliberate risk taking, this was influenced by the English idea of recklessness. At the moment gross negligence would appear to cover this form of fault, but its separate identification in French law as a more serious form of fault would appear to be desirable.

The maximum sentences for involuntary manslaughter appear relatively light with one of the offences having a maximum of five years compared with life in England.

---

[31] *'Les violences ayant entraîné la mort sans intention de la donner sont punies de quinze ans de réclusion criminelle.'*

11

Non-fatal offences against the person

Introduction

This chapter will look first at voluntary non-fatal offences against the person and secondly at involuntary non-fatal offences against the person.

Voluntary non-fatal offences against the person

A distinction can be drawn between crimes of violence and crimes involving threats, and these will be considered in turn.

Violent offences

These offences share certain common elements in their *actus reus* and *mens rea* and these will be discussed first, and then the individual offences analysed.

Actus reus

The old Criminal Code originally referred to *coups et blessures volontaires*. A *coup* required a direct application of force, while a *blessure* required a breaking of the skin causing a bleeding. The courts took the view that the concepts did not extend to such conduct as throwing a victim on the ground, spitting on their face or pulling their hair.[1] Legislation was therefore passed in 1863 to introduce the offence of *violences ou voies de fait*. The latter offence was interpreted as extending to where there was contact between the author and the victim (so as to cause the victim psychological

---

[1] Crim. 7 avr. 1967, *D.* 1967.601.

harm, for example), so that there was a significant overlap between this and *coups et blessures*.[2] The offence was committed where a person received threatening telephone calls,[3] and anonymous letters containing drawings of swastikas and coffins.[4]

The new Code simply refers to *violences*. It was repeated during the preparation of the legislation and the accompanying circular that this terminology was intended to confirm and follow all the earlier legislative and case law developments and to incorporate the old concepts of *coups et blessures* and *voie de fait*.

The concept of violence includes direct and indirect applications of force, as well as conduct that causes psychological harm. A case involving psychological harm arose where a driver had driven his car in the direction of the victim.[5] It can be committed at a distance, through telephone harassment[6] and the sending of anonymous letters.[7]

The gravity of these offences is determined according to the duration of a total incapacity to work. This does not refer to an individual's inability to carry out their work in the strict sense, instead the *Cour de cassation* has interpreted it as covering the impossibility for the victim of carrying out their normal personal activities such as doing the shopping or accomplishing their household tasks.[8] This interpretation avoids the offence being randomly dependent on the particular profession of the individual, instead of being determined objectively by the seriousness of the injuries inflicted. Medical certificates have to be obtained so that the trial judge can determine in each case the duration of the incapacity.[9]

There must be a causal link between the harmful act and the harm caused. The violence must have been directed against a person. If the violence was originally directed against an object but a person is injured by ricochet this will not be sufficient. In one case, a door was broken by the defendant's fist and a piece of glass went into the eye of a young girl situated three metres away, no offence against the person was committed.[10] For a full discussion of causation see p. 61.

The classification of the offences is determined according to the gravity of the harm caused. The gravity of the harm is calculated according to the duration of the victim's incapacity to work.

---

[2]   Crim. 7 mars 1972, *B* 85; 17 juill.1984, *B*. 259; 21 nov. 1988, *B*. 392.
[3]   Crim. 3 janv. 1969, *B*.1, *R.S.C.* 1969.406 obs. Levasseur; 4 janv. 1974, *J.C.P.* 1974.II.17731, note Lindon, *R.S.C.* 1974.774, obs. Levasseur.
[4]   Crim. 9 juin 1991, *B*. 253.
[5]   Crim. 9 mars 1961, *B*. no. 150.
[6]   Crim. 17 juill. 1984, *B*. no. 259 and *R.S.C.* 1985. 297, obs. Levasseur.
[7]   Crim. 13 juin 1991, *B*.. no. 253 and *R.S.C.* 1992. 74, obs. Levasseur.
[8]   Crim. 22 nov. 1982, *B*. no. 263 and *R.S.C.* 1983, 479, obs. Levasseur.
[9]   Crim. 20 fév. 1995, *Dr. pén* 1995, comm. 138.
[10] Crim. 3 oct. 1991, *Dr. pén*, 1992, comm. 57.

Mens rea

An intention is required, and it is this intention that distinguishes offences of voluntary violence from offences of involuntary violence. The legislation does not specify what form of intention is required. Under the old Code, case law considered that the requisite intention could be found in the fact that the defendant wanted to commit the act that caused the harm, and it was not necessary to show that the defendant wanted to cause the harm that was actually caused. In a classic statement of the law, the *Cour de cassation* observed:

> A major offence is committed when there is a voluntary act of violence even though its author may not have wanted the harm that resulted from it.[11]

This means that no special intent was required. The defendant would be punished for a voluntary violence which caused more harm than they had wanted to cause.[12] This interpretation is in accordance with the wording of the new Code which simply refers to violence 'having led to' the harm incriminated. This is a very low threshold of *mens rea* for some very serious offences. As with voluntary homicide, the motive of the defendant is irrelevant.

The individual offences

Incapacity to work

A minor offence of the fourth class is committed where the violence has caused an incapacity to work. Article R.624–1 states:

> Except for the cases provided for in articles 222–13 and 222–14, voluntary violence not causing any total incapacity to work is punished by the fine laid down for minor offences of the fourth class.[13]

This is the least serious offence of violence.

Incapacity to work for eight days

A minor offence is committed where violence has caused an incapacity to

---

[11] *'le délit est constitué lorsqu'il existe un acte volontaire de violence alors même que son auteur n'aurait pas voulu le dommage qui en est résulté'*: Crim. 21 oct. 1969, *B.* 258; 29 nov. 1972, *B.* 368, *R.S.C.* 1975.408, obs. Levasseur; 5 févr.1979, *B.* 49; 3 oct. 1991, *Dt pén.*1991, comm. 57; 6 juill. 1993, *Dt pén.* 1993, comm. 254.

[12] Crim. 29 nov. 1972, *Gaz. pal.* 1973. 1.109 and *R.S.C.* 1973, 408, obs. Levasseur.

[13] *'Hors les cas prévus par les articles 222-13 et 222-14, les violences volontaires n'ayant entraîné aucune incapacité totale de travail sont punies de l'amende prévue pour les contraventions de la 4e classe.'*

work for eight days or less. Article R.625–1 states:

> Except for the cases provided for in articles 222–13 and 222–14, voluntary violence causing a total incapacity to work for a period of eight days or less is punished by the fine laid down for minor offences of the fifth class.[14]

Under the old Code this offence was punished with imprisonment, but the new Code removed this power to imprison.

Incapacity to work for eight days with an aggravating circumstance

Where violence has caused an incapacity to work for eight days and is accompanied by an aggravating circumstance the sentence is increased to three years imprisonment and FF300,000 fine.[15]

The sentence is further increased where two or three of a selection of these aggravating circumstances exist. Paragraph 2 of article 222–13 states:

> The sentences incurred are increased to five years imprisonment and FF500,000 fine when the offence defined in the first paragraph is committed on a minor under fifteen years old by a legitimate, natural or adoptive parent or by any other person having authority over the minor. The sentences are also increased to five years imprisonment and FF500,000 fine when this offence, having caused a total incapacity to work of eight days of less, is committed in two of the circumstances laid down in points 1 to 10 of this article. The sentences are increased to seven years imprisonment and FF700,000 fine when it is committed in three of these circumstances.[16]

Incapacity to work of more than eight days

Under article 222-11:

> Violence leading to a total incapacity to work for more than eight days is punished by three years imprisonment and a FF300,000 fine.[17]

---

[14] 'Hors les cas prévus par les articles 222–13 et 222–14, les violences volontaires ayant entraîné une incapacité totale du travail d'une durée inférieure ou égale à huit jours sont punies de l'amende prévue pour les contraventions de la 5e classe.'

[15] Art. 222–13 para. 1.

[16] 'Les peines encourues sont portées à cinq ans d'emprisonnement et à 500 000F d'amende lorsque l'infraction définie au premier alinéa est commise sur un mineur de quinze ans par un ascendant légitime, naturel ou adoptif ou par toute autre personne ayant autorité sur le mineur. Les peines sont également portées à cinq ans d'emprisonnement et 500 000F d'amende lorsque cette infraction, ayant entraîné une incapacité totale de travail inférieur ou égale à huit jours, est commise dans deux des circonstances prévues aux 1 à 10 du présent article. Les peines sont portées à sept ans d'emprisonnement et 700 000 F d'amende lorsqu'elle est commise dans trois de ces circonstances.'

[17] 'Les violences ayant entraîné une incapacité totale de travail pendant plus de huit jours sont punies de trois ans d'emprisonnement et de 300 000F d'amende.'

The distinction between this offence and article R.625–1 rests exclusively on the duration of the incapacity to work.

More than eight days incapacity to work

A major offence is committed where a person suffers more than eight days incapacity to work. The maximum sentence that can be given is three years imprisonment and FF300,000 fine. Under article 222–12, the sentence can be increased to five years and FF500,000 in the presence of one of the ten aggravating circumstances cited in the article which are identical to those mentioned in article 222–13. It can be further increased to seven years and FF700,000 in the presence of two of these circumstances and ten years and FF1,000,000 in the presence of three of them. This last punishment is also imposed where the victim is under fifteen and the offender is their parent.

Mutilation or permanent infirmity

A major offence is committed under article 222–9 when violence causes a mutilation or permanent infirmity.[18] It is punished by up to ten years imprisonment and FF1,000,000 fine. The drafting of this provision is simpler than under the old Code[19] and will avoid some of the finer distinctions on interpretation that had been developed under the old law, where for example, a simple reduction in the ability to see or hear was not sufficient. A serious offence is committed under article 222–10 where one of the ten aggravating circumstances exist, with a maximum sentence of fifteen years imprisonment. In addition, a serious offence with a maximum sentence of 20 years imprisonment is committed when the victim is under fifteen years old and the offender was in a position of authority over him or her. For the two latter forms of this offence, a minimum period is laid down which must be spent in prison.

Violence habitually exercised on a vulnerable person

Article 222–14 states:

> Habitual violence on a minor under fifteen or on a person whose particular vulnerability, due to their age, an illness, an infirmity, a physical or mental disability or a pregnancy, is apparent or known to their author is punished by:
>
> 1. Twenty years imprisonment when it has led to a mutilation or permanent infirmity;
> 2. Ten years imprisonment and FF1,000,000 fine when they have led to a total incapacity to work for more than eight days;

---

[18] *'une mutilation ou une infirmité permanente.'*
[19] Art. 310 of the old Criminal Code.

3. Five years imprisonment and F500,000 fine when they have not led to a total incapacity to work of more than eight days.[20]

On the meaning of habitual violence see p. 156. Habitual violence on a vulnerable person is treated as a major offence where the violence caused less than eight days incapacity to work with a maximum sentence of five years and a fine of FF500,000. The sentence is increased to ten years if the incapacity is for eight days or more. It becomes a serious offence punishable with up to 30 years imprisonment (including a minimum time to be spent in prison) if the violence caused either a mutilation, permanent infirmity or death.

Torture and inhumane acts

Under the old Code, torture and inhumane acts were treated as an aggravating circumstance. Under the new Code they are treated as offences in their own right, though they remain aggravating circumstances for certain specific offences, such as rape,[21] murder[22] and theft.[23]

The basic offence is contained in article 222–1 which lays down that:

The fact of submitting a person to torture or inhumane acts is punished by fifteen years imprisonment.[24]

No definition is provided for the meaning of 'torture' and 'inhumane acts', but they are accepted to be particularly serious forms of violence.[25] The basic offence is punished with fifteen years imprisonment. The sentence can be increased to 20 years in the presence of one of the ten aggravating circumstances discussed above.[26] The sentence can be increased to 30 years where the violence caused a mutilation or permanent infirmity.[27] The sentence is 30 years where the victim was under fifteen years old, the

---

[20] *'Les violences habituelles sur un mineur de quinze ans ou sur une personne dont la particulière vulnérabilité, due à son âge, à une maladie, à une infirmité, à une déficience physique ou psychique ou à un état de grossesse, est apparente ou connue de leur auteur sont punies:'*
  1. *De vingt ans de réclusion criminelle lorsqu'elles ont entraîné une mutilation ou une infirmité permanente;*
  2. *De dix ans d'emprisonnement et de 1 000 000F d'amende lors qu'elles ont entraîné une incapacité totale de travail pendant plus de huit jours;*
  3. *De cinq ans d'emprisonnement et de 500 000F d'amende lors qu'elles n'ont pas entraîné une incapacité totale de travail pendant plus de huit jours.'*

[21] Art. 222. 6.

[22] Art. 221.2.

[23] Art. 311.10.

[24] *'Le fait de soumettre une personne à des tortures ou à des actes de barbarie est puni de quinze ans de réclusion criminelle.'*

[25] Crim. 9 juin 1977, *B.* no. 211.

[26] Art. 222–3

[27] Art. 222–5.

offender was in a position of authority over the minor and the violence was habitually carried out.[28] The sentence is raised to life imprisonment where the acts have preceded, accompanied or followed another serious offence or have been habitually carried out, or where death has been caused without the intention to kill.[29]

Threats

Threat to commit an offence against the person

According to article 222–17:

> A threat to commit a serious crime or major offence against the person of which the attempt is punishable is punished by six months imprisonment and a F50,000 fine when it is either repeated or substantiated in a written document, a picture or any other object.
>
> The punishment is increased to three years imprisonment and to a fine of FF300,000 if it involves a threat of death.[30]

The threat must not be ambiguous. It must be aimed at an identified or identifiable person. It is not necessary that the threats be addressed directly at the person to whom they are aimed, they can be addressed to a third party with a view to this person passing on the threat to the intended victim.[31] As regards the more serious offence where there is a threat to kill, the statement 'Go before the worst happens to you'[32] has been found to be sufficient.

The *mens rea* for this offence and the offences contained in articles 222–18 and R623–1 (discussed below) is that the defendant must have issued the threat voluntarily while being aware of the disturbance it would cause to the peace of mind of the victim. The motive is irrelevant and it does not matter that the threat was in some way justified.

Threat with an order to fulfil a condition

Article 222–18 states:

---

[28] Art. 222–4.

[29] Art. 222-2.

[30] '*La menace de commettre un crime ou un délit contre les personnes dont la tentative est punissable est punie de six mois d'emprisonnement et de F50,000 d'amende lorsqu'elle est, soit réitérée, soit matérialisée par un écrit, une image ou tout autre objet.*

> *La peine est portée à trois ans d'emprisonnement et à 300 000F d'amende s'il s'agit d'une menace de mort.*'

[31] Crim. 21 fév. 1991, *Dr. pén.* 1991, comm. 226.

[32] Crim. 4 juin 1966, *Gaz. pal.* 1966. 2. 138, note Hugueney.

A threat, in whatever form, to commit a serious crime or major offence against the person, is punished by three years imprisonment and a FF300,000 fine when it is made with an order to fulfil a condition.

The punishment is increased to five years imprisonment and a F500,000F fine if it involves a threat of death.[33]

Article 222–18 punishes the threat, by whatever means, to commit a serious crime or a major offence against people when it is done in order to obtain the satisfaction of a condition. In this case, the threat does not need to be repeated or put into a substantive form, though proof of a single verbal threat will be difficult to prove in practice. The defendant may be demanding that a positive act be carried out or that a person abstain from carrying out an act. An example of this offence was where a prisoner threated to kill a friend unless she hurried up and wrote to him.[34]

Threat of violence

Under article R623–1:

> Except in the cases laid down in articles 222–17 and 222–18, a threat to commit violence against a person, when this threat is either repeated, or substantiated in a written document, a picture or any other object, is punished by a fine laid down for minor offences of the third class.[35]

Malicious telephone calls

There is a specific offence of malicious telephone calls which is punishable with one year in prison or a FF100 000 fine. Article 222–16 states:

> Malicious telephone calls and oral attacks, repeated with a view to disturbing someone's peace of mind, are punished by one years imprisonment and a FF100,000 fine.[36]

This offence does not require that any physical harm was caused by the defendant's behaviour. The circular comments that telephone harassment

---

[33] *'La menace, par quelque moyen que ce soit, de commettre un crime ou un délit contre les personnes, est punie de trois ans d'emprisonnement et de 300 000F d'amende, lorsqu'elle est fait avec l'ordre de remplir une condition.*
La peine est portée à cinq ans d'emprisonnement et à 500 000F d'amende s'il s'agit d'une menace de mort.'

[34] Crim. 25 avril 1990, Dr. pén. 1990 no. 289.

[35] *'Hors les cas prévus par les articles 222-17 et 222-18, la menace de commettre des violences contre une personne, lorsque cette menace est soit réitérée, soit matérialisée par un écrit, une image ou toute autre object, est punie de l'amende prévue pour les contraventions de la 3e classe.'*

[36] *'Les appels téléphoniques malveillants ou les agressions sonores, réitérés en vue de troubler la tranquillité d'autrui, sont punis d'un an d'emprisonnement et de 100 000F d'amende.'*

could fall within one of the more serious offences where it has given rise to physical harm.

Involuntary non-fatal offences against the person

For a discussion of the *mens rea* of these offences see the discussion of the *mens rea* of involuntary homicide discussed on page 161.

Total incapacity to work of more than three months

Article 222–19 states:

> The fact of causing to another, in the conditions and according to the distinctions laid down by article 121–3, by ineptitude, carelessness, inattention, negligence or a breach of an obligation of security or of care imposed by legislation or regulation, a total incapacity to work for more than three months is punishable by two years imprisonment and a FF200,000 fine.
>
> In the case of an obviously deliberate breach of a particular obligation of security or of care imposed by legislation or regulation, the punishments incurred are increased to three years imprisonment and a FF300,000 fine.[37]

Total incapacity to work of up to three months

Article 222–20 provides:

> The fact of causing another, by an obviously deliberate breach of a particular obligation of security or of care imposed by legislation or regulation, a total incapacity to work of up to three months, is punished by one year imprisonment and a FF100,000 fine.[38]

This offence is only committed where there is an obviously deliberate breach of an obligation of security or of care. For a discussion of this form of *mens rea* see p. 80.

---

[37] *'Le fait de causer à autrui, dans les conditions et selon les distinctions prévues à l'article 121–3 par maladresse, imprudence, inattention, négligence ou manquement à une obligation de sécurité ou de prudence imposée par la loi ou le règlement, une incapacité totale de travail pendant plus de trois mois est puni de deux ans d'emprisonnement et de FF200 000 d'amende.*

En cas de violation manifestement délibérée d'une obligation particulière de sécurité ou de prudence imposée par la loi ou le règlement, les peines encourues sont portées à trois ans d'emprisonnement et à FF300 000 d'amende.'

[38] *'Le fait de causer à autrui, par la violation manifestement délibérée d'une obligation particulière de sécurité ou de prudence imposée par la loi ou le règlement, une incapacité totale de travail d'une durée inférieure ou égale à trois mois, est puni d'un an d'emprisonnement et de FF100 000 d'amende.'*

Deliberate breach of an obligation causing no incapacity to work

Article R625–3 states:

> The fact, by a deliberate breach of an obligation of security or of care imposed by legislation or regulations, of attacking another without a total incapacity to work resulting is punished by a fine laid down for minor offences of the fifth class.[39]

Attack causing no incapacity to work

Article R622–1 creates an offence of carelessly attacking another, where no incapacity to work is caused. The article states:

> Except the case laid down in article R625–3, the fact of attacking another through ineptitude, carelessness, inattention, negligence or breach of an obligation of security or of care imposed by legislation or regulations, without any total incapacity to work resulting is punished by a fine laid down for minor offences of the second class.[40]

Comparative analysis

The structure of these offences is much more complex than English law, particularly due to the re-occurring range of ten aggravating circumstances, though this does mean that the judge is provided by the legislature with greater guidance on sentencing. There is a very low threshold of *mens rea* for the non-fatal offences against the person, compared with the approach in English law.

---

[39] *'Le fait, par un manquement délibéré à une obligation de sécurité ou de prudence imposée par la loi ou les règlements, de porter atteinte à l'intégrité d'autrui sans qu'il en résulte d'incapacité totale de travail est punie de l'amende prévue pour les contraventions de la 5e classe.'*

[40] *'Hors le cas prévu par l'article R625–3, le fait, par maladresse, imprudence, inattention, négligence ou manquement à une obligation de sécurité ou de prudence imposée par la loi ou les règlements, de porter atteinte à l'intégrité d'autrui sans qu'il en résulte d'incapacité totale de travail est puni de l'amende prévue pour les contraventions de la 2e classe.'*

12

Rape

Introduction

Significant reforms were made to the sexual offences by the Act of 23 December 1980. One of the main aims of this Act was to remove the discrimination in the definition of the offences based on the sex of the offender or victim. These reforms have largely been included in the new Code. The Code divides sexual offences between sexual aggressions and sexual violations. The former are committed with the use of violence, constraint, a threat or deception,[1] the latter are committed without the use of one of these means. Rape is categorised as a sexual aggression.

The current definition of the offence of rape is contained in article 222–23:

> Any act of sexual penetration, of whatever nature it may be, committed on another person by violence, constraint, threat or abuse is a rape.
>
> Rape is punished by fifteen years imprisonment.[2]

Actus reus

The *actus reus* of rape consists of the exercise of violence, constraint, a threat or abuse in order to commit a sexual penetration.

---

[1] 'Art. 222–22: *Constitue une agression sexuelle toute, atteinte sexuelle commise avec violence, contrainte, menace ou surprise.*'

[2] '*Tout acte de pénétration sexuelle, de quelque nature qu'il soit, commis sur la personne d'autrui par violence, contrainte, menace ou surprise est un viol.*

  Le viol est puni de quinze ans de réclusion criminelle.'

Violence, constraint, a threat or abuse

In order for a rape to be committed, the offender must have used either violence, constraint, a threat or abuse[3] to achieve sexual penetration without the consent of the victim. The scope of these concepts overlap.

Violence refers to the use of physical force on the victim and violence against property or another person is not sufficient.

The constraint can be either physical or psychological. Physical constraint is the same as violence. Psychological constraint consists of threatening the victim with harm to themselves, their property, or to someone they are close to. The *Cour de cassation* has ruled that a court of first instance was entitled to find a psychological constraint where the victim had submitted to sexual intercourse due to the fact that she feared the defendant. He was her manager, had a tyrannical personality and considerable physical strength.[4] Though the mere fact that a person exercises authority over the victim, or that the victim was very young, is not in itself sufficient for a finding of psychological constraint.[5] A victim was found to have been subjected to psychological constraint where the defendant threatened that unless she had sexual intercourse he would abandon her in the middle of nowhere in the depths of the night when the weather was very cold.[6]

The concept of a threat overlaps with the idea of psychological constraint. A court of appeal refused to take into account a threat to put a spell on the victim and their family by using supposed supernatural powers.[7]

Abuse occurs where a person obtains sexual favours by deceiving the victim as to the real situation or by taking advantage of the difficulties the victim has in understanding the situation due to their age or physical or mental state. The incapacity need not be permanent, so a rape can be committed on a person who is under the influence of drink or drugs or under hypnosis.[8] When dealing with a young victim, the issue is determined not by looking at their age, but by looking at their level of understanding.[9] The Civil Division of the *Cour de cassation* found that a rape had been committed where the sixteen-year-old victim had not resisted the defendant, suffered from a mental disability and was deaf.[10]

---

[3] 'Abuse' is a loose translation of the concept of *'la surprise'* as there is no directly equivalent concept in English law.

[4] Crim. 8 févr. 1995: *Dr. pén.* 1995, comm. no. 171, obs. M. Véron.

[5] Crim. 21 oct. 1998: *JCP* G 1998 II, 10215, note D. Mayer; *Dr. pén.* 1999, comm. no. 5, note M. Véron; *B.* no. 274; *D.* 1999, jurispr. p. 75, note Y. Mayaud.

[6] Crim. 11 févr. 1992, *Dr. pén* 1992, comm. 174.

[7] CA Caen, 23 mars 1987: *Juris-Data* no. 050299.

[8] Crim. 3 sept. 1991: *Juris-Data* no. 003783.

[9] Crim. 11 juin 1992: *B.* No. 228.

[10] Cass. 1er civ., 6 nov. 1961: *Gaz. Pal.* 1962, 1, p. 195; *D.* 1961, p. 733, note Holleaux; *R.S.C.* 1962, p. 98, obs. Hugueney; Crim. 8 juin 1994: *B.* no. 226.

Unlike the English law, the definition of the offence of rape contains no direct reference to the requirement that the victim was not consenting. Instead, the absence of consent is implied from the presence of one of the four vitiating factors listed above.

In the past a conviction for rape would only be made where it was established that:

• the victim had consistently resisted the defendant;

• there was an obvious inequality in strength between the victim and the defendant

• the victim had screamed

• there were traces of violence on her body.

Modern case law no longer applies these strict rules, with the judges focusing on the absence of the victim's consent.[11] The fact that the victim is reputed to have a 'loose' reputation cannot be a basis for a finding that she consented to the sexual intercourse.[12] Unfortunately, it may be treated as a basis for reducing the sentence.[13]

Sexual penetration

Under the old code, rape consisted of the penetration by the man's penis of a woman's vagina. The defendant had to be male and the victim female, though a woman could be an accomplice to a rape. The Act of 1980 broadened the definition of rape and made it less gender specific. This reform has been followed by the new Code. A father has been convicted of raping his son[14] and a mother of raping her daughter.[15] Rape now extends to any act of sexual penetration of whatever nature committed on another person. Thus it includes penetration by an object, such as a bottle or a finger, and not just by the penis. It covers oral[16] and anal[17] intercourse. However, in a case where a group of young people put a stick into the anus of their victim in order to extort money from him, the *Cour de cassation* took the view that the appropriate label was not rape.[18] It stated that

---

[11] Crim. 10 juill. 1973: *B*. no. 322; *R.S.C.* 1974, p. 594, obs. G. Levasseur. ; 4 mai 1993: *Dr. pén.* 1993 comm. 179.

[12] CA Versailles, 26 févr. 1988: *Juris-Data* no. 040295.

[13] CA Nancy, 9 mars 1988: *Juris-Data*, no. 045890.

[14] Crim. 3 juill. 1991, *Gaz. Pal.* 1992, chron. Dr. crim. p. 39; *Dr. pénal.* 1991, comm. 314.

[15] Crim. 4 janv. 1985, *B*. no. 10; *R.S.C.* 1984.814, obs. Levasseur.

[16] Crim. 22 févr. 1984, *B*. no. 71; *R.S.C.* 1984.743, obs. Levasseur; 9 juill. 1991, *B*. no. 294.

[17] Crim. 27 avr. 1994: *B*. no. 157.

[18] Crim. 9 déc. 1993: *B*. no. 383; *Dr. pén.* 1994, somm. no. 83, obs. M. Véron, chron. no. 26, rapp. L.-M. Niyose.

penetration of the anus would constitute a rape where there was a sexual motive,[19] which is a debatable distinction, as the motive of the offender is normally irrelevant in determining criminal liability. It also ignores the nature of the offence, which is essentially an offence of violence that seeks to humiliate the victim. The court has less controversially ruled that no rape was committed by a doctor who had been appointed as an expert by an investigating judge, when he carried out an internal inspection of a person's anus after this person had swallowed sachets containing heroin.[20]

In the past a husband could not be liable for raping his wife. The *Cour de cassation* appeared to shift in its position in 1990 but the facts of that case were exceptional.[21] In 1992 the *Cour de cassation* made it clear that the presumption that a spouse has consented to sexual intercourse is rebuttable.[22]

Mens rea

Only a general intent, and no special intent is required for this offence. Defendants must be aware of the illegal character of their actions. The *mens rea* will therefore not exist if they thought the victim was consenting. There will be no *mens rea* where defendants can satisfy the court that they made a genuine mistake and thought that the potential victim was consenting.

Sentencing

The ordinary offence of rape is punishable with a maximum sentence of fifteen years imprisonment. Under the old Code the maximum had been 20 years and this had been reduced to ten years by the 1980 Act. The current maximum is therefore a compromise between these two positions.

The maximum sentence is increased in a number of circumstances. Rape will be punished with a maximum of 20 years imprisonment[23] where it is committed:

- and leads to a mutilation or permanent infirmity;

- on a person under fifteen;

[19] Crim. 6 déc. 1995, *B.* no. 372; *Dr pén.* 1996, comm. 101.

[20] Crim. 29 janv. 1997: *JCP* G 1997, IV, 1169.

[21] Crim. 5 sept. 1990, *B.* no. 313; *D.* 1991.13, note Angevin; *JCP* 1991.II.21629, note M.-L. Rassat; *Gaz. Pal.* 1991.1.58 note Doucet; *R.S.C.* 1991.348, obs. Levasseur.

[22] Crim. 11 juin 1992: *B.* no. 232; *D.* 1993, p. 118, note M-L Rassat.

[23] Art. 222–24.

- on a person whose particular vulnerability, due to their age, illness, infirmity, physical or mental deficiency or pregnancy, is apparent or known to the offender.[24]

- by a parent or any other person having authority over the child;

- by people who abuse the authority which their functions confer on them. This was the case where the manager of a refuge centre raped the victim who had been placed in his care;[25]

- by several people acting as principal offenders or accomplices;

- with the use or threat of a weapon;[26]

- by an offender who was placed in contact with the victim by a telecommunications network diffusing messages to the general public. This aggravating circumstance was added to the Code by the Act of 17 June 1998 following public concern on the issue.

The maximum sentence is increased to 30 years imprisonment where the rape has led to the death of the victim.[27] It is raised to life imprisonment when it has been preceded, accompanied or followed by torture or inhumane acts.[28]

Comparison with English law

Both the English and French law on rape have been subject to recent legislative and judicial reform to bring them closer to the expectations of modern society. The shift by the courts to allowing matrimonial rape occurred at a surprisingly similar time.

The French offence of rape is now both wider and narrower than that of its English counterpart. It is wider in that it includes penetration by an object and can therefore be committed by a female defendant. It is narrower in that the defendant must have used violence, constraint, a threat or abuse, while the focus of the English law is on the fact that the victim was not consenting for whatever reason. The English law would appear to provide in this respect greater protection for victims of penetrative violence.

---

[24] Crim. 4 janv. 1990, *Gaz. Pal.* 1990.2.387; *R.S.C.* 1990.341, obs. Levasseur; 3 sept. 1991, *Gaz Pal.* 1992 chron. Cr, crim. 38, note Doucet.
[25] Crim. 3 mai 1989, *Dr pén.* 1990, no. 52.
[26] On the definition of a weapon see art. 132–75.
[27] Art. 222–25.
[28] Art. 222–26.

13

Property offences

Introduction

There are three key property offences in French criminal law: theft (*le vol*), abuse of confidence (*l'abus de confiance*) and fraud (*l'escroquerie*). These offences are well established in the law and can be found in the original Criminal Code of 1810. Each will be considered in turn.

Theft

The legislative provisions relating to theft are contained in articles 311–1 to 311–16 of the new Criminal Code. The classic definition of theft contained in the old Code[1] has remained unchanged by the new Code. Article 311–1 states:

> Theft is the appropriation of the thing of another with guilty intent.[2]

Thus, the offence consists of four elements:

- Appropriation (*la soustraction*)
- A thing (*la chose*)
- Belonging to another (*d'autrui*)
- Guilty intent (*l'intention frauduleuse*)

The first three elements form part of the *actus reus*, and the latter the *mens rea*.

---

[1] Art. 379.
[2] 'Art. 311–1. Le vol est la soustraction frauduleuse de la chose d'autrui.'

Actus reus

Appropriation

The concept of appropriation is not defined by the legislation, and it has been left to the case law to clarify its meaning. Traditionally appropriation has been restricted to where there had been a physical removal[3] of an object but in recent years this has been found to be inadequate to cope with modern criminal activity. It has therefore been extended to include the legal transfer[4] of property.

Physical removal

In the past there could only be a theft where there was a physical removal of property, and this approach still heavily influences the current law. According to the classic formula 'one must take, remove, carry off'.[5] Thus a seller was found not guilty of theft when he refused to hand over some goods to the purchaser who had paid for them.[6]

Legal transfer

Recent case law has established that there can be an appropriation without a physical taking where there has been instead a legal transfer of the property. This will frequently arise where the owner has handed over their property without the intention of passing ownership to the receiver. If the receiver subsequently chooses to keep it against the will of the actual owner then the courts are prepared to find an appropriation despite the fact that the receiver was given the property, rather than physically removing it themselves.[7] For example, in one case the victim gave an acquaintance their wallet to hold temporarily because their arms were full of shopping bags. The acquaintance then refused to return the wallet and this constituted an appropriation.[8] Other examples would be handing over a product to be tried before completing a sale, or the employer giving various pieces of equipment to employees to be used during the course of their employment.

A complication arose for the criminal courts in relation to sale transactions because in civil law, following article 1583 of the Civil Code, a purchaser acquires ownership in the property 'as soon as they are agreed on the property and the price, even though the thing has not been handed

---

[3] *le déplacement matériel.*
[4] *le maniement juridique.*
[5] *'Il faut prendre, enlever, ravir'*: Crim. 18 nov. 1837: *B* no. 405.
[6] Crim. 15 nov. 1850, *S.* 1851.1.453.
[7] Crim. 30 nov. 1977, *B. no.* 381; Crim. 3 mars 1993, *Dr. pén.* 1993, comm. 254 and *R.S.C.* 1993, 546, obs. Bouzat.
[8] Crim. 21 avril 1964, *B.* no. 121.

over nor the price paid'. This civil principle has effectively been ignored by the criminal courts in determining liability for theft for non-payment for goods where the transaction required an immediate payment. The criminal courts take the view that the final transfer of the thing is suspended until the price has been paid, until that point there is merely a provisional transfer which does not change the legal rights of the seller.[9] This is the analysis applied in the context of a self-service supermarket. If a person takes an item from the shelf and then fails to pay for it, this amounts to a usurpation of the rights of the owner and constitutes an appropriation. Thus, a theft is committed when a person walks past a cash till without paying for goods. If a person is caught in the process of hiding items on their person before going past the cash till, this also amounts to an attempted theft.[10] The exception to the general civil law principle does not apply where payment for the goods is not required immediately. If payment can be deferred or staggered over a period of time then the ordinary civil principles apply. There will be an immediate transfer of ownership in the property once the price and property have been agreed upon and there will be no theft if the purchaser subsequently fails to pay. If the seller later tries to take back the goods that have not been paid for he or she will themselves be liable for theft.[11]

Consent of the owner

The property must have been removed against the will of its legitimate owner or possessor. There is therefore no appropriation where the property has been voluntarily handed over[12] by its owner to the defendant, even when this has occurred by mistake or as the result of dishonesty.[13] There is, therefore, no theft where a person is given too much change by a cashier, or too much cash from a cash point machine, and decides to keep it.[14] In this situation there is merely a potential breach of contract, and criminal liability will not normally be imposed.

The courts will find that the property was handed over involuntarily where the victim was unable to give a genuine consent to the transfer of their property due to their age, their intellectual faculties[15] or because they were acting out of fear (where, for example, they had been threatened with

[9] Crim. 4 juin 1915, *D.* 1921, 1, 57, note Nast.
[10] Crim. 3 janv. 1973, *Gaz. pal.* 1973, 1. 290.
[11] Crim. 12 oct. 1976, *B.* no. 289.
[12] *la remise volontaire.*
[13] For decisions to the contrary see Crim. 24 oct. 1972, *B.* 306, *R.S.C.* 1973.417, obs. Bouzat; Crim. 4 nov. 1977, *B.* 330 which concerned the head of the warehouse of a shop found to be an accomplice to the thief.
[14] Crim. 24 novembre 1983, *D.* 1984, 465, note Lucas de Leyssac; Crim. 1er juin 1988, *J.C.P.* 1989.II.21172, note Devèze.
[15] Crim. 18 janv. 1978, *B..* no. 20; Crim 16 mars 1989, *G.P.* 1989. 2. somm. 379, obs. Doucet; Crim. 16 mars 1989, G.P. 1989.2.somm.379, obs. Doucet and *R.S.C.* 1980. 80, obs. Bouzat.

a weapon.[16]) So, there can be an appropriation where a person has handed over their property when under the influence of alcohol.

Temporary appropriation

The traditional view was that there could be no theft if the property was handed back to the owner. As a result there was no theft when a person took a bicycle for a bike ride and then left it by the side of the road.[17] This position had to be reconsidered with the increased problem of joyriding, as cars were only temporarily taken from their owners. The *Cour de cassation* accepted that property could be appropriated temporarily by using it[18] in 1959.[19] The concept of 'theft by use' has been applied where documents have been photocopied and the originals returned to the owner.[20]

The thing appropriated

In the context of theft the legislature refers to a 'thing' (*la chose*) while for fraud and abuse of confidence it refers to 'property' (*le bien*). The former must have a physical existence, it must be moveable, but need not have any economic value. The latter must have economic value but need not have a physical existence. As a thing need not have pecuniary value, a love letter can be stolen.

Immoveable property

Under Roman law it was established that only moveable property could be the subject of an offence which attacked legal rights over property. This position has been accepted by the French law for the offence of theft. Thus, there cannot be a theft of immoveable property, though there can be theft of pieces detached from immoveable property.[21] One cannot steal a house, but one can be liable for stealing the bricks that make up the house.[22] Plants growing in a field cannot be stolen, but once they have been harvested they can be stolen. In one case a piece of stalactite was removed from a cave and this amounted to theft.[23]

---

[16] Crim. 22 févr. 1894, *B*. 51; 4 mai 1973, *G.P.* 1973.1.612.

[17] T. corr. Saint-Claude, 7 janv. 1954: *JCP* G 1954, II, 7938, note Chambon.

[18] *le vol d'usage*.

[19] Crim. 28 oct. 1959, *D*. 1960.314, note A. Chavanne.

[20] Crim. 8 janv. 1979, *D*. 1979.509, note P. Corlay; 29 avr. 1986, *D*. 1987.131, note Lucas de Leyssac; *R.S.C.* 1987.701, obs. Bouzat; 24 oct. 1990 *B*. no.355; Crim. 8 déc. 1998: *B*. no. 336; *R.S.C.* 1999, p. 67, obs. R. Ottenhof; Crim. 16 mars 1999: *J.C.P.* G 1999, II, 10166, note S. Bouretz.

[21] Crim. 19 juin 1975, *G.P.* 1975.2.660.

[22] Crim. 27 avr. 1866: *D*. 1866, jurspr. p. 288.

[23] Crim. 5 avr. 1948, *G.P.* 1948.1.253.

Intangible property[24]

Until recently it was unanimously accepted that the object of a theft could not be intangible property. The physical support for intangible property could be stolen. For example, an exam paper could be stolen, but not the information it contained.[25] It is not possible, therefore, to steal a credit, though one can steal the physical document[26] that represents the credit.[27] With the computerisation of economic life, there were a number of products which had significant economic value but which were intangible, for example, computer software. The owner could be deprived of such property without there being a physical removal. It has therefore been argued by some academic writers that theft extends to the appropriation of intangible property, while others maintain that it does not, but might fall within one of the other property offences, particularly fraud.

In an important judgement, known as the *Bourquin* case, the Court of Appeal of Reims convicted two company employees of stealing 70 floppy disks and the contents of 47 of these. In 1989 the Criminal Division of the *Cour de cassation* rejected an appeal against this decision.[28]

In another case, known as the *Antoniolli* case, an employee had used financial information from his company to create tables and graphs which he passed on to a competitor. He was convicted of theft and his conviction was upheld by the *Cour de cassation*.[29]

It would appear from these cases that the *Cour de cassation* is prepared to find theft of information, which is intangible property, though it may only be prepared to do this where there is a temporary appropriation of the physical support to this information. Thus, merely memorising information would not probably be sufficient. This is the approach taken in the context of the neighbouring offences of abuse of confidence,[30] and handling.[31] The *Cour de cassation* was also not prepared to find a theft where television programmes were decoded without permission.[32]

The new Code makes it clear in article 311–2 that energy, such as electricity or gas, can be the subject of a theft, an approach that had been accepted by the earlier case law.

---

[24] *les biens incorporels.*
[25] CA Paris, 24 juin 1965: *JCP* G 1966, II, 14700, note Bécourt.
[26] *le titre.*
[27] Crim. 30 janv. 1846.1.127.
[28] Crim. 12 janv. 1989, *B.* no. 14, Dt de l'informatique, 1989.34, obs.Devèze.
[29] Crim. 1er mars 1989, *B.* no. 100.
[30] Crim. 9 mars 1987, *J.C.P.* 1988.II.20913, note Devèze.
[31] Crim. 3 avr. 1995: *B..* no. 142: *J.C.P.* G 1995, II, 22429, note Deneux: *R.S.C.* 1995, p. 599, obs. Francillon et 821 obs. Ottenhof.
[32] Paris, 24 June 1987, *G.P.* 1987.2.3, note J-P Marchi.

Belonging to another

The object of the theft must belong to another. The documents in a medical file belong to the patient. A doctor was found to have committed a theft where he had removed a patient's medical file to avoid incurring liability following the patient's death.[33]

A person cannot steal something that they own, even if someone else has rights over it.[34] If a person agrees to lend someone property and then takes it back before the agreed time of return, they may commit a civil wrong, such as a breach of contract, but they will not incur criminal liability for theft. One can, however, steal something from a joint owner. So if one sells property that is jointly owned, one is treated as having stolen the part that belonged to the other joint owner.[35]

The thing must belong to someone, and certain things belong to no-one, such as the sea, rivers, and wild life. As a person belongs to no-one, they cannot be stolen. Wild animals and plants on private property can be stolen.[36]

There is no theft where someone has abandoned property,[37] but this must not be confused with property that has merely been lost. Objects of value and which are new are presumed to be lost rather than abandoned.[38] Where a wallet containing a sum of money is found the courts takes the view that the wallet may have been abandoned but that the money was lost and thus stolen by the person who kept both.[39] In one case a railway truck containing rum had been damaged and the rum was pouring out of the vehicle. The defendant had collected some of the rum in a container and was found not guilty of theft, as by failing to collect the rum themselves the train company had abandoned the drink.[40]

Mens rea

The *mens rea* of theft is a guilty intent.

General intention

The defendant must have known that the property belonged to another and have intended to act against the will of the owner. If the person has

---

[33] Crim. 12 janv. 1994, *B*. no. 16.
[34] Crim. 13 janv. 1971 *D*. 1971.J.191; Pau 18 déc. 1950 *J.C.P.* 1952 II.6684, note Hubrecht.
[35] Crim. 25 mai 1988, *B*. no. 223; *G.P.* 1989.1, somm. 4, obs. Doucet.
[36] Crim. 3 avril 1903, *B*. 148; 12 févr. 1948, *D*. 1948.J.242, *R.S.C.* 1948.534,obs. Bouzat.
[37] Crim. 12 avril. 1850, *D*. 1850.1.112.
[38] Crim. 31 mai 1978, *G.P.* 1979, somm 150: rolls of copper wire belonging to the telephone company left in the street had not been abandoned.
[39] Trib. Correct. Seine 9 mars 1956, *G.P.* 1956.2.56.
[40] CA Rennes, 22 juin 1926: *D.H.* 1927, 2 p. 23.

made a mistake of fact they may lack this knowledge. There is no theft if the person thought they owned the property, or that nobody owned it.[41] A classic example would be where someone has accidentally taken another's coat from a cloakroom. A case involving a mistake occurred where a man had in the past the permission of a landowner to look for truffles on his land. He had gone looking for truffles unaware that the land had been rented out to another person. No theft of truffles had occurred due to the absence of *mens rea*.[42] The defendant must have known that the owner of the property had not consented to the appropriation of their property.[43]

Special intention

Theft requires a special intention which consists in the intention to treat the property as one's own.[44] In practice, it is difficult to distinguish the general intention from the special intention as the two concepts are almost identical. The question has arisen as to whether there needs to be an intention to permanently deprive the owner of their property. The issue was first highlighted during the 1950s when there started to be a growing problem with 'joyriding'. Initially, the case law refused to recognise a theft of the car[45] and the prosecution sought to punish for theft of the petrol.[46] Then, in 1959, the Criminal Division of the *Cour de cassation* ruled that borrowing a car amounted to a theft of the car, as the defendant intended, at least momentarily, to behave as if they owned the car.[47] It is therefore now established that there is no need to intend to permanently deprive the owner of their property.

It suffices to intend to usurp one of the rights of an owner, such as the right to reproduce documents.[48]

The *Cour de cassation* found that there was insufficient evidence of a dishonest intention at the time of the appropriation in a case where a car driver had noticed that the petrol pump meter went back to zero after having reached FF999. He helped himself to FF1,200 worth of petrol and only paid FF200. His conviction for theft was quashed by the *Cour de cassation*.[49]

The motive of the defendant is, of course, irrelevant. The offender need not intend their personal enrichment. Thus a creditor who seeks to gain

---

[41] Crim. 12 févr. 1864, *B*. 39; 25 juin 1901, *B*. 213.
[42] CA Grenoble, 11 juill. 1896: *S*. 1897, 2, p. 269.
[43] Crim. 4 mai 1995, *B*. 165.
[44] *la volonté d'appropriation*.
[45] Cass. Civ.7 juill.1953, *R.S.C.* 1953.671.
[46] Trib. Correct. Nantes 31 oct. 1930, *S*. 1931.2.83.
[47] Crim. 19 févr. 1959, *S*. 1959. J. 21 note M.R.M.P., *D*. 1959.J.331, note R. Boubée, *J.C.P.* 1959.II.11178, note Chambon.
[48] Crim. 24 oct. 1990, *G.P..* somm. ann. 167, *B*. no. 335.
[49] Crim. 1er juin 1988, *G.P.* 1988.2.763; *JCP* 1989.II.21.172, note Devèze; *R.S.C.* 1989.512, obs. Bouzat.

repayment by taking property belonging to the debtor is guilty of theft.[50] A theft was committed where pig farmers intercepted a lorry transporting pork from abroad, removed the contents of the lorry and poured diesel oil over it.[51]

Sentence

The sentencing structure was modernised and simplified by the 1981 Act on Security and Liberty,[52] though the law is still relatively complex in this field.

Ordinary theft

Article 311–3 of the Criminal Code lays down that ordinary theft is subject to a maximum sentence of three years and a fine of FF300,000.

Aggravated theft

The relevant aggravating circumstances are listed in article 311–4. The legislature has abolished the aggravating circumstance that the theft was committed at night. The aggravating circumstances can relate to the offender, the victim, the means used to commit the offence, or the place where the offence took place.

• The offender
The offence of theft is rendered more serious where it was committed by several people, by a State employee, or someone who pretends to be a State employee.

• The victim
Following an innovation of the new Criminal Code, the theft is rendered more serious where it has been facilitated by a vulnerability of the victim. This vulnerability must have been due to their age, illness, infirmity, physical or psychological weakness or pregnant condition which was apparent or known to the offender.

• The means used
There are three aggravating circumstances that relate to the means used to commit the theft. The theft is rendered more serious, firstly where violence is exercised against the person (violence against property, or threatened violence against the person are not sufficient); secondly, where the theft

---

[50] Crim. 21 nov, 1979,*D*. 1980.I.R.444, *R.S.C.* 1980.991, obs. Bouzat.
[51] Crim. 14 janv. 1986: *D*. 1986, inf. rap. p. 405, obs. R. Boubèe.
[52] Act February 2 1981.

was accompanied by destruction or damage to property; thirdly, where a weapon was used or shown, or if the weapon requires authorisation (primarily guns), where it is simply in the possession of the offender[53]. The notion of a weapon is given a wide definition in article 132–75.[54] Under the old case law the violence had to be committed at the time of the theft. Now article 311–11 makes it clear that these aggravating circumstances can precede, accompany or follow the appropriation.

- The means used and place committed

The offence is rendered more serious where the thief tricked,[55] climbed[56] or broke his way into[57] an inhabited building, or a place used to store property. The concept of trickery is not defined by the Criminal Code. Article 132–73[58] states that a break-in consists of forcing, damaging or destroying any locking or closing mechanism. It includes the use of a set of keys obtained dishonestly which are used to open a door. The concept of *'une escalade'* which we have loosely translated here as 'climbing' into a building is defined by article 132–74.[59] This states that it is the fact of entering a place either by climbing an area that is closed or by entering any opening not destined to be used as an entrance.

- The place

The offence is aggravated where the theft takes place on public transport or a place destined for access to public transport. At the time of passing this legislation the legislature was particularly concerned with the rise in thefts occurring on the Paris metro trains and stations.

The effect of the aggravating circumstance

The existence of aggravating circumstances can lead either to three levels of major offences or three levels of serious offences. The legislature has treated more seriously thefts accompanied by violence or the use or possession of a weapon. Looking first at the major offences, theft is punished by five years imprisonment and FF500,000 fine when it is committed with one of the eight aggravating circumstances listed by article 311–4. The maximum sentence is increased to seven years and a

---

[53] Art. 311–8.

[54] See p. 147.

[55] *la ruse.*

[56] *l'escalade.*

[57] *l'effraction.*

[58] 'Art. 132–73. *L'effraction consiste dans le forcement, la dégradation ou la destruction de tout dispositif de fermeture ou de toute espèce de clôture. Est assimilé à l'effraction l'usage de fausses clefs, de clefs indûment obtenues ou de tout instrument pouvant être frauduleusement employé pour actionner un dispositif de fermeture sans le forcer ni le dégrader.'*

[59] 'Art. 132–74. *L'escalade est le fait de s'introduire dans un lieu quelconque, soit par-dessus un élément de clôture, soit par toute ouverture non destinée à servir d'entrée.'*

FF700,000 in the case of a combination of two of these circumstances and to ten years and a FF1,000,000 fine when the theft is accompanied by three of these circumstances.

Turning now to the serious offences, the maximum fine for these offences is always a FF1,000,000 fine. A maximum sentence of fifteen years imprisonment can be imposed where violence has led to a mutilation or permanent infirmity. There is a maximum sentence of twenty years imprisonment where a weapon has been involved. Life imprisonment can be imposed if the theft has led to the death of someone or involved the use of torture or inhumane acts.

As regards theft accompanied by violence, the legislature distinguishes according to the gravity of the violence used. Under article 311–5 the maximum sentence is increased to seven years imprisonment and a FF700,000 fine when the violence has led to a total incapacity to work of up to eight days. Article 311–6 increases the maximum sentence to ten years and FF1,000,000 when the incapacity to work is more than eight days.

Fraud

The basic offence of fraud (*l'escroquerie*) is defined in article 313–1 of the Criminal Code:

> Art. 313–1. Fraud is the fact of tricking a physical or moral person, either by the use of a false name, or of a false characteristic, or by abuse of a real characteristic, or by the use of fraudulent tactics, and to induce them thereby, to their detriment or to the detriment of a third party, to hand over funds, valuables or any property, to provide a service or to consent to an act creating an obligation or a discharge of an obligation.
>
> Fraud is punished by five years imprisonment and a FF2,500,000 fine.[60]

Both theft and fraud involve the appropriation of property belonging to another. The difference in the offences arises from the means used to appropriate the property. For theft, the property is taken against the owner's will. For fraud, the owner is tricked by the defendant into handing over the property.

---

[60] 'Art. 313–1. *L'escroquerie est le fait, soit par l'usage d'un faux nom ou d'une fausse qualité, soit par l'abus d'une qualité vraie, soit par l'emploi de manoeuvres frauduleuses, de tromper une personne physique ou morale et de la déterminer ainsi, à son préjudice ou au préjudice d'un tiers, à remettre des fonds, des valeurs ou un bien quelconque, à fournir un service ou à consentir un acte opérant obligation ou décharge.*
L'escroquerie est punie de cinq ans d'emprisonnement et de 2 500 000F d'amende.'

Actus reus

Property

The Criminal Code refers to the owner handing over 'funds, valuables or any property,' which is the same formula used in the old Code. There is some overlap in the choice of words as funds are also valuables and both could be described as property.

While theft refers to 'a thing', fraud focuses on 'property'. Immoveable property cannot be the subject of the offence.[61] The property need not be tangible, but it must have some pecuniary value. Thus information can be the subject of a fraud offence.

A major innovation of the new Code is that the offence extends to the obtaining of a service. While under the old Code using someone else's season ticket did not constitute a fraud, it would now fall within the offence.

Deception

The defendant must have lied or used fraudulent tactics in order to obtain the property. Omissions are not sufficient to give rise to liability, so a person will not be guilty of fraud where they have simply failed to reveal a fact to the victim, or have allowed the victim to deceive themselves. Liability was imposed where a person failed to provide certain information in an application to obtain welfare benefits.[62] A son who continued to receive his father's pension after his father's death was found to have committed a positive act.[63]

The deception must have induced the owner to hand over their property,[64] and it must therefore have preceded the handing over of the property.[65] Thus in a case in 1978 an individual was found not liable for fraud where he had claimed invalidity benefit when he had lost his sight, and continued to receive the money after he had recovered his sight.[66] In certain exceptional cases where the handing over preceded the deception, the *Cour de cassation* has still upheld a conviction for fraud because the deception was intended to induce the victim to continue to hand over their property. Thus, in one case the defendant had presented a bank with false accounts so that the bank would continue to give him credit.[67]

[61] Crim. 15 juin 1992, *Dr. pén.* 1992, comm. 281.
[62] Crim. 26 avr. 1994, *Dr pén.* 1994, comm. 181; *R.S.C.* 1994.773, obs. Giudicellidelage.
[63] Crim. 20 mars 1997, *Dr. pén* 1997, comm. 93.
[64] Crim. 14 mai 1990, *B.* 187; *Dr. pén* 1990, comm 255.
[65] Crim. 8 nov. 1988, *B.* 381.
[66] Crim. 2 oct. 1978, *D.* 1979 IR.116.
[67] Crim. 31 oct. 1981, *D.* 1982 IR, 124, obs. Vasseur.

To determine whether the deception was sufficient the courts take a subjective rather than an objective approach. Thus, the courts must take into account the actual intellectual capacity and vulnerability of the victim.[68]

A lie

Only certain types of lies are sufficient to constitute the offence.[69] The defendant must have lied about their name or one of their characteristics, or they must have abused the confidence that their real status affords. The latter was not expressly included in the old Code but had been accepted by the case law.

A mere oral or written lie alone is not sufficient, so the simple fact of claiming to have forgotten one's wallet in order to be lent money or to promise marriage in exchange for the handing over of some property does not constitute a fraud.[70] For a lie to become effective for the purposes of the offence the simple oral or written lie must be accompanied by an external fact or physical act destined to give it force or credit. In practice, some recent decisions have taken a fairly relaxed view as to what would be sufficient to constitute this external fact or physical act.[71] In addition the case law has been prepared to give greater weight to certain types of written documents which are of a sort to inspire confidence in the public. Such documents, including official documents,[72] computerised documents[73] or accounts[74] will be treated in themselves as sufficient for the purposes of the offence of fraud.

• A false name

The false name can be an imaginary name or the name of another person. It can be a false surname, first name or pseudonym. A person will be treated as having used a false name where they have used a stolen credit card to buy goods.[75]

• A false characteristic

The characteristic that is the subject of a deception might, for example, be the person's age, matrimonial status or profession. It cannot be a mental

[68] Crim. 5 oct. 1871, *D.* 1872.1.382.
[69] Paris, 16 janv. 1960, *J.C.P.* 1960. II.11473; Crim. 7 oct. 1969, *B.* no. 242, *R.S.C.* 1970.398, obs. Bouzat.
[70] Crim. 23 juin 1883, *B.*161; 20 juill. 1960, *D.* 1961.J.191, note Chavanne, *J.C.P.* 1961.II.11973, note Guyon; Crim. 16 oct. 1957, *B.* 636; 11 févr. 1976, *D.* 1976. J. 295, Rapport Dauvergne; 3 nov. 1983, *B.* 277.
[71] Crim. 3 juin 1985, *B.* 211.
[72] Crim. 22 mars 1978, *B.* 114, concerning the *'carte grise'* of a vehicle.
[73] Crim. 16 mars 1976, *B.* 97.
[74] Crim. 8 nov. 1976, *B.* 317.
[75] Crim. 19 mai 1987, *G.P.* 1988, somm. 5, obs. Doucet; *R.S.C.* 1988.534, obs. Bouzat.

characteristic, so no fraud is committed if a person falsely claims that they are hardworking or serious. Examples of where a person has deceived another by assuming a false characteristic are where a person claimed that they had a university qualification,[76] were a member of a regulated profession,[77] holder of a public office,[78] a Michelin Guide inspector[79] or the pope.[80]

A person will normally assume a false characteristic by lying orally or in writing but it is also possible to do this by one's conduct. This would be the case where a person withdraws money from a cash point machine using someone else's card.[81]

- Abuse of a real characteristic

Here fraudsters use one of their actual characteristics to give force and credit to their lies due to the confidence it inspires. This occurred where a nurse defrauded a health insurance organisation by making a claim for professional work she had not carried out.[82]

Fraudulent tactics

This is the most common form of fraud and the most difficult to define. The tactics used serve to corroborate the defendant's lie. There are three main fraudulent tactics that the courts will uphold as giving rise to criminal liability.

1. Production of a written document

The production of a written document attesting the truth of a falsehood amounts to the use of fraudulent tactics. The written document must be separate from the expression of the lie itself. For example, a person might provide false pay slips in order to obtain social security benefits, while lying that they were on a low income.

2. Scheming[83]

There is a fraud when a defendant supports a lie with a scheme to trick the victim into believing the lie. The scheme might consist of using marked playing cards;[84] changing the price tag on a product before taking it to the

---

[76] Crim. 23 oct. 1956, *B*. 65.
[77] Crim. 30 oct. 1903, *B*. 350.
[78] Crim. 15 déc. 1943, *D*. 1945.J.131, note Donnedieu de Vabres.
[79] Crim. 26 juin 1974, *B*. no. 243.
[80] Crim. 11 oct. 1966, *JCP* 1980.11.19308, note R de Lestang.
[81] Bordeaux, 25 mars 1987, *D*. 1987.424, note Pradel.
[82] Crim. 10 janv. 1990, *Dr. pén*. 1990, comm. 187.
[83] *la machination; la mise en scène.*
[84] Crim. 19 mars 1971, *B*. 165.

checkout;[85] or inserting a coin of no value into a parking meter.[86] Going to sign on every fortnight to claim unemployment benefit was sufficient to amount to a scheme supporting the original lie that the person was unemployed.[87]

3. Intervention of a third party

A fraud is committed when the initial lie of the defendant is corroborated by a third party. If the third party is aware that they are providing support for a deception they will be liable as a secondary party.[88] Frequently the third party will not be aware of the deception, for example in the case known as the *King of the Gypsies*.[89] In this case the leader of a group of gypsies had produced a concoction that was capable of plunging a person into a state of complete physical incapacity for a limited time. Various gypsies got themselves run over by cars to incur minor injuries, and then made claims for compensation. Before they were examined by doctors appointed by the insurance companies they drank some of the concoction. The doctors then attested in good faith that the victims were suffering from a total permanent incapacity.

The case law has also applied this principle where no third party actually exists but the fraudster has invented a fictitious third party to provide support for their lie.[90] This would occur for example where the fraudster has produced letters that are supposed to be from satisfied clients.

The third person must in law be autonomous from the defendant, which is not the case of an employee of the defendant.[91]

Handing over the property

The owner of the property must have handed it over to the defendant. This handing over can take a range of forms. It can occur simply in a conversation when the victim provides valuable information to the defendant.

Physical or psychological harm

The fraudster need not get any personal benefit from the fraud. Because

[85] Crim. 9 mars 1983, *D.* 1984.J.209, note Devéze.
[86] Crim. 20 déc. 1970, *D.* 1972.155, note Boubée.
[87] Paris, 27 sept. 1978, *D.* 1979.I.R. 178, obs. Boubée, *R.S.C.* 1979. 576, obs. Bouzat.
[88] Crim. 5 oct. 1967, *G.P.* 1967.2.308.
[89] *l'affaire du roi des gitans*, Crim. 20 déc. 1967, *D.* 1969.J.309, note Lepointe.
[90] Crim. 5 nov. 1903, *D.* 1904.1.25.
[91] Crim. 2 nov. 1936, *G.P.* 1937.1.100.

the harm can consist of psychological harm, the defendant can be liable where they have paid the correct price for the property, but the owner would not have handed over the property if they had known the true situation.[92] Thus the courts have in the past accepted that the mere fact that the victim did not act of their own free will is sufficient.[93] Recent cases have taken a more lenient view on this issue. For example, the *Cour de cassation* approved the acquittal of a man who had been accused of an insurance fraud, where he had legitimately claimed money for a broken windscreen, but then not spent the insurance money on repairing the windscreen, but on removing a dent in the car's bodywork. The court concluded that no harm had been caused by the defendant's acts.[94]

The harm can consist of knowingly deceiving a court to obtain a favourable judgement, either by the production of false documents, or by the use of false witnesses.[95]

Mens rea

The defendant must have intended to defraud the victim. No offence is committed where the defendant mistakenly believes they had a right to use the false name or false characteristic.

Sentencing

Ordinary fraud incurs a maximum sentence of five years imprisonment and a fine of FF2,500,000. Unlike theft, fraud can never become a serious offence, it is always a major offence. There are five aggravating circumstances for fraud, which can increase the maximum sentence to seven years imprisonment (reduced from ten under the old Code) and a fine of FF5,000,000. These occur where the fraud has been committed:

- by a person in public authority or who is charged with a mission of public service;

- by a person who pretends to be acting as an agent of the State;

- in the context of a public call for savings;

- on a person who was particularly vulnerable;

- by an organised gang. The concept of an organised gang is defined in

[92] Crim. 30 oct. 1936, *D.* 1936.590; 29 déc. 1949, *J.C.P.* 1950.II.5582, note A.C.
[93] Crim. 15 déc. 1943, *D.* 1945.J.131, note Donnedieu de Vabres.
[94] Crim. 3 avr. 1991, *D.* 1992, 400 note C. Mascala.
[95] Crim. 3 nov. 1978, *B.* no. 299; 19 sept. 1995, *B.* no 274; 26 mars 1998, *B.* no. 117.

article 132–71 and has been interpreted as including where two people act together.

Abuse of confidence

The offence of abuse of confidence[96] occurs where property has been handed over to the defendant under a contract for a specific purpose, but the defendant has misappropriated[97] it. The offence is laid down in article 314–1:

> Abuse of confidence is the fact of a person misappropriating to the detriment of another funds, valuables or any property which has been handed over to him and which he has accepted on condition of giving them back, of exhibiting them or of using them in a specific way.
>
> Abuse of confidence is punished by three years imprisonment and a FF2,500,000 fine.[98]

Actus reus

A contract

The old Code stated that the property must have been handed over under one of six types of contract.[99] This limitative list caused significant problems in practice, with the courts sometimes artificially labelling certain transactions to fit one of the six categories in order to be able to impose criminal liability. The new Code no longer contains such a list. It makes no direct reference to the need for a contract, though an implied contract will exist where the property has been handed over under one of the conditions mentioned in the new Code and discussed below. Normally a violation of a contract will only give rise to civil liability, but criminal liability will be imposed for abuse of confidence where the defendant had an obligation to treat the property in a particular way and acted with the necessary criminal intent.

---

[96]   *l'abus de confiance.*
[97]   *détourné.*
[98]   'L'abus de confiance est la fait par une personne de détourner au préjudice d'autrui des fonds, des valeurs ou un bien quelconque qui lui ont été remis et qu'elle a acceptés à charge de les rendre, de les représenter ou d'en faire un usage déterminé.
      L'abus de confiance est puni de trois ans d'emprisonnement et de 2 500 000F d'amende.'
[99]   Art. 408 of the old Criminal Code: 'à titre de louage, de dépôt, de mandat, de nantissement, de prêt à usage, ou pour un travail salarié ou non salarié.'

Property

The Criminal Code of 1810 provided a list of the types of property that were susceptible of being the subject of an abuse of confidence.[100] This list was limited to certain forms of moveable property with monetary value. As a result, some property of no pecuniary value, such as a love letter, could be the subject of a theft or a fraud, but not an abuse of confidence.[101] On the other hand, intangible property could be the subject of an abuse of property while it could not be the subject of a theft. The new Code contains no limitative list of what can be the subject of an abuse of confidence, it restricts it instead to 'funds, valuables or any property'. Thus immoveable property, and property with no pecuniary value, are still excluded, while intangible property is included.

It does not matter that the property has an illegal origin or destination. The earlier dishonesty of the victim or even their dishonest collaboration with the defendant does not excuse the additional dishonest conduct of the defendant in misappropriating the property for their own profit. For example, there can be an abuse of confidence where a person misappropriates the profits from smuggling or from illegal bets.[102]

Conditional handing over

The property must have been handed over on condition that it will be given back, exhibited or used in a specific way. The offence will not be committed where there has been a complete transfer of the property. Thus an employee who was paid in advance was not liable when he took the money but failed to carry out the work.[103] The offence was committed by an employee who made personal use of the company stamping machine.[104]

There is no misappropriation where the owner has left the defendant the possibility of taking the property. Therefore, a farmer who sold manure produced by the property rather than using it to develop the property was acquitted of abuse of confidence,[105] as was the mistress who kept property that had been brought to her house by her companion for her personal use.[106]

---

[100] 'les effets, deniers, marchandises, billets, quittances ou tous autres écrits contenant ou opérant obligation ou décharge'.
[101] Crim. 21 août 1940, S. 1840.1.703.
[102] Crim. 9 juill. 1857, D. 1857.1.379.
[103] Crim. 21 avr. 1898, D. 1898.1.433; 17 juin 1991, B. 257.
[104] Crim. 16 janv. et 13 févr. 1984, D. 1984, IR 224, obs. Boubée; R.S.C. 1984.749 et 1985.307 obs. Bouzat.
[105] Crim. 17 août 1843, S. 1844.1.82.
[106] Crim. 17 févr. 1949, S. 1949.1.149, note Lemercier.

The property must have been voluntarily handed over, otherwise there will be a theft at this initial stage. Where a locked container has been handed over without its key this is not treated as a voluntary handing over and if the contents are appropriated this will be a theft rather than an abuse of confidence.[107]

Misappropriation[108]

The misappropriation occurs where the defendant prevents the victim from exercising any of their rights over the property.[109] The defendant has in effect ignored the fact that the property was only handed over to them under certain conditions. A misappropriation does not occur through the mere failure to carry out a contract. It can occur in one of three ways:

Squandering the property

The defendant may have squandered the property, making it impossible for the property to be returned to its owner. The squandering can take the form of physically consuming, destroying or abandoning the property. Alternatively, the defendant may commit a legal act that is incompatible with the victim's rights over the property, by for example, selling it or giving it away.[110]

If the squandered property was a determined piece of property, the squandering suffices in itself to constitute an abuse of confidence, as due to the specific nature of the property the defendant is not in a position to hand it back. It does not matter that the defendant has the means to compensate the victim for their loss.[111] As a result, if a person sells a Picasso which had been temporarily deposited with him or her, then liability will not be avoided by simply paying the price of the picture. Nor does it matter if the defendant later succeeds in regaining possession of the picture and returning it to its previous owner, because the offence has already been committed, their conduct will merely be relevant to the issue of mitigating the sentence.[112]

If the property was not a fixed item, then the squandering alone will not constitute the offence, but in addition it must be impossible for the defendant to return equivalent property to the owner. Thus, if money has been deposited with the defendant, then the defendant can spend the

---

[107] Crim. 10 nov. 1855, *D.* 1864.5.300; 12 avr. 1930, *S.* 1931.1.73, note Roux.
[108] *le détournement.*
[109] Crim. 15 mai 1968, *D.* 1968.594.
[110] Crim. 23 août 1879, *B.* no. 169.
[111] Crim. 24 juill. 1956, *B.* no. 568.
[112] Crim. 8 avr. 1967, *J.C.P.* 1967.II.15248, note Gavalda.

money without incurring any liability, provided that they are able to pay back later an equivalent sum.[113]

Refusing to hand back the property

The defendant may refuse to hand back the property, for example, where a person denies ever having received the property. Simply delaying handing back property is not sufficient to amount to a misappropriation; where a defendant returned a rented car later than the agreed time no offence was committed.[114]

Using the property abusively

Property is used abusively when the defendant uses it for a purpose other than the agreed purpose. This occurred when an employee used a company car for his personal use.[115]

Harm

The Code expressly refers to the requirement that harm must have resulted from the misappropriation of the property. It is not necessary that the offender have received any personal benefit from their conduct.[116] The victim need not have been permanently deprived of their property, even a temporary deprivation of their rights over the property will be sufficient.[117] The prosecution do not need to prove actual harm, it is sufficient to show that the victim might suffer a loss. In one case a former employee was found liable for abuse of confidence where he had removed documents belonging to his former employer, though it had not been shown that these documents had actually been used by his new employers.[118]

It is not necessary that the person with whom the defendant made the contract has suffered the harm, the harm could be caused to another person. For example, the defendant could have contracted with the seller to deliver the goods to the purchaser. If the defendant fails to carry out the delivery the harm will have been suffered by the purchaser and this will be sufficient for criminal liability to be imposed.[119] The victim of the harm need not be clearly identified, so the civil servant who squandered money

---

[113] Crim. 8 janv.1969, *B.* no. 15.
[114] Crim. 21 mars 1971, *B.* no. 99.
[115] Crim. 16 janv. et 13 févr. 1984, *D.* 1984, IR 225, obs. Boubée; R.S.C. 1984. 749 et 1985.307, obs. Bouzat.
[116] Crim. 8 juin 1977, *B.* no. 207.
[117] Crim. 16 févr. 1977, *B.* no. 61.
[118] Crim. 3 janv. 1979. *D.* 1979, IR 258.
[119] Crim. 25 oct. 1935, *D.H.* 1935.557.

that had been collected to help the victims of a flood was liable for abuse of confidence.[120]

The actual owner of the property can be liable for abuse of confidence where they have breached the rights of another over the property, such as the person who had the right to possession of the property.

Mens rea

The Code provides no reference to the form of *mens rea* required, but the courts have implied that defendants must intend to do wrong. They must know that the property has been handed to them under a condition and be aware of the illegality of their conduct.

Sentencing

Abuse of confidence is punishable with a maximum of three years imprisonment and a fine of FF2,500,000. Two aggravating circumstances can increase the maximum sentence to seven years imprisonment and a FF5,000,000 fine:

- the offence was committed in the context of a public call for savings in the industrial and commercial context (though not for humanitarian purposes);

- the offence was committed by a person who habitually helps the misappropriation of property belonging to third parties. This targets the criminal activities of professionals.

A third aggravating circumstance increases the maximum sentence to ten years imprisonment and a fine of FF10,000,000. It applies where the offence was committed by an officer of the law[121] or a public officer.

Family immunity

All three of these property offences have a defence of family immunity. The defence is contained in article 311–2, to which article 313–3 refers for the purposes of fraud and article 314–4 refers for the purposes of abuse of confidence. Article 311–12 states:

> *Art. 311–12.* Theft cannot give rise to a criminal prosecution where it has been committed by a person:

---

[120] Crim. 18 août 1877, *D.* 1878.1.285.
[121] *le mandataire de justice.*

1. To the detriment of his ascendant or descendant;
2. To the detriment of his spouse, except when the spouses are separated or authorised to reside separately.[122]

This defence applies where the victim of the offence is, for example, the defendant's grandfather or daughter. The new Code has removed the immunity from those individuals who are related through marriage, other than the spouses themselves. The defence exists to protect the social unity of the family, though this can look rather artificial in the context of the modern family. In practice, it has the advantage of avoiding difficulties of proof that frequently exist when dealing with offences committed between family members.

Proposals for reform produced in the 1980s would have removed this immunity if the victim made a formal complaint to the public authorities.

Distinction between theft, fraud and abuse of confidence

The three key property offences discussed above each cover their own domain of criminal activity. Theft is the appropriation[123] of a thing belonging to another without the owner's consent. Fraud consists of deceiving a person to hand over property. Abuse of confidence is committed by misappropriating property voluntarily handed over by its owner. Thus a key distinction between the three offences lies in the attribute that the fact that the owner handed over their property is merely a preliminary condition for the occurrence of an abuse of confidence (and must be followed by a misappropriation), while it is central to the commission of a fraud and prevents the occurrence of a theft.

Abuse of confidence revolves around a dishonest failure to carry out a contract, while no contractual relationship is required for the other two offences. Fraud requires the use of deception, which is not required for the other two offences, and would actually prevent the occurrence of a theft. Finally, while theft is concerned with the appropriation of a 'thing' the other two offences are concerned with the handing over or misappropriation of 'property'. Thus a love letter with no pecuniary value can be the subject of a theft, but it cannot be the subject of the other two offences.

---

[122] 'Art. 311–12. *Ne peut donner lieu à des poursuites pénales le vol commis par une personne:*
   1. *Au préjudice de son ascendant ou de son descendant;*
   2. *Au préjudice de son conjoint, sauf lorsque les époux sont séparés de corps ou autorisés à résider séparément.*'
[123] *la soustraction matérielle.*

Comparison with English law

There are significant differences between these key property offences in French law and the principal property offences in English law. For a start, there is no English equivalent of the offence of abuse of confidence, and one is tempted to conclude that this leaves no significant gap in the imposition of criminal liability in English law.

As regards theft, this is defined as having a narrower *actus reus* in French law than in English law. Under French law there is no appropriation where the victim consented to handing over their property, essentially where deception has been used. This means that the French law has succeeded in maintaining a clear distinction between theft and fraud, which the English law has failed to do since the decision of *R v Gomez*.[124] In English law a person can be guilty of appropriating property when they keep property that has been handed over by mistake,[125] while this falls outside the scope of theft in French criminal law. Under French law you cannot steal your own property, though you might commit a specific offence created to fill the gap.[126]

French law does not have separate offences of burglary and robbery instead these are expressly treated as aggravated forms of theft with increased sentences. The French equivalent to robbery extends to where the force has been used after the theft occurred, which is not the case under English law.[127]

As regards the offence of fraud, this extends to include the obtaining of a service, while in English law two separate offences have been created: the obtaining of property by deception[128] and the obtaining of a service by deception.[129] Apart from this, the *actus reus* of fraud has a narrower definition than its English equivalent, since only a limited number of lies suffice and these must frequently be supported by external physical evidence. In English law any lie will be sufficient provided it induced the obtaining of the property or the service.

Finally there is no equivalent in English law to the defence of family immunity.

---

[124] [1991] 3 All ER 394; [1991] 1 WLR 1334.
[125] Theft Act 1968 s. 5(4). See, for example, *Attorney-General's Reference (No. 1 of 1983)*[1985] QB 182.
[126] *le détournement d'objets gagés ou d'objets saisis.*
[127] Theft Act 1968 s. 8. See, for example, *R v Hale* [1979] Crim. LR 596.
[128] Theft Act 1968 s. 15.
[129] Theft Act 1978 s. 1.

14

Drug offences

Introduction

Until 1994, the drug offences were found in the Code of Public Health, but faced with an increasing drug problem, the French government decided to move the more serious offences into the new Criminal Code. Two minor offences remain in the Code of Public Health: illegally using drugs[1] and provoking the use of or trafficking in drugs.[2]

After looking at the meaning of 'drugs'[3] for the purposes of the criminal law, the key offences will be examined, looking first at the serious drug offences and then the major drug offences.

Drugs

Article 222–41 provides that for the purposes of the criminal law 'drugs' means those substances or plants referred to in article L. 627 of the Code of Public Health. Article L. 627 itself refers to those substances and plants that are listed as drugs in the relevant regulations.

The serious drug offences

Controlling or organising a group destined for drug trafficking

Article 222–34 provides:

> The fact of controlling or organising a group having for object the illegal production, manufacture, import, export, transport, possession, offer, supply,

[1] Art. L. 628 Code of Public Health.
[2] Art. L. 630 Code of Public Health.
[3] *les stupéfiants.*

acquisition or use of drugs is punished by life imprisonment and a FF50,000,000 fine.[4]

This offence targets the leaders of Mafia-type organisations and should only be used sparingly by the courts.

Production or manufacture of drugs

Article 222–35 provides:

> The illegal production or manufacture of drugs is punished by twenty years imprisonment and a FF50,000,000 fine.
> These facts are punished by thirty years imprisonment and a FF50,000,000 fine when they are committed by an organised gang.[5]

While the previous offence targets the organisers of a group involved in drug trafficking, this offence is aimed at the members of the group.

The major offences

Import or export of drugs

Article 222–36 provides:

> The illegal import or export of drugs is punished by ten years imprisonment and FF50,000,000 fine.
> These facts are punished by thirty years imprisonment and a FF50,000,000 fine when they are committed as part of an organised gang.[6]

Before 1994, this was a serious offence triable before the *Cour d'assises*. While over 2,000 people were convicted of this offence each year, only a dozen were sentenced to more than ten years imprisonment and these were convictions against individuals involved in organised gangs. The legislature therefore decided to reduce the offence to a major offence, to

---

[4] '*Art. 222–34. Le fait de diriger ou d'organiser un groupement ayant pour objet la production, la fabrication, l'importation, l'exportation, le transport, la détention, l'offre, la cession, l'acquisition ou l'emploi illicites de stupéfiants est puni de la réclusion criminelle à perpetuité et de 50 000 000F d'amende.*'

[5] '*Art. 222–35. La production ou la fabrication illicites de stupéfiants sont punies de vingt ans de réclusion criminelle et de FF50 000 000 d'amende.*
   Ces faits sont punis de trente ans de réclusion criminelle et de FF50 000 000 d'amende lorsqu'ils sont commis en bande organisée.'

[6] '*Art. 222-36. L'importation ou l'exportation illicites de stupéfiants sont punies de dix ans d'emprisonnement et de FF50 000 000 d'amende.*'
   Ces faits sont punis de trente ans de réclusion criminelle et de 50 000 000 F d'amende lorsqu'ils sont commis en bande organisée.'

avoid over use of the *Cour d'assises*. It becomes a serious offence when it is committed by an organised gang. In 1982 a boat was found containing cannabis and hashish, which was held to be both a violation of the laws on customs and the commission of the offence contained in the Code of Public Health[7] that preceded article 222–36.[8]

The defendant need not have had physical possession of the drug in order to incur liability. Thus the *Cour de cassation* has found that a court of appeal was correct to convict a defendant who had bought drugs that had been carried into the country by his mistress.[9]

Transport, possession, offer or supply of drugs

The offence contained in paragraph 1 of article 222–37 is aimed at intermediaries who work as 'wholesalers' in the drug trade, rather than the actual drug user or the dealer who sells directly to the drug user. Paragraph 1 of article 222–37 states:

> The illegal transport, possession, offer, supply, acquisition or use of drugs is punished by ten years imprisonment and a FF50,000,000 fine.[10]

Though this offence is primarily targeted at intermediaries, a defendant was held to be liable for possession where one gram of hashish was found in his prison cell. He claimed that it had been hidden there by another prisoner whose conduct he had not dared to prevent because he feared reprisals.[11]

A conviction was upheld when the presence of drugs were found in the urine of the defendant, who had been arrested in a car where the passenger was found in possession of varying quantities of different drugs and the co-defendants accused each other of instigating the journey to buy drugs.[12]

On the other hand, the mere fact of being found in possession of an average amount of drugs when in the company of a group of addicts was not sufficient to justify a finding that the defendant had offered or supplied the drug.[13]

Facilitating the illegal use of drugs

Paragraph 2 of article 222–37:

[7] Art. L. 627.
[8] Crim. 3 juin 1982: *B.* no. 141.
[9] Crim. 13 juin 1991: *Juris-Data* no. 003457.
[10] '*Art. 222–37 para. 1. Le transport, la détention, l'offre, la cession, l'acquisition ou l'emploi illicites de stupéfiants sont punis de dix ans d'emprisonnement et de FF50 000 000 d'amende.*'
[11] Crim. 17 oct. 1994: *B.* no. 334; *Dr. pén* 1995, comm. 61 obs. Véron.
[12] CA Douai, 3 juin 1992: *Juris-Data* no. 049433.
[13] CA Aix-en-Provence, 1er févr. 1993: *Juris-Data* no. 041603.

The fact of facilitating, by whatever means, the illegal use of drugs, the obtaining of drugs by means of false or inappropriate prescriptions, or to hand over drugs on presentation of such prescriptions knowing their false or inappropriate character, is punished by [ten years imprisonment and a FF50,000,000 fine].[14]

This offence cannot be committed by an omission. It applies, for example, to the provision of premises in which drugs can be consumed or the loaning of money for the purchase of drugs. In a recent case, the owner of a bar was convicted of this offence, where he deliberately allowed his establishment to be used as a meeting place for drug users and dealers to buy, sell and consume drugs, and sometimes even took orders for a dealer, or loaned money to drug addicts to buy drugs. His motive appears to have been to increase the business in his bar.[15]

The offence targets pharmacists who hand over drugs knowing that a prescription is false. In order to be liable for issuing an inappropriate prescription, a doctor must know that the drug prescribed is destined for illegal consumption. A conviction for issuing an inappropriate prescription will not be made simply on the basis that the doctor failed to examine the patient before prescribing a controlled drug.[16]

In a tragic case, a woman had been treated with a controlled drug following several surgical operations. She had become addicted to this drug and a doctor continued to prescribe the substance despite the fact that it was for illegal consumption rather than for therapeutic purposes. He issued a large number of prescriptions without carrying out any prior medical examination and was found liable for inappropriately prescribing the drug.[17]

Where the drug supplied by the defendant has led to the drug user's death, the defendant can be liable not only for this offence, but also for involuntary homicide.[18]

Money laundering[19]

Article 222–38 states:

The fact of facilitating, by whatever means, the false justification of the origin of property or revenue of the author of one of the offences mentioned in articles

---

[14] 'Art. 222–37 para 2. Est puni des mêmes peines le fait de faciliter, par quelque moyen que ce soit, l'usage illicite de stupéfiants, de se faire délivrer des stupéfiants au moyen d'ordonnances fictives ou de complaisance, ou de délivrer des stupéfiants sur la présentation de telles ordonnances en connaissant leur caractère fictif ou complaisant.'

[15] Crim. 27 févr. 1997: *B*. no. 81.

[16] Toulouse, 2 déc. 1982: *G.P.* 1983, 1 somm. 47.

[17] Crim. 10 janv. 1984: *D*. 1985. IR 464, obs. Penneau.

[18] Chambéry 25 mars 1987: *G.P.* 1987. 2. 603; *R.S.C.*. 1988.86, obs. Levasseur.

[19] *le blanchiment du produit des infractions*.

222–34 to 222–37 or of helping in the placing, hiding or conversion of the product of one of these offences is punished by ten years imprisonment and a FF5,000,000 fine. The fine can be increased to half the value of the property or funds which were the subject of the money laundering.

When the offence was concerned with the property or funds coming from one of the serious offences mentioned in articles 222–34, 222–35 and the second paragraph of article 222–36 the offender is subject to the punishments laid down for the serious offences of which he had knowledge.[20]

In the context of international banking, it will frequently be difficult to prove the *mens rea* of this offence: that the defendant knew the origin of the property. In a recent case, a lawyer[21] was convicted of money laundering where he had assisted an international drug trafficker to buy a flat in the name of the trafficker's mistress and advised the man to pay for the flat by an international bank transfer rather than cash to make the transaction look more legitimate. The drug trafficker had used a false name but the lawyer was aware of his true identity and of his involvement in drug trafficking.[22]

False justification of resources

Art. 222–39–1 was added to the Code by the Act of 13 May 1996[23]. It states:

The fact of not being able to justify resources corresponding to one's way of life, while being in regular contact with one or several people involved in one of the activities incriminated in this section, or with several people involved in the use of drugs, is punished by five years imprisonment and a fine of FF500,000.

The punishment is increased to ten years when one or more of the people referred to in the preceding paragraph are minors.[24]

---

[20] '*Art. 222–38. Est puni de dix ans d'emprisonnement et de FF5 000 000 d'amende le fait de faciliter, par tout moyen, la justification mensongère de l'origine des biens ou des revenus de l'auteur de l'une des infractions mentionnées aux articles 222–34 à 222–37 ou d'apporter son concours à une opération de placement, de dissimulation ou de conversion du produit de l'une de ces infractions. La peine d'amende peut être élevée jusqu'à la moitié de la valeur des biens ou des fonds sur lesquels ont porté les opérations de blanchiment.*
Lorsque l'infraction a porté sur des biens ou des fonds provenant de l'un des crimes mentionnés aux articles 222-34, 222-35 et 222-36, deuxième alinéa, son auteur est puni des peines prévues pour les crimes dont il a eu connaissance.'

[21] *un notaire.*

[22] Crim. 7 déc 1995: *B.* no. 375; *R.S.C.*1996. 666, obs. Delmas Saint-Hilaire; *Dr pén* 1996. comm. 139, obs. Véron.

[23] Act no. 96–392.

[24] '*Art. 222–39–1. Le fait de ne pas pouvoir justifier de resources correspondant à son train de vie, tout en étant en relations habituelles avec une ou plusieurs personnes se livrant à l'une des activités réprimées par la présente section, ou avec plusieurs personnes se livrant à l'usage de stupéfiants, est puni de cinq ans d'emprisonnement et de FF500,000 d'amende.*
La peine d'emprisonnement est portée à dix ans lorsqu'une ou plusieurs personnes visées à l'alinéa précédent sont mineures.'

This offence essentially reverses the ordinary burden of proof in a criminal trial. It targets people who make a profit from drug trafficking, without directly handling the drugs. The second paragraph is concerned with the growing problem of drug traffickers using young people to supply drugs to drug users, taking advantage of the fact that young people are treated more leniently by the criminal justice system and attempting to avoid criminal liability themselves.

Supply or offer with a view to personal consumption

This offence targets the dealer at the end of the trafficking chain. Article 222–39 states:

> The illegal supply or offer of drugs to a person with a view to its personal consumption is punished by five years imprisonment and a FF500,000 fine.
>
> The punishment of imprisonment is increased to ten years when the drugs are offered or supplied, in the conditions defined by the preceding paragraph, to minors or in educational establishments or in premises of the administration.[25]

Use of drugs

Article L. 628 of the Code of Public Health punishes with one year's imprisonment and/or a fine of FF25,000, those who have illegally used drugs. The existence of this offence has been criticised by those in favour of legalising the use of soft drugs. But in a recent case the *Cour de cassation* ruled that the offence did not breach the right to manifest one's convictions contained in article 9 of the European Convention on Human Rights.[26] Medical treatment can be ordered to replace the criminal sanction in appropriate cases.[27]

Provocation to use or deal in drugs

Article L. 630 of the Code of Public Health lays down an offence of provoking the use of or dealing in drugs, such as through presenting such conduct in a favourable light. The offence extends to provoking people to use substances which are presented as having the same effect as controlled drugs.[28] It is punished by five years imprisonment and a fine of FF500,000.

---

[25] 'Art. 222–39. *La cession ou l'offre illicites de stupéfiants à une personne en vue de sa consommation personelle sont punies de cinq ans d'emprisonnement et de FF500 000 d'amende.*
　　La peine d'emprisonnement est portée à dix ans lorsque les stupéfiants sont offerts ou cédés, dans les conditions définies à l'alinéa précédent, à des mineurs ou dans des centres d'enseignement ou d'éducation ou dans les locaux de l'administration.'

[26] Crim. 5 févr. 1998, *B.* no. 49.

[27] Code of Public Health, art. L. 355–14 to L. 355–21.

[28] TGI Paris, 24 févr. 1984: *J.C.P.* 1985, éd. G, IV, 217.

This offence was found to have been committed where an individual had sold postcards with the words 'LSD j'aime' printed on the front, with a drawing of a heart and a hypodermic syringe.[29] On the other hand, the offence was not committed by manufacturing and selling perfume or cosmetic products under the name of opium.[30]

If the provocation is committed by the media, the Act on Freedom of the Press is applied to determine the person who is responsible for the publication.[31] Where a newspaper published a reader's letter which could be viewed as portraying drug use in a positive light, the editor was acquitted of this offence as it was found that he simply wanted to inform his readers of the opinion of a drug addict on the subject, in the context of a wider investigation into drugs.[32]

Specific defence

Due to the difficulties of detecting the commission of a drug offence, article 222–43 provides that a person's prison sentence will be reduced by half where they have provided information which has facilitated the detection of other drug offenders. According to the terms of article 222–43:

> Art. 222–43. The sentence of imprisonment incurred by a principal offender or an accomplice of the offences laid down in articles 222–34 to 222–40 is reduced by half if, having alerted the administrative or legal authorities, he has permitted the termination of criminal conduct and the identification, in appropriate cases, of the other guilty people.[33]

Sentencing drug offences

The sentence for several of the offences is increased where they are committed by an organised gang. The concept of an organised gang for these purposes is defined by article 132–71.[34] In addition to the sentences laid down for each offence, the guilty person can also incur certain supplementary sentences listed in the Criminal Code.[35] Property belonging to a convicted person or to a person who knows that it has been used in the commission of a drug offence, can be confiscated.[36]

---

[29] Crim. 9 janv. 1974; *B*. no. 15; *G P*. 1974, 1, p. 201.

[30] CA Paris, 7 mai 1979: *JCP* 1980, éd. G, IV, 136.

[31] Art. 42, Act on Freedom of the Press of 1881; Crim. 7 avr. 1998, *B*. no. 137.

[32] Crim. 20 avr. 1982: *G.P.* 1982, 2, p. 538, note Doucet.

[33] 'Art. 222–43. *La peine privative de liberté encourue par l'auteur ou le complice des infractions prévues par les articles 222–34 à 222–40 est réduite de moitié si, ayant averti les autorités administratives ou judiciaires, il a permis de faire cesser les agissements incriminés et d'identifier, le cas échéant, les autres coupables.*'

[34] See p. 101.

[35] Art. 222–44, 222–45 and 222–47.

[36] Art. 222–35, 222–36 and 222–38.

Appendix 1

Key provisions of the French Criminal Code in English and French

Art. 111–3

No one can be punished for a serious crime or for a major offence whose elements are not defined by an Act or for a minor offence whose elements are not defined by a regulation.

Nul ne peut être puni pour un crime ou pour un délit dont les éléments ne sont pas définis par la loi ou pour une contravention dont les éléments ne sont pas définis par le règlement.

Art. 121–3

There is no serious crime or major crime in the absence of an intention to commit it.

However, when the law so provides, a major offence can be committed by imprudence, negligence or by deliberately putting another in danger.

There is also a major offence, when the law so provides, where there is carelessness, negligence or a failure to fulfil an obligation of care or of security laid down by legislation or regulation, if it is established that the person who carried out this conduct did not exercise normal care taking into account, where appropriate, the nature of his mission, functions and competence as well as the power and the means at his disposal.

In the case foreseen by the preceding paragraph, physical people who have not directly caused the harm, but who have created or contributed to creating the situation which has permitted the realisation of the harm or who have not taken the measures permitting its avoidance, are criminally responsible if it is established that they have, either obviously deliberately breached a particular obligation of care or security laid down by legislation or regulation, or committed an established fault and who exposed another to a particularly serious risk of which they could not have been unaware.

Il n'y a point de crime ou de délit sans intention de le commettre.

Toutefois, lorsque la loi le prévoit, il y a délit en cas d'imprudence, de négligence ou de mise en danger délibérée de la personne d'autrui.

Il y a également délit, lorsque la loi le prévoit, en cas de faute d'imprudence, de négligence ou de manquement à une obligation de prudence ou de sécurité prévue par la loi ou le règlement, s'il est établi que l'auteur des faits n'a pas accompli les diligences normales compte tenu, le cas échéant, de la nature de ses missions ou de ses fonctions, de ses compétences ainsi que du pouvoir et des moyens dont il disposait.

Dans le cas prévu par l'alinéa qui précède, les personnes physiques qui n'ont pas causé directement le dommage, mais qui ont créé ou contribué à créer la situation qui a permis la réalisation du dommage ou qui n'ont pas pris les mesures permettant de l'éviter, sont responsables pénalement s'il est établi qu'elles ont, soit violé de façon manifestement délibérée une obligation particulière de prudence ou de sécurité prévue par la loi ou le règlement, soit commis une faute caractérisée et qui exposait autrui à un risque d'une particulière gravité qu'elles ne pouvaient ignorer.

Art. 121–4

The principal offender is the person who:
1. Commits the criminal conduct;
2. Attempts to commit a serious offence or, in the cases provided for by the legislation, a major offence.

Est auteur de l'infraction la personne qui:
1. *Commet les faits incriminés;*
2. *Tente de commettre un crime ou, dans les case prévus par la loi, un délit.*

Art. 121–5

An attempt is constituted when the defendant has started to execute the full offence, which was only suspended or failed to achieve its result because of circumstances independent of the will of the defendant.

La tentative est constituée dès lors que, manifestée par un commencement d'exécution, elle n'a été suspendue ou n'a manqué son effet qu'en raison de circonstances indépendantes de la volonté de son auteur.

Art. 121–6

The accomplice of the offence, as defined in article 121–7, will be punished as a principal offender.

Sera puni comme auteur le complice de l'infraction, au sens de l'article 121–7.

Art. 121–7

An accomplice to a serious or major offence is the person who knowingly, by help or assistance, facilitated its preparation or commission.

A person is also an accomplice who by gift, promise, threat, order, abuse of authority or power has provoked an offence or given instructions to commit it.

Est complice d'un crime ou d'un délit la personne qui sciemment, par aide ou assistance, en a facilité la préparation ou la consommation.

Est également complice la personne qui par don, promesse, menace, ordre, abus d'autorité ou de pouvoir aura provoqué à une infraction ou donné des instructions pour la commettre.

Art. 122–1

A person is not criminally liable who was affected at the time of the facts by a psychological or neuro-psychological illness which had removed his discernment or his control over his acts.

A person suffering, at the time of the facts, from a psychological or neuro-psychological illness which altered his discernment or impeded his control over his acts remains punishable; however, the case law takes account of this circumstance when it determines the length and mode of punishment.

N'est pas pénalement responsable la personne qui était atteinte au moment des faits, d'un trouble psychique ou neuropsychique ayant aboli son discernement ou le contrôle de ses actes.

La personne atteinte, au moment des faits, d'un trouble psychique ou neuropsychique ayant altéré son discernement ou entravé le contrôle de ses actes demeure punissable; toutefois, la jurisprudence tient compte de cette circonstance lorsqu'elle détermine la peine et en fixe le régime.

Art. 122–2

A person is not criminally liable who acted under the influence of a force or a constraint which they could not resist.

N'est pas pénalement responsable la personne qui a agi sous l'empire d'une force ou d'une contrainte à laquelle elle n'a pas pu résister.

Art. 122–3

A person is not criminally liable if they prove that they believed, due to an error of law that they were not in a position to avoid, they were allowed to legally carry out the act.

N'est pas pénalement responsable la personne qui justifie avoir cru, par une erreur sur le droit qu'elle n'était pas en mesure d'éviter, pouvoir légitimement accomplir l'acte.

Art. 122–4

A person is not criminally liable who carries out an act ordered or authorised by legislative or regulatory provisions.

A person who carries out an act ordered by a legitimate authority is not criminally liable, except if this act is obviously illegal.

N'est pas pénalement responsable la personne qui accomplit un acte prescrit ou autorisé par des dispositions législatives ou règlementaires.

N'est pas pénalement responsable la personne qui accomplit un acte commandé par l'autorité légitime, sauf si cet acte est manifestement illégal.

Art. 122–5

A person who, faced with an unjustified attack against themselves or another, carries out at that time an act required by the necessity of the legitimate defence of themselves or another is not criminally liable, except if there is a disproportion between the means of defence used and the gravity of the attack.

A person who, in order to prevent the commission of a serious or major offence against property, carries out an act of defence, other than voluntary homicide, when this act is strictly necessary for the goal sought is not criminally liable when the means used are proportionate to the gravity of the offence.

N'est pas pénalement responsable la personne qui, devant une atteinte injustifiée envers elle-même ou autrui, accomplit dans le même temps, un acte commandé par la nécessité de la légitime défense d'elle-même ou d'autrui, sauf s'il y a disproportion entre les moyens de défense employés et la gravité de l'atteinte.

N'est pas pénalement responsable la personne qui, pour interrompre l'exécution d'un crime ou d'un délit contre un bien, accomplit un acte de défense, autre qu'un homicide volontaire, lorsque cet acte est strictement nécessaire au but poursuivi dès lors que les moyens sont proportionnés à la gravité de l'infraction.

Art. 122–6

A person is presumed to have acted in a state of legitimate defence when they carry out the act:
1. To repel, at night, an entrance by force, violence or fraud into inhabited premises;
2. To defend themselves against the authors of theft or looting executed with force.

Est présumé avoir agi en état de légitime défense celui qui accomplit l'acte:
1. *Pour repousser, de nuit, l'entrée par effraction, violence ou ruse dans un lieu habité;*
2. *Pour se défendre contre les auteurs de vols ou de pillages exécutés avec violence.*

Art. 122–7

A person is not criminally liable who, faced with an existing or imminent danger which threatens themselves, another or property, carries out a necessary act to safeguard the person or property, except if there is disproportion between the means used and the gravity of the threat.

N'est pas pénalement responsable la personne qui, face à un danger actuel ou imminent qui menace elle-même, autrui ou un bien, accomplit un acte nécessaire à la sauvegarde de la personne ou du bien, sauf s'il y a disproportion entre les moyens employés et la gravité de la menace.

Art. 122–8

Minors found guilty of criminal offences are the subject of measures of protection, assistance, supervision and education according to the conditions fixed by a special law.

This law also determines the conditions in which punishment can be imposed on minors over thirteen.

Les mineurs reconnus coupables d'infractions pénales font l'objet de measures de protection, d'assistance, de surveillance et d'éducation dans les conditions fixées par une loi particulière.

Cette loi détermine également les conditions dans lesquelles des peines peuvent être prononcées à l'encontre des mineurs de plus de 13 ans.

Art. 131–10

When the legislation so provides, a serious or major offence can be sanctioned by one of several complementary punishments which, being imposed on physical people, involve the banning, disqualification, incapacity or removal of a right, freezing or confiscation of assets, closure of an establishment or publication of the decision given or diffusion of this either through the written press, or by any means of audiovisual communication.

Lorsque la loi prévoit, un crime ou un délit peut être sanctionné d'une ou de plusieurs peines complémentaires qui, frappant les personnes physiques, emportent interdiction, déchéance, incapacité ou retrait d'un droit, immobilisation ou confiscation d'un objet, fermeture d'un établissement ou affichage de la décision prononcée ou diffusion de celle-ci soit par la presse écrite, soit par tout moyen de communication audiovisuelle.

Art. 132–72

Premeditation is the plan formed before the action to commit a particular serious or major offence.

La préméditation est le dessein formé avant l'action de commettre un crime ou un délit déterminé.

Art. 132–75

A weapon is any object conceived to kill or injure.

Any other object susceptible of presenting a danger to people is classed as a weapon when it is used to kill, injure or threaten or it is destined by the person carrying it, to kill, injure or threaten.

Any object which resembles and can be confused with a weapon defined in the first paragraph, and that is used to threaten, kill or injure or is destined, by the person carrying it, to threaten, kill or injure, is classed as a weapon.

The use of an animal to kill, injure or threaten is classed as using a weapon. Where the owner of the animal is convicted or if the owner is not known, the court can decide to hand over the animal to an animal refuge, which can dispose of it as they wish.

Est une arme tout objet conçu pour tuer ou blesser.

Tout autre objet susceptible de présenter un danger pour les personnes est assimilé à une arme dès lors qu'il est utilisé pour tuer, blesser ou menacer ou qu'il est destiné, par celui qui en est porteur, à tuer, blesser ou menacer.

Est assimilé à une arme tout objet qui, présentant avec l'arme définie au premier alinéa une ressemblance de nature à créer une confusion, est utilisé pour menacer de tuer ou de blesser ou est destiné, par celui qui en est porteur, à menacer de tuer ou de blesser.

L'utilisation d'un animal pour tuer, blesser ou menacer est assimilée à l'usage d'une arme. En cas de condamnation du propriétaire de l'animal ou si le propriétaire est inconnu, le tribunal peut décider de remettre l'animal à une oeuvre de protection animale reconnue d'utilité publique ou déclarée, laquelle pourra librement en disposer.

Art. 211–1

Genocide consists in the execution of a concerted plan aimed at the total or partial destruction of a national, ethnic, racial or religious group, or of a group determined by any other arbitrary criteria, to commit or to have committed, against members of this group, one of the following acts:

- A voluntary attack on life;
- A serious attack on their physical or psychological integrity;
- Submission to living conditions likely to lead to the total or partial destruction of the group;
- Measures aiming to prevent reproduction;
- Forced transfer of children…

Constitue un génocide le fait, en exécution d'un plan concerté tendant à la destruction totale ou partielle d'un groupe national, ethnique, racial ou religieux, ou d'un groupe déterminé à partir de tout autre critère arbitraire, de commettre ou de faire commettre, à l'encontre de membres de ce groupe, l'un des actes suivants:

- *Atteinte volontaire à la vie;*
- *Atteinte grave à l'intégrité physique ou psychique;*
- *Soumission à des conditions d'existence de nature à entrainer la destruction totale ou partielle du groupe;*
- *Mesures visant à entraver les naissance;*
- *Transfer forcé d'enfants …*

Art. 212–1

Deportation, slavery or the massive and systematic practice of summary executions, the abduction of people followed by their disappearance, torture or inhuman acts, inspired by political, philosophical, racial or religious motives and organised in the execution of a concerted plan against a group of the civil population are punished by life imprisonment.

La déportation, la réduction en esclavage ou la pratique massive et systématique d'exécutions sommaires, d'enlèvements de personnes suivis de leur disparition, de la torture ou d'actes inhumains, inspirées par des motifs politiques, philosophiques, raciaux ou religieux et organisées en exécution d'un plan concerté à l'encontre d'un groupe de population civile sont punies de la réclusion criminelle à perpétuité...

Art. 212–2

The acts referred to in article 212–1 are punished by life imprisonment when committed in times of war in the execution of a concerted plan against those who are fighting against the ideological system in the name of which are perpetrated crimes against humanity...

Lorsqu'ils sont commis en temps de guerre en exécution d'un plan concerté contre ceux qui combattent le système idéologique au nom duquel sont perpétrés des crimes contre l'humanité, les actes visés à l'article 212–1 sont punis de la réclusion criminelle à perpétuité...

Art. 221–1

The fact of voluntarily killing another constitutes murder. It is punished by 30 years imprisonment.

Le fait de donner volontairement la mort à autrui constitue un meurtre. Il est puni de trente ans de réclusion criminelle.

Art. 221–2

A murder which precedes, accompanies or follows another serious offence is punished by life imprisonment.

A murder that aims to prepare or facilitate a major offence, either to enable the escape or to assure the impunity of the author or the accomplice of a major offence is punished by life imprisonment.

Le meurtre qui précède, accompagne ou suit un autre crime est puni de la réclusion criminelle à perpétuité.

Le meurtre qui a pour objet soit de préparer ou de faciliter un délit, soit de favoriser la fuite ou d'assurer l'impunité de l'auteur ou du complice d'un délit est puni de la réclusion criminelle à perpétuité.

Art. 221–3

Murder committed with premeditation constitutes an assassination. It is punished with life imprisonment.

The two first paragraphs of article 132–23 relating to the minimum period to be spent in prison are applicable to the offence laid down by this article. However, when the victim is under fifteen-years-old and the assassination is preceded or accompanied by a rape, torture or inhumane acts the *Cour d'assises* can, by a special decision, either increase the minimum time to be spent in prison to 30 years, or, if it hands down a life sentence, decide that none of the measures listed in article 132–23 can be granted to the convicted person; ...

Le meurtre commis avec préméditation constitue un assassinat. Il est puni de la réclusion criminelle à perpétuité.

Les deux premiers alinéas de l'article 132–23 relatif à la période de sûreté sont applicables à l'infraction prévue par le présent article. Toutefois, lorsque la victime est un mineur de quinze ans et que l'assassinat est précédé ou accompagné d'un viol, de tortures ou d'actes de barbarie, la cour d'assises peut, par décision spéciale, soit porter la période de sûreté jusqu'à trente ans, soit, si elle prononce la réclusion criminelle à perpétuité, décider qu'aucune des mesures énumérées à l'article 132–23 ne pourra être accordée au condamné; ...

Art. 221–4

Murder is punished with a life sentence when it is committed:

1. On a minor under fifteen;
2. On a legal or natural parent or on the adoptive mother or father;
3. On a person whose particular vulnerability, due to their age, to an illness, to an infirmity, to a physical or psychological deficiency or to a pregnancy, is apparent or known to its author;
4. On a judge, juror, an *avocat*, an *officier public* or an *officier ministériel*, an official of the *gendarmerie*, a member of the national police, customs, the prison service or any other person having public authority or charged with a mission of public service, in the exercise or on the occasion of their exercise of their functions or of their mission, when the status of the victim is apparent or known to the author;
5. On a witness, a victim or a private claimant, either to prevent him from denouncing the facts, reporting an offence or giving evidence in court, or because of their denunciation, complaint or deposition.

Le meurtre est puni de la réclusion criminelle à perpétuité lorsqu'il est commis:

1. *Sur un mineur de quinze ans;*
2. *Sur un ascendant légitime ou naturel ou sur les père ou mère adoptifs:*
3. *Sur une personne dont la particulière vulnérabilité, due à son âge, à une maladie, à une infirmité, à une déficience physique ou psychique ou à un état de grossesse, est apparente ou connue de son auteur;*
4. *Sur un magistrat, un juré, un avocat, un officier public ou ministériel, un militaire de la gendarmerie, un fonctionnaire de la police nationale, des douanes, de l'administration pénitentiaire ou toute autre personne dépositaire de l'autorité publique ou chargée d'une mission de service public, dans l'exercice ou à l'occasion de l'exercice de ses fonctions ou de sa mission, lorsque la qualité de la victime est apparente ou connue de l'auteur;*
5. *Sur un témoin, une victime ou une partie civile, soit pour l'empêcher de dénoncer les faits, de porter plainte ou de déposer en justice, soit en raison de sa dénonciation de sa plainte ou de sa déposition.*

Art. 221–5

The fact of attacking the life of another through the use or administration of substances that cause death constitutes a poisoning …

Le fait d'attenter à la vie d'autrui par l'emploi ou l'administration de substances de nature à entrainer la mort constitue un empoisonnement…

Art. 221–6

The fact of causing, in the conditions and according to the distinctions laid down by article 121–3, by ineptitude, carelessness, inattention, negligence or a breach of an obligation of security or of care imposed by legislation or regulation, the death of another constitutes an involuntary homicide punishable by three years imprisonment and a FF300,000 fine.

In the case of an obviously deliberate breach of a particular obligation of security or of care imposed by legislation or regulation, the punishments incurred are increased to five years imprisonment and a FF500,000 fine.

Le fait de causer, dans les conditions et selon les distinctions prévues à l'article 121–3, par maladresse, imprudence, inattention, négligence ou manquement à une obligation de sécurité ou de prudence imposée par la loi ou le règlement, la mort d'autrui constitue un homicide involontaire puni de trois ans d'emprisonnement et de FF300 000 d'amende.

En cas de violation manifestement délibérée d'une obligation particulière de sécurité ou de prudence imposée par la loi ou le règlement, les peine encourues sont portées à cinq ans d'emprisonnement et à FF500 000 d'amende.

Art. 222–1

The fact of submitting a person to torture or inhumane acts is punished by fifteen years imprisonment.

Le fait de soumettre une personne à des tortures ou à des actes de barbarie est puni de quinze ans de réclusion criminelle.

Art. 222–7

Violence leading to death without the intention of doing so is punished with fifteen years imprisonment.

Les violences ayant entraîné la mort sans intention de la donner sont punies de quinze ans de réclusion criminelle.

Art. 222–8

The offence defined in article 222–7 is punished by 20 years imprisonment when it is committed:
1. On a minor under fifteen;
2. On a person whose particular vulnerability, due to their age, illness, infirmity, physical or mental disability, or pregnancy, is known or apparent to the offender;
3. On the legitimate or illegitimate parent or on the adoptive mother or father;
4. On a judge, juror, *avocat*, *officier public* or *officer ministériel*, an official of the *gendarmerie*, a police officer, a customs officer, a prison officer, or any other holder of public authority or person charged with carrying out the public service, in the exercise or during the exercise of his functions, when the quality of the victim is apparent or known to the offender;
5. On a witness, a victim or civil party, either to stop the denouncing of the facts, or the making of a complaint or the giving of evidence;
6. By the spouse or partner of the victim;
7. By a person holding public authority or charged with carrying out a public service in the exercise or during the exercise of their functions or of their mission;
8. By several people acting as principal offenders or as accomplices;
9. With premeditation;
10. With the use or threat of a weapon.

L'infraction définie à l'article 222–7 est punie de vingt ans de réclusion criminelle lorsqu'elle est commise:

1. *Sur un mineur de quinze ans;*
2. *Sur une personne dont la particulière vulnérabilité, due à son âge, à une maladie, à une infirmité, à une déficience physique ou psychique ou à un état de grossesse, est apparente ou connue de leur auteur;*
3. *Sur un ascendant légitime ou naturel ou sur les père ou mère adoptifs;*
4. *Sur un magistrat, un juré, un avocat, un officier public ou ministériel, un militaire de la gendarmerie, un fonctionnaire de la police nationale, des douanes, de l'administration pénitentiaire ou toute autre personne dépositaire de l'autorité publique ou chargée d'une mission de service public, dans l'exercice ou à l'occasion de l'exercice de ses fonctions ou de sa mission, lorsque la qualité de la victime est apparente ou connue de l'auteur;*
5. *Sur un témoin, une victime ou une partie civile, soit pour l'empêcher de dénoncer les faits, de porter plainte ou de déposer en justice, soit en raison de sa dénonciation, de sa plainte ou de sa déposition;*
6. *Par le conjoint ou le concubin de la victime;*
7. *Par une personne dépositaire de l'autorité publique ou chargée d'une mission de service public dans l'exercice ou à l'occasion de l'exercice de ses fonctions ou de sa mission;*
8. *Par plusieurs personnes agissant en qualité d'auteur ou de complice;*
9. *Avec préméditation;*
10. *Avec usage ou menace d'une arme.*

Art. 222–11

Violence leading to a total incapacity to work for more than eight days is punished by three years imprisonment and a FF300,000 fine.

Les violences ayant entraîné une incapacité totale de travail pendant plus de huit jours sont punies de trois ans d'emprisonnement et de FF300 000 d'amende.

Art. 222–13

… The sentences incurred are increased to five years imprisonment and FF500,000 fine when the offence defined in the first paragraph is committed on a minor under fifteen years old by a legitimate, natural or adoptive parent or by any other person having authority over the minor. The sentences are also increased to five years imprisonment and FF500,000 fine when this offence, having caused a total incapacity to work of eight days or less, is committed in two of the circumstances laid down in points 1 to 10 of this article. The sentences are increased to seven years imprisonment and FF700,000 fine when it is committed in three of these circumstances.

... Les peines encourues sont portées à cinq ans d'emprisonnement et à FF500 000 d'amende lorsque l'infraction définie au premier alinéa est commise sur un mineur de quinze ans par un ascendant légitime, naturel ou adoptif ou par toute autre personne ayant autorité sur le mineur. Les peines sont également portées à cinq ans d'emprisonnement et FF500 000 d'amende lorsque cette infraction, ayant entraîné une incapacité totale de travail inférieur ou égale à huit jours, est commise dans deux des circonstances prévues aux 1 à 10 du présent article. Les peines sont portées à sept ans d'emprisonnement et FF700 000 d'amende lorsqu'elle est commise dans trois de ces circonstances.

Art. 222–14

Habitual violence on a minor under fifteen or on a person whose particular vulnerability, due to their age, an illness, an infirmity, a physical or mental disability or a pregnancy, is apparent or known to their author is punished by:
1. Thirty years imprisonment when it has led to the death of the victim;
2. Twenty years imprisonment when it has led to a mutilation or permanent infirmity;
3. Ten years imprisonment and FF1,000,000 fine when it has led to a total incapacity to work for more than eight days;
4. Five years imprisonment and FF500,000 fine when it has not led to a total incapacity to work of more than eight days.

Les violences habituelles sur un mineur de quinze ans ou sur une personne dont la particulière vulnérabilité, due à son âge, à une maladie, à une infirmité, à une déficience physique ou psychique ou à un état de grossesse, est apparente ou connue de leur auteur sont punies:
1. *De trente ans de réclusion criminelle lorsqu'elles ont entraîné la mort de la victime;*
2. *De vingt ans de réclusion criminelle lorsqu'elles ont entraîné une mutilation ou une infirmité permanente;*
3. *De dix ans d'emprisonnement et de FF1 000 000 d'amende lors qu'elles ont entraîné une incapacité totale de travail pendant plus de huit jours;*
4. *De cinq ans d'emprisonnement et de FF500 000 d'amende lors qu'elles n'ont pas entraîné une incapacité totale de travail pendant plus de huit jours.*

Art. 222–16

Malicious telephone calls and oral attacks, repeated with a view to disturbing someone's peace of mind, are punished by one year's imprisonment and a FF100,000 fine.

Les appels téléphoniques malveillants ou les agressions sonores, réitérés en vue de troubler la tranquillité d'autrui, sont punis d'un an d'emprisonnement et de FF100 000 d'amende.

Art. 222–17

A threat to commit a serious crime or major offence against the person of which the attempt is punishable is punished by six months imprisonment and a FF50,000 fine when it is either repeated or substantiated in a written document, a picture or any other object.

The punishment is increased to three years imprisonment and to a fine of FF300,000 if it involves a threat of death.

La menace de commettre un crime ou un délit contre les personnes dont la tentative est punissable est punie de six mois d'emprisonnement et de F50,000 d'amende lorsqu'elle est, soit réitérée, soit matérialisée par un écrit, une image ou tout autre objet.

La peine est portée à trois ans d'emprisonnement et à 300 000F d'amende s'il s'agit d'une menace de mort.

Art. 222–18

A threat, in whatever form, to commit a serious crime or major offence against the person, is punished by three years imprisonment and a FF300,000 fine when it is made with an order to fulfil a condition.

The punishment is increased to five years imprisonment and a FF500,000 fine if it involves a threat of death.

La menace, par quelque moyen que ce soit, de commettre un crime ou un délit contre les personnes, est punie de trois ans d'emprisonnement et de 300 000F d'amende, lorsqu'elle est fait avec l'ordre de remplir une condition.

La peine est portée à cinq ans d'emprisonnement et à 500 000F d'amende s'il s'agit d'une menace de mort.

Art. 222–19

The fact of causing to another, in the conditions and according to the distinctions laid down by article 121–3, by ineptitude, carelessness, inattention, negligence or a breach of an obligation of security or of care imposed by legislation or regulation, a total incapacity to work for more than three months is punishable by two years imprisonment and a FF200,000 fine.

In the case of an obviously deliberate breach of a particular obligation of security or of care imposed by legislation or regulation, the punishments incurred are increased to three years imprisonment and a FF300,000 fine.

Le fait de causer à autrui, dans les conditions et selon les distinctions prévues à l'article 121–3 par maladresse, imprudence, inattention, négligence ou manquement à une obligation de sécurité ou de prudence imposée par la loi ou le règlement, une incapacité totale de travail pendant plus de trois mois est puni de deux ans d'emprisonnement et de FF200 000 d'amende.

En cas de violation manifestement délibérée d'une obligation particulière de sécurité ou de prudence imposée par la loi ou le règlement, les peines encourues sont portées à trois ans d'emprisonnement et à FF300 000 d'amende.

Art. 222–20

The fact of causing another, by an obviously deliberate breach of a particular obligation of security or of care imposed by legislation or regulation, a total incapacity to work of up to three months, is punished by one year's imprisonment and a FF100,000 fine.

Le fait de causer à autrui, par la violation manifestement délibérée d'une obligation particulière de sécurité ou de prudence imposée par la loi ou le règlement, une incapacité totale de travail d'une durée inférieure ou égale à trois mois, est puni d'un an d'emprisonnement et de FF100 000 d'amende.

Art. 222–23

Any act of sexual penetration, of whatever nature it may be, committed on another person by violence, constraint, threat or abuse is a rape.
Rape is punished by fifteen years imprisonment.

Tout acte de pénétration sexuelle, de quelque nature qu'il soit, commis sur la personne d'autrui par violence, contrainte, menace ou surprise est un viol.
Le viol est puni de quinze ans de réclusion criminelle.

Art. 222–34

The fact of controlling or organising a group having for object the illegal production, manufacture, import, export, transport, possession, offer, supply, acquisition or use of drugs is punished by life imprisonment and a FF50,000,000 fine.

Le fait de diriger ou d'organiser un groupement ayant pour objet la production, la fabrication, l'importation, l'exportation, le transport, la détention, l'offre, la cession, l'acquisition ou l'emploi illicites de stupéfiants est puni de la réclusion criminelle à perpetuité et de FF50 000 000 d'amende.

Art. 222–35

The illegal production or manufacture of drugs is punished by twenty years imprisonment and a FF50,000,000 fine.

These facts are punished by 30 years imprisonment and a FF50,000,000 fine when they are committed by an organised gang.

La production ou la fabrication illicites de stupéfiants sont punies de vingt ans de réclusion criminelle et de FF50 000 000 d'amende.

Ces faits sont punis de trente ans de réclusion criminelle et de FF50 000 000 d'amende lorsqu'ils sont commis en bande organisée.

Art. 222–36

The illegal import or export of drugs is punished by ten years imprisonment and 50,000,000FF fine.

These facts are punished by 30 years imprisonment and a FF50,000,000 fine when they are committed as part of an organised gang.

L'importation ou l'exportation illicites de stupéfiants sont punies de dix ans d'emprisonnement et de FF50 000 000 d'amende.

Ces faits sont punis de trente ans de réclusion criminelle et de FF50 000 000 d'amende lorsqu'ils sont commis en bande organisée.

Art. 222–37

The illegal transport, possession, offer, supply, acquisition or use of drugs is punished by ten years imprisonment and a FF50,000,000 fine.

The fact of facilitating, by whatever means, the illegal use of drugs, the obtaining of drugs by means of false or inappropriate prescriptions, or to hand over drugs on presentation of such prescriptions knowing their false or inappropriate character, is punished by [ten years imprisonment and a FF50,000,000 fine].

Le transport, la détention, l'offre, la cession, l'acquisition ou l'emploi illicites de stupéfiants sont punis de dix ans d'emprisonnement et de 50 000 000F d'amende.

Est puni des mêmes peines le fait de faciliter, par quelque moyen que ce soit, l'usage illicite de stupéfiants, de se faire délivrer des stupéfiants au moyen d'ordonnances fictives ou de complaisance, ou de délivrer des stupéfiants sur la présentation de telles ordonnances en connaissant leur caractère fictif ou complaisant.

Art. 222–38

The fact of facilitating, by whatever means, the false justification of the origin of property or revenue of the author of one of the offences mentioned in articles 222–34 to 222–37 or of helping in the placing, hiding or conversion of the product of one of these offences is punished by ten years imprisonment and a FF5,000,000 fine. The fine can be increased to half the value of the property or funds which were the subject of the money laundering.

When the offence was concerned with the property or funds coming from one of the serious offences mentioned in articles 222–34, 222–35 and the second paragraph of article 222–36 the offender is subject to the punishments laid down for the serious offences of which he had knowledge.

Est puni de dix ans d'emprisonnement et de FF5 000 000 d'amende le fait de faciliter, par tout moyen, la justification mensongère de l'origine des biens ou des revenus de l'auteur de l'une des infractions mentionnées aux articles 222–34 à 222–37 ou d'apporter son concours à une opération de placement, de dissimulation ou de conversion du produit de l'une de ces infractions. La peine d'amende peut être élevée jusqu'à la moitié de la valeur des biens ou des fonds sur lesquels ont porté les opérations de blanchiment.

Lorsque l'infraction a porté sur des biens ou des fonds provenant de l'un des crimes mentionnés aux articles 222–34, 222–35 et 222–36, deuxième alinéa, son auteur est puni des peines prévues pour les crimes dont il a eu connaissance.

Art. 222–39

The illegal supply or offer of drugs to a person with a view to its personal consumption is punished by five years imprisonment and a FF500,000 fine.

The punishment of imprisonment is increased to ten years when the drugs are offered or supplied, in the conditions defined by the preceding paragraph, to minors or in educational establishments or in premises of the administration.

La cession ou l'offre illicites de stupéfiants à une personne en vue de sa consommation personelle sont punies de cinq ans d'emprisonnement et de FF500 000 d'amende.

La peine d'emprisonnement est portée à dix ans lorsque les stupéfiants sont offerts ou cédés, dans les conditions définies à l'alinéa précédent, à des mineurs ou dans des centres d'enseignement ou d'éducation ou dans les locaux de l'administration.

Art. 222–39–1

The fact of not being able to justify resources corresponding to one's way of life, while being in regular contact with one or several people involved in one of the activities incriminated in this section, or with several people involved in the use of drugs, is punished by five years imprisonment and a fine of FF500,000.

The punishment is increased to ten years when one or more of the people referred to in the preceding paragraph are minors.

Le fait de ne pas pouvoir justifier de resources correspondant à son train de vie, tout en étant en relations habituelles avec une ou plusieurs personnes se livrant à l'une des activités réprimées par la présente section, ou avec plusieurs personnes se livrant à l'usage de stupéfiants, est puni de cinq ans d'emprisonnement et de 500,000F d'amende.

La peine d'emprisonnement est portée à dix ans lorsqu'une ou plusieurs personnes visées à l'alinéa précédent sont mineures.

Art. 222–43

The sentence of imprisonment incurred by a principal offender or an accomplice of the offences laid down in articles 222–34 to 222–40 is reduced by half if, having alerted the administrative or legal authorities, he has permitted the termination of criminal conduct and the identification, in appropriate cases, of the other guilty people.

La peine privative de liberté encourue par l'auteur ou le complice des infractions prévues par les articles 222–34 à 222–40 est réduite de moitié si, ayant averti les autorités administratives ou judiciaires, il a permis de faire cesser les agissements incriminés et d'identifier, le cas échéant, les autres coupables.

Art. 311–1

Theft is the appropriation of the thing of another with guilty intent.

Le vol est la soustraction frauduleuse de la chose d'autrui.

Art. 311–12

Theft cannot give rise to a criminal prosecution where it has been committed by a person:
1. To the detriment of his ascendant or descendant;
2. To the detriment of his spouse, except when the spouses are separated or authorised to reside separately.

Ne peut donner lieu à des poursuites pénales le vol commis par une personne:
1. *Au préjudice de son ascendant ou de son descendant;*
2. *Au préjudice de son conjoint, sauf lorsque les époux sont séparés de corps ou autorisés à résider séparément.*

Art. 313–1

Fraud is the fact of tricking a physical or moral person, either by the use of a false name, or of a false characteristic, or by abuse of a real characteristic, or by the use of fraudulent tactics, and to induce them thereby, to their detriment or to the detriment of a third party, to hand over funds, valuables or any property, to provide a service or to consent to an act creating an obligation or a discharge of an obligation.

Fraud is punished by five years imprisonment and a FF2,500,000 fine.

L'escroquerie est le fait, soit par l'usage d'un faux nom ou d'une fausse qualité, soit par l'abus d'une qualité vraie, soit par l'emploi de manoeuvres frauduleuses, de tromper une personne physique ou morale et de la déterminer ainsi, à son préjudice ou au préjudice d'un tiers, à remettre des fonds, des valeurs ou un bien quelconque, à fournir un service ou à consentir un acte opérant obligation ou décharge.

L'escroquerie est punie de cinq ans d'emprisonnement et de FF2 500 000 d'amende.

Art. 314–1

Abuse of confidence is the fact of a person misappropriating to the detriment of another funds, valuables or any property which has been handed over to him and which he has accepted on condition of giving them back, of exhibiting them or of using them in a specific way.

Abuse of confidence is punished by three years imprisonment and a FF2,500,000 fine.

L'abus de confiance est la fait par une personne de détourner au préjudice d'autrui des fonds, des valeurs ou un bien quelconque qui lui ont été remis et qu'elle a acceptés à charge de les rendre, de les représenter ou d'en faire un usage déterminé.

L'abus de confiance est puni de trois ans d'emprisonnement et de FF2 500 000 d'amende.

Art. 450–1

A conspiracy consists of any group formed or understanding established with a view to the preparation, evidenced by one or more physical fact, of one or more serious offences or one or more major offences punishable by ten years imprisonment.

Participation in a conspiracy is punishable by ten years imprisonment and a FF1,000,000 fine.

Constitue une association de malfaiteurs tout groupement formé ou entente établie en vue de la préparation, caractérisée par un ou plusieurs faits matériels, d'un ou plusieurs crimes ou d'un ou plusieurs délits punis de dix ans d'emprisonnement.

La participation à une association de malfaiteurs est punie de dix ans d'emprisonnement et de FF1 000 000 d'amende.

Art. 450–2

Any person having participated in a group or an understanding defined by article 450–1 is exempt from punishment if he has, before any prosecution, revealed the group or understanding to the competent authorities and enabled the identification of the other participants.

Toute personne ayant participé au groupement ou à l'entente définis par l'article 450–1 est exempte de peine si elle a, avant toute poursuite, révélé le groupement ou l'entente aux autorités compétentes et permis l'identification des autres participants.

Art. R.622–1

Except the case laid down in article R.625–3, the fact of attacking another through ineptitude, carelessness, inattention, negligence or breach of an obligation of security or of care imposed by legislation or regulations, without any total incapacity to work resulting is punished by a fine laid down for minor offences of the second class.

Hors le cas prévu par l'article R.625–3, le fait, par maladresse, imprudence, inattention, négligence ou manquement à une obligation de sécurité ou de prudence imposée par la loi ou les règlements, de porter atteinte à l'intégrité d'autrui sans qu'il en résulte d'incapacité totale de travail est puni de l'amende prévue pour les contraventions de la 2e classe.

Art. R. 623–1

Except in the cases laid down in articles 222–17 and 222–18, a threat to commit violence against a person, when this threat is either repeated, or substantiated in a written document, a picture or any other object, is punished by a fine laid down for minor offences of the third class.

Hors les cas prévus par les articles 222–17 et 222–18, la menace de commettre des violences contre une personne, lorsque cette menace est soit réitérée, soit matérialisée par un écrit, une image ou toute autre object, est punie de l'amende prévue pour les contraventions de la 3e classe.

Art. R.624–1

Except for the cases provided for in articles 222–13 and 222–14, voluntary violence not causing any total incapacity to work is punished by the fine laid down for minor offences of the fourth class.

Hors les cas prévus par les articles 222–13 et 222–14, les violences volontaires n'ayant entraîné aucune incapacité totale de travail sont punies de l'amende prévue pour les contraventions de la 4e classe.

Art. R.625–1

Except for the cases provided for in articles 222–13 and 222–14, voluntary violence causing a total incapacity to work for a period of eight days or less is punished by the fine laid down for minor offences of the fifth class.

Hors les cas prévus par les articles 222–13 et 222–14, les violences volontaires ayant entraîné une incapacité totale du travail d'une durée inférieure ou égale à huit jours sont punies de l'amende prévue pour les contraventions de la 5e classe.

Art. R.625–3

The fact of, by a deliberate breach of an obligation of security or of care imposed by legislation or regulations, attacking another without a total incapacity to work resulting is punished by a fine laid down for minor offences of the fifth class.

Le fait, par un manquement délibéré à une obligation de sécurité ou de prudence imposée par la loi ou les règlements, de porter atteinte à l'intégrité d'autrui sans qu'il en résulte d'incapacité totale de travail est punie de l'amende prévue pour les contraventions de la 5e classe.

Appendix 2

Sample French judgment

French judgments are much shorter than the judgments of English common law courts, often fitting onto a single page. Traditionally they consist of only one sentence with a single full stop to be found at the end. The judgment is divided into two parts: the grounds for the court's decision (*les motifs*) and the court's verdict (*le dispositif*). Each paragraph forming part of the *motifs* usually starts with the phrase *attendu que*, meaning 'whereas', or 'given that'. The verdict constitutes the most important part of the judgement for the litigants, while it is the paragraph(s) of the *motifs* containing the specific reasoning of the court which is the most important for lawyers.

Below is an example of a judgment of the Criminal Division of the *Cour de cassation*, along with a possible translation of that judgment. The case is based on the principle that the motive of the defendant is irrelevant to the *mens rea* of the offence. The background facts to the case are that the mistress of the deceased, Mr Moricau-Clos, had put flowers and vases on his grave. His daughter and her husband had removed these flowers and vases and thrown them onto a rubbish dump. The Court of Appeal acquitted them of theft of these objects on the basis that they had acted out of hate and had simply thrown away the objects. The matter was appealed to the *Cour de cassation*.

Chambre criminelle, 8 février 1977

Lahore

Attendu que le délit de vol est constitué quel que soit le mobile qui a inspiré son auteur dès lors que la soustraction frauduleuse de la chose d'autrui est constatée;

Attendu qu'il résulte de l'arrêt attaqué et du jugement dont il a adopté les motifs non contraires qu'après avoir arraché les fleurs et les vases dont la demoiselle Amouroux avait orné la tombe de Moricau-Clos, les époux Lahore les ont jetés dans une décharge;

Attendu, en l'état de ces constations, qu'en se bornant à énoncer pour écarter la prévention de vol desdits époux Lahore, que les agissements de ces derniers avaient été inspirés par la haine, la cour d'appel n'a pas donné une base légale à sa décision;

Qu'en effet, en s'emparant pour les détruire, d'ornements qu'ils savaient ne pas leur appartenir, les prévenus, qui se sont appropriés ces biens sans droit, ont commis une soustraction frauduleuse, leur mobile ne pouvant être retenu autrement que pour l'application de la peine;

Qu'ainsi l'arrêt encourt la cassation;

Translation

Criminal Division, 8 February 1977

Lahore

Whereas the major offence of theft is constituted whatever may have been the motive that inspired its author from the moment that the appropriation of the thing of another with guilty intent is proven;

Whereas it results from the appellate decision that is the subject of this appeal and from the judgement of first instance whose reasoning it adopted that after having grabbed the flowers and vases with which Miss Amouroux had decorated the tomb of Moricau-Clos, Mr and Mrs Lahore threw them on a rubbish dump;

Whereas, in the light of these facts, by simply stating as the basis of rejecting the charge of theft of the aforementioned Mr and Mrs Lahore, that the acts of the latter had been inspired by hate, the court of appeal has not given a legal basis for its decision;

That in effect, by seizing in order to destroy ornaments that they knew they did not own, the defendants, who took this property without the right to do so, have committed an appropriation with guilty intent, their motive only being relevant in determining the punishment;

Thus the appellate decision is quashed;

Glossary of criminal legal terms

A

à huis clos	in camera
à perpetuité	life, for life
à temps	fixed term
abus (m) d'autorité	abuse of authority
abus (m) de confiance	abuse of confidence
abus (m) de pouvoir	abuse of power
accomplir les diligences normales	to exercise normal care
accusatoire	adversarial
accusé (e)	accused, defendant
acte (m) de barbarie	inhumane act
action (f) publique	public prosecution
administration (f) pénitentiaire	prison service
affaire (f)	case
affichage (f)	publication
agent (m) de police judiciaire	police officer
agir sous l'empire de	to act under the influence of
agissements (m) incriminés	criminal conduct
alinéa (m)	paragraph
amende (f)	fine
amende (f) honorable	public confession, apology
appel (m)	appeal (on facts and/or law)
appel (m) téléphonique malveillant	malicious telephone call
arme (f)	weapon
arrestation (f)	arrest
assassinat (m)	assassination
association (f) de malfaiteurs	conspiracy
atteinte (f)	attack
attendu que	whereas, given that
audience (f)	court hearing
auteur (m)	principal offender, defendant, author

auteur (m) intellectuel	a person who is treated as the principal offender, though he/she did not personally carry out the *actus reus* of the offence; also known as *l'auteur moral*
auteur (m) matériel	principal offender
auteur (m) moral	a person who is treated as the principal offender, though he/she did not personally carry out the *actus reus* of the offence; also known as *l'auteur intellectuel*
autorité (f) légitime	legitimate authority
avertir les autorités judiciaires	to alert the legal authorities

B

bande (f) organisée	organised gang
baïonettes (f) intelligentes	principle according to which subordinates are expected to ensure the legality of an order before executing it
bien (m)	property
bien (m) incorporel	intangible property
blanchiment (m)	money laundering
blesser	to injure
bon père de famille	reasonable person
bourreau (m)	state executioner

C

carcan (m)	iron collar
cause (f) de non-imputabilité	defence which is directly linked to the defendant; subjective defence; excuse
céder	to supply
cession (f) de stupéfiants	supply of drugs
Chambre (f) de l'instruction	the name given to the old *Chambre d'accusation* following the Act of 15 June 2000
Chambre (f) correctionnelle	Criminal Division (of the *Tribunal correctionnel, Tribunal de grande instance* or *Cour d'assises*)
Chambre (f) criminelle	Criminal Division (of the *Cour de cassation*)
Chambre (f) d'accusation	division of the appeal court concerned with controlling the judicial investigation, now known as the *Chambre de l'instruction*
coauteur (m)	joint principal
Code (m) d'instruction criminelle	Code of Criminal Procedure
Code (m) pénal	Criminal Code
commettre	to commit
complice (m)	accomplice
complicité (f) corespective	analysis according to which the joint principal is also automatically an accomplice
complot (m)	conspiracy

condamnation (f)	conviction
condamné(e)	convicted person
confiscation (f) d'un objet	confiscation of assets
consommation (f)	commission
contrainte (f)	constraint
contravention (f)	minor offence
coupable	guilty
coupable (m)	guilty person
coups et blessures volontaires	crime of intentionally injuring another
Cour d'appel	court of appeal
Cour d'assises	court that tries serious offences
Cour d'assises des mineurs	court that tries serious offences where the accused is a minor
Cour de cassation	court that hears final appeals on points of law only
crime (m)	serious offence, serious crime
crime (m) contre l'humanité	crime against humanity
crime (m) de guerre	war crime
culpabilité (f)	guilt

D

déchéance (f)	disqualification
décision (f) de condamnation	conviction and sentencing
décision (f) de relaxe	acquittal
décision de renvoi	decision to send the defendant for trial
déclencher l'action publique	to institute criminal proceedings
décolation (f)	decapitation
défendeur (m)	defendant
se défendre	to defend oneself
défit (m)	wrongful conduct
délai (m) de prescription	limitation period
délit (m)	major offence, intermediate offence
délit (m) matériel	major offence which only required as a *mens rea* that the defendant's conduct be voluntary
déni (m) de justice	miscarriage of justice
se dépêcher sur les lieux	to hasten to the scene of a crime
déportation (f)	deportation
déposer en justice	to give evidence in court
détention (f)	detention
détention (f) provisoire	remand in custody
détournement (m)	misappropriation
détournement (m) de fonds	embezzlement, misappropriation of funds
détourner	to misappropriate
diligences (f)	care
dispositif (m)	court's finding (stated at the end of the decision)
dol (m)	fault
dol (m) aggravé	additional *mens rea* beyond general or special intention

dol (m) éventuel	oblique intention, indirect intention
dol (m) dépassé	the result caused goes beyond the intention and foresight of the defendant
dol (m) général	general intention
dol (m) imprécis	where a person does an act seeking a result without being able to foresee what exactly the result will be. Also known as *dol indéterminé*
dol (m) indéterminé	where a person does an act seeking a result without being able to foresee what exactly the result will be. Also known as *dol imprécis*
dol (m) spécial	special intention
donner volontairement la mort à autrui	to kill voluntarily another person

E

écartèlement	quartering
élément (m) intellectuel	*mens rea*
élément (m) matériel	*actus reus*
élément (m) moral	*mens rea*
élément (m) psychologique	*mens rea*
élus par leurs pairs	elected by their peers
empoisonnement (m)	poisoning
emprisonnement (m)	imprisonment
en matière contraventionnelle	for minor offences, in cases involving minor offences
en matière correctionnelle	for major offences, in cases involving major offences
encombrement (m) de la voie publique	obstructing the highway
encourir une peine	to incur a punishment
enfeindre les prohibitions légales	to break the law
engager une action	to bring an action
enlèvement (m)	abduction
enquête (f)	investigation
enquête (f) de flagrance	expedited investigation (with extended powers)
enquête (f) préliminaire	ordinary investigation (without special powers)
entraver	to impede
entrée (f) par effraction	entrance by force
erreur (f) sur le droit	error of law
escroquerie (f)	fraud
être astreinte aux obligations du contrôle judiciaire	to be subjected to conditional bail
être assimilé à une arme	to be classed as a weapon
être atteinte de	to be affected by, to suffer from
être défendu	to be forbidden
être poursuivi	to be prosecuted

être puni de	to be punished with
être reconnu coupable	to be found guilty
être responsable pénalement	to be criminally responsible
exercer l'action publique	to bring a prosecution

F

fait (m) incriminé	criminal conduct
fait (m) justificatif	a defence that provides a justification for the criminal conduct which ceases to be viewed as anti social; justification; objective defence
faire l'objet de mesures	to be the subject of measures
faute (f) d'imprudence	carelessness
faute (f) caractérisée	established fault
faute (f) contraventionnelle	the *mens rea* of minor offences
force (f)	force
fouet (m)	flogging
frapper quelqu'un d'une peine	to impose a punishment on someone
frauduleux	with guilty intent
fuite (f)	escape

G

garde à vue (f)	police custody
génocide (m)	genocide

H

homicide (m)	homicide
homicide (m) volontaire	voluntary homicide
homicide (m) involontaire	involuntary homicide, involuntary manslaughter

I

immobilisation (f) d'un objet	freezing of assets
impossibilité (f) matérielle	physical impossibility
imprudence (f)	imprudence
impunité (f)	impunity
incapacité (f)	incapacity
incapacité (f) totale de travail	total incapacity to work
in concreto	subjective
infraction (f)	offence
infraction (f) contre un bien	offence against property
infraction (f) contre la personne	offence against the person
infraction (f) flagrante	offence giving rise to an expedited investigation complete offence that does not require a result offence which only requires as a *mens rea* that the defendant's conduct be voluntary. The nearest English equivalent is a strict liability offence
infraction (f) formelle	
infraction (f) matérielle	
infraction (f) pénale	criminal offence

injustifié	unjustified
inquisitoire	inquisitorial
instruction (f)	judicial investigation
intention (f)	intention
intention (f) frauduleuse	guilty intent
interdiction (f)	banning
interrompre l'exécution d'une infraction	to prevent the commission of an offence
intime conviction (f)	personal conviction

J

jour (m) amende	daily fine
juge (m) d'instruction	judge in charge of the judicial investigation; sometimes translated as examining magistrate or investigating judge
juge (m) des libertés et de la détention	judge responsible for deciding whether to grant bail or to place on remand
juré(e)	juror
juridiction (f) pénale	criminal court
juridiction (f) répressive	criminal court
jury (m)	jury

L

légitime défense	legitimate defence
légitimement	legally
lettre (f) de rémission	pardon
lien (m) de causalité	causal link

M

machination (f)	scheming
magistrature (f) du parquet	public prosecutor's office; the prosecution
maladresse (f)	ineptitude
maniement (m) juridique	legal transfer
manifestement	obviously
manoeuvre (f) frauduleuse	fraudulent tactic
manquement (m) à une obligation de prudence ou de sécurité	failure to fulfil an obligation of care or of security
marque (m) au fer rouge	branding with a red hot iron
massacre (m)	massacre
menace (f)	threat
menacer	to threaten
meurtre (m)	murder
mineur (m)	minor
ministère (m) publique	public prosecutor's office, the prosecution
mise (f) en accusation	bringing charges
mise (f) en danger délibérée de la	

personne d'autrui	deliberately putting another in danger
mise (f) en examen	charging of the suspect
mise (f) en scène	scheming
motif (m)	ground, reason, motive

N

nécessité (f)	necessity
négligence (f)	negligence
nul n'est censé ignorer la loi	ignorance of the law is no defence

O

Officier (m) de police judiciaire	senior police officer

P

parquet (m)	public prosecutor's office, the prosecution
partie (f) civile	civil party, private claimant
peine (f)	sentence
peine (f) complémentaire	complementary punishment
peine (f) de sûreté	minimum period to be spent in prison
peine (f) de mort	death penalty
peine (f) privative de liberté	sentence of imprisonment
pénal	criminal
période (f) de sûreté	minimum period to be spent in prison
perpétration (f)	commission
perquisition (f)	search of property
personne (f) mise en examen	accused (n)
pillage (m)	looting
plan (m) concerté	concerted plan
police (f) administrative	crime prevention police
police (f) judiciaire	criminal investigation police
porter à	to increase to
porter atteinte à l'intégrité d'autrui	to attack another
porter une arme	to carry a weapon
porter plainte	to report an offence
potence (f)	gallows
poursuite (f)	prosecution, decision to bring charges
poursuite (f) pénale	criminal prosecution
poursuivre	to bring charges
poursuivre au pénal	to prosecute
préméditation (f)	premeditation
prescrire	to order
se prescrire	to be subject to a limitation period
présomption (f) d'innocence	presumption of innocence
prévoir	to provide, to lay down
prévenu(e)	defendant
procédure (f) pénale	criminal procedure
procureur (m) de la République	senior public prosecutor
prononcer une peine à l'encontre de	to impose a punishment on

prononcer la réclusion criminelle à perpétuité	hand down a life sentence
provoquer	to provoke
puni de	punishable by
punir	to punish
punissable	punishable

R

réclusion (f)	imprisonment
réclusion (f) criminelle	imprisonment
réclusion (f) criminelle à perpétuité	life imprisonment
remise (f)	handing over
réprimer	to incriminate
réquisitoire (m)	submission (by the prosecution)
réquisitoire (m) introductif	application for judicial investigation
résolution (f) de mise en accusation	decision to bring charges
responsabilité (f) pénale	criminal liability
ruse (f)	fraud

S

sciemment	knowingly
soustraction (f)	appropriation
stupéfiant (m)	drug
supplice (m) de la roue	torture on the wheel
surprise (f)	abuse
surveillance (f)	supervision

T

talion (m)	law of retaliation
témoin (m)	witness
témoin (m) assisté	represented witness
tentative (f)	attempt
tentative (f) achevée	failed attempt
tentative (f) stérile	failed attempt
tenter	to attempt
tirage (m) au sort	random selection
torture (f)	torture
travail (m) d'intérêt général	work in the community
se transporter sur les lieux	to go to the scene of the crime
tribunal (m) correctionnel	court that tries major offences
tribunal (m) de police	court that tries minor offences
tribunal (m) pour enfants	juvenile court, youth court
tribunal (m) répressif	criminal court
tromper	to trick, to deceive
trouble (m) psychique	psychological illness
trouble (m) neuropsychique	neuro-psychological illness
troubler la tranquillité d'autrui	to disturb someone's peace of mind
tuer	to kill

V

victime (f)	victim
viol (m)	rape
violation (f)	breach
violence (f)	violence, force
violer	to breach
visite (f) domiciliaire	house search
voie (m) de fait	offence of violence
vol (m)	theft
vol (m) d'usage	theft by temporarily using property
volontairement	intentionally
volonté (f)	will

Index